MW01256361

Mapping
Information
Landscapes

Every purchase of a Facet book helps to fund CILIP's advocacy, awareness and accreditation programmes for information professionals.

Mapping Information Landscapes

New methods for exploring the development and teaching of information literacy

Andrew Whitworth

facet
publishing

Published by Facet Publishing
7 Ridgmount Street, London WC1E 7AE
www.facetpublishing.co.uk

Facet Publishing is wholly owned by CILIP: the Library and Information Association.

British Library Cataloguing in Publication Data
A catalogue record for this book is available from the British Library.

ISBN 978-1-78330-417-2 (hardback)
ISBN 978-1-78330-418-9 (e-book)

First published 2020

Text printed on FSC accredited material.

Typeset from author's files in 10.5/13pt Elegant Garamond and Myriad Pro by Flagholme Publishing Services.
Printed and made in Great Britain by CPI Group (UK) Ltd, Croydon, CR0 4YY.

Contents

Appendices

List of figures

Foreword

Ground-breaking can be an overused and hackneyed phrase but it is entirely true in this case, and an apt pun, for a book that focuses on information landscapes in their infinite variety. But that's not to say that it is narrow in view, this is a much broader treatment on the discourse of information literacy – it is a sure-footed and forensic exploration of the topic. Drew's discussion on the history of information literacy is a very clear break with received wisdom of the past and especially questions the hegemony of thought embodied in powerful Western voices. Drew provides us with a critical overview, in a sense an information literacy of information literacy, which has been sadly lacking but now rectified in this volume. However, it is the notion of the information landscape that defines this work.

When Mark Hepworth and I wrote our book on information literacy, we were very conscious of the 'information character' of an information source (whatever that might be), but never fully developed what we meant by that. Drew gives us a clear notion of what information character is through this notion of an information landscape (not as metaphor but as embodied social practice); how we inhabit, map and navigate it to become, not just informed, but to make well-calibrated judgements of the information we encounter. It is notable that Drew draws our attention to the overlooked, and often misunderstood issue by those outside the information profession, that information literacy is not simply about technical competencies, no, it is much more than this. Indeed, it is about our practice as we move through, encounter and use information for whatever purpose.

Information literacy is a social and cognitive set of practices which help us locate ourselves in the world. These practices are contextual (work, education or play), negotiated and re-negotiated and, are not entirely rational. Therein lies a problem, which Drew highlights very eloquently, in effect the limited perspective that information literacy taught in higher education brings. Educators are excellent at enabling or even empowering students to become information literate within the educational context but this does not translate well to the workplace because, like the geographical landscape where mountains and valleys are very different places, the information landscapes of education and work are entirely different too. What this book gives us is a set of road maps (literally and figuratively) to a complete and thorough unpacking of our lived experience as navigators of the multitude of information landscapes we encounter as we move through time. By exploring the history of maps and cartography, Drew supplies us with a new way of envisaging information and its relationship with power, knowledge and resistance.

This work will challenge your existing knowledge, especially about notions of authority and the very nature of what constitutes the most credible information and, how it is produced and reproduced. In other words, there is no correct way to respond to a text. Drew brings new perspectives which will open your mind to fresh ways of thinking about a very familiar topic. I hope you find it as thought-provoking as I did!

Geoff Walton, Manchester Metropolitan University

Introduction

This book is a study of how educators and learners can use the practice and process of *mapping* in developing their information and digital literacy, and of the centrality of *place* and *time* to these notions. Mikhail Bakhtin used the term *chronotope* (1981), derived from the Greek words for time and place, to describe the unique moments that we all continuously experience, the differing qualities of which irrevocably shape our encounters with information. The information landscapes (Lloyd, 2010a) which we inhabit can be and, due to our individuality, must be viewed from a multitude of different chronotopes, and thus from a multitude of differing perspectives. And in any decision-making process, whether individual, organisational or societal, judgements are more *informed* when decision-makers can effectively navigate the information they must draw upon, discern the contours and nuances of these landscapes, map them and learn how to acknowledge difference in how these processes are perceived, and how they subsequently manifest in practice.

The effective use of information to learn and to take informed decisions, and the effective navigation of information landscapes, have been termed *information literacy*, though as Chapter 1 will discuss, this term has by no means achieved universal acceptance and can mean quite different things depending on the perspective from which one attempts to describe it. Nevertheless, informed judgements are always made against the background of information landscapes that intersect at the here and now – that is, at given *chronotopes* – and which are organised across both the physical, geographical realm and the virtual, informational one. One of this book's principal arguments is that these two realms are indivisible and the techniques we use to navigate each are essentially similar.

Based on this fundamental indivisibility of the geographical and information landscape, I present mapping as an educational approach that can help us, as individuals and as members of groups, better learn how to navigate the information landscapes that are relevant at our (constantly shifting) chronotope and, as a result, develop and sustain information literacy (IL). To explore this proposition requires defining IL as more than just a set of technical competencies, but as a practice that is embodied in a multitude of social sites that shape how we relate to, and use, information. Thus, the 'information landscape' (Lloyd, 2010a) is not just a metaphor, but a notion that must be fully integrated with the social theories we use to explain human activity (Harvey, 1996, 46). Information landscapes are rooted in physical landscapes and are made navigable by how we organise and represent these landscapes, their elements and their relationships to ourselves and to others. In other words, IL becomes evident in how we draw maps of these landscapes and how these maps serve as utterances in ongoing dialogues. As Lloyd notes (2010a, 2):

> ... the process of becoming information literate requires the whole person to be aware of themselves within the world (Csordas, 1994); to experience information through the opportunities that are furnished by the landscape or context; to recognise these experiences as contributing to learning; and, to take into account how the context and its sanctioned practices, sayings and doings enable and constrain information use.

Thanks to the work of authors such as Lloyd, the idea that information, and IL, is specific to context is well established in the literature, but what has not necessarily been so well developed is the impact of *spatiality*. Contexts are not 'spaceless abstractions' (Crang and Thrift, 2000, 2), nor are the social theories that help explain action within these contexts, including information literacy and how it is manifested and taught. Crang and Thrift emphasise that 'no social process exists without geographical extent and historical duration... we need to consider the embeddedness of action in the world' (2000, 3). This means understanding how the concepts of space and place (an essential distinction to be explored further) are both shapers of, and shaped by, the ways we understand and work with information and IL.

And time is a factor as well. All informed judgements must be made in a present that is structured by judgements and utterances made in the past (Bakhtin, 1986, 93) and against goals that will be achieved, if at all, at some indefinite point in the future. What is relevant today may not have been relevant yesterday, yet the ways our information landscapes are organised and represented may have been determined months, years or decades ago. The persistence of cognitive schema (Bartlett, 1932), or what I will term *discursive maps*, that shape and guide our interactions with information landscapes is both essential to our being able to engage with the world and a potential block on our being able to perceive the importance of information that is new or different, and hence is not represented on the maps we bring into play in a given place and time. Can the maps we are using be reviewed and revised when necessary? Can the claims they make be scrutinised? Are maps the locus of authority and power in a given place and time or means by which authority can there be distributed more equably (Whitworth, 2014)?

There are other reasons to be concerned about our relationship to place in the 21st century. David Barrie has recently expressed the same concerns as raised in Whitworth (2009, 59) regarding how an increased reliance on satellite navigation systems, as opposed to our own navigational skills, might retard the development of the hippocampus, the region of the brain which orients us and helps us establish direction. Barrie (2019) suggested that the 'acute sense of their surroundings and place in the world' that people have established through history is now so frequently delegated to technological aids like Google Maps that the hippocampus is simply not being used as much as in the past.

Maps have been part of public discourse for centuries (see Chapter 2) and a good map can supplement one's own navigational skills, but it is still up to the user of a paper map to be aware of where *they* are in relation to the world as represented thereon. Google Maps takes this responsibility away. The 'blue dot' is an aid of great accuracy, but it removes the need to be aware of one's own positionality vis-à-vis the map in use. In short, we no longer need to remember where we are and how we reached there; the need to *learn pathways through the landscape*, and to use a map to do so, has reduced markedly in the era of the global positioning system (GPS). If this means that people, particularly younger people, are not 'exercising' their hippocampuses, what if this also affects our ability to navigate information, to follow pathways and establish position in landscapes that are predominantly virtual? Reducing the idea of 'navigation' to an archaism, something we can afford to leave behind as we move forward into the digital future, may be leading to deeper problems than we know.

In this book I investigate mapping as a *practice* and like all practices this means it has both technical and social aspects. Mapping is something that is *done* and there are techniques, skills and ways of using particular equipment to map that one can learn and apply. But it is also something that is *said*; to 'be mapping' means to have positioned oneself with relation to these practices in particular ways: one will have a goal in mind and a belief (whether consciously articulated or not) that mapping is an appropriate way of achieving this goal. The products of mapping – whether these be maps themselves as graphical artefacts or the broader learning outcomes of the process, the changes it has wrought in perceptions of the world around us – become utterances in the ongoing dialogues by which we shape the world (Bakhtin, 1986). This gives maps *discursive force* (Kitchin, Perkins and Dodge, 2009, 3) and thus mapping is a process that can generate *power* to act in the world.

How different understandings of maps, mapping and information landscapes come together, and how apparent tensions between them may be resolved, are key themes running through this book. One particular tension needs highlighting early on. If IL is manifested in specific chronotopes, it gives rise to an essential practical question for any educator. In its very first paragraph, Lloyd's *Information Literacy Landscapes* (2010a, xv) immediately contrasts an understanding of IL developed from the formal educational context with one developed from a study of workplace learning. Typically, IL in the higher education (HE) context is focused on the transition of learners into university and is aimed at establishing in them what are considered appropriate academic practices: learning how to use the library and online databases, understanding and avoiding plagiarism; in short, knowing how to navigate the academic information landscape (e.g. Rockman, 2004).

These are different skills than those useful in a workplace setting where learning and informational needs are by no means as clear-cut and learning much more often takes place in social groups (what Wenger (1999) calls *communities of practice*). But if Lloyd is right – and there is plenty of evidence to suggest that, at least, her model of IL is a highly compelling one – what damage does this do to not only the aspirations of IL educators, but any HE educator? Must we accept the existence of an irresolvable schism between what we do in the lecture theatre, seminar room and (increasingly) online teaching settings, and what we know our eventual graduates will be expected to do in their later lives (not only 'work', but community and civic life)? Is this why the notion of *transfer* – 'the ability to apply or adapt knowledge to novel contexts' (Pai, Sears and Maeda, 2015, 82) – is so problematic?

For all their richness, Lloyd's theories are not a theory of IL *education*. Nor does she say much about what it actually means to 'map a landscape', despite several references to the process. This book therefore asks how can we teach people to become better navigators of information landscapes and to develop tools – in this case, maps – that help them do so and might help others do so? Can this be done in ways that contribute to the armamentarium of tools and practices that learners will need once the teaching is over? What is happening when students are learning IL in this way – and what facilitates the dialogue between the teacher and the learner?

In *Radical Information Literacy* (2014) I suggested the value of a model of IL that distributed authority over information practices, whether between teachers and learners or among members of communities of practice. However, the pedagogical implications of this stance – in other words, what can be done to teach IL in this way? – were underdeveloped in that book (Pilerot, 2015). In this book, I therefore undertake a detailed investigation of mapping's value to the IL educator. What mapping practices have been developed through history? What representations of physical and information landscapes exist and how do these become the basis for judgements made within these landscapes at given chronotopes? How can mapping be used to empower the learner and how can mapping practice become a constitutive part of the disciplinary and IL knowledge they develop?

Outline

The book's structure is as follows (see also Appendix 2, which displays a concept map of key ideas drawn whilst the book was being written). **Chapter 1** begins with a summary of the diverse ways in which IL has been characterised and then attends in detail to the implications of the strand of IL that defines it as *practice*. Important ideas drawn out in this chapter include the notion that all practices (including IL) take place in sites that are structured by practice architectures defined in the past and are then manifested through embodied action by practitioners, which (at least potentially) impacts upon both the geographic and informational landscapes that intersect at these social sites. Practice has an innately *affective* element and our reactions and judgements made in context can never be reduced entirely to 'rational' or 'objective' judgements. Practice is also innately *social* and this reveals a tension with how IL, as an educational endeavour, has defined itself more as an individual, cognitive capacity rather than a characteristic of groups and communities.

Once these key ideas are established, **Chapter 2** presents a history of mapping practice as it has applied to geographical landscapes. What actually *are* maps, in cognitive and informational terms? What techniques have been developed to represent the world around us and to communicate these representations to others? What impact have these representations – maps – had on education, culture and our collective sense of place and time? The focus in this chapter is on the graphical map, that is, the map as an illustration or visualisation of a landscape, but it is in this chapter that the indivisibility of geographical and information landscapes becomes apparent.

Chapter 3 takes the discussion forward by offering the notion of the *discursive map*, meaning those cognitive schema that structure our thinking and become the basis for judgements about information but which do not necessarily exist in graphical form, instead using more textual and discursive ways of defining and representing certain resources within a landscape and the particular relations between them. This discussion is based on the work of critical geographer David Harvey (1996), whose work also compels attention to how these discursive maps become loci of power and authority. The notion of the discursive map is crucial to understanding how it is not just the production of a map but the *process of mapping* itself that has the greatest impact on learning, for better or worse.

The next three chapters focus on different empirical studies into how graphical and discursive mapping can be used in navigating information landscapes. **Chapter 4** examines these processes at an individual and affective level, drawing on three self-reflective 'psychogeographies': the first of a landscape, and the mental map of this landscape, that are very familiar and up-to-date; the second, a landscape very familiar in the past but not the present; and the third, an unfamiliar landscape. What navigational and mapping techniques come into play in each of these types?

If geographical and information landscapes are indivisible, then mapping should also be able to represent relations between informational concepts that are not necessarily affixed to particular geographical locations: something manifested in the notion of mind, or concept, maps. These types of map are discussed in **Chapter 5,** which reviews a selection of prior studies that have used mapping in IL-based research and teaching. These studies confirm that, at least in a preliminary way, mapping has been shown to have value when it comes to understanding how individuals and small groups make judgements about information. The chapter then looks in more detail at a specific concept mapping technique and explores the outcomes of applying this in a workplace, investigating the impact that mapping had on the collective IL of a group of workplace learners faced with changes to practice that were simultaneously both spatial and informational. How are maps 'talked into being' and so serve as the record of a group judgement? How do less measurable factors, particularly emotion and other affects, come into play?

Chapter 6 then investigates how discursive mapping techniques are evident in how students in an HE setting perceive and structure their information landscapes and how a particular approach to teaching and assessment can help them do so in ways that, at least to some extent, distribute authority over these landscapes. It is in this study that the operations of power are most apparent, particularly through the assessment regime operating in this setting. Yet the study also shows that students can themselves draw on this to *empower* themselves, both individually and as a group. Mapping allows the judgements that have been made within and around this landscape to be *scrutinised* and this is an essential characteristic of more participatory and democratic forms of IL, or what I have previously called 'radical IL' (Whitworth, 2014).

Chapter 7 reviews what has been learned from each of these three empirical chapters and concludes the book by summarising the key arguments.

Acknowledgements

I must acknowledge the many people whose support and encouragement has allowed this book to come into being. Like all workers, academics are busy people, but we are luckier than some in that the institution of the academic sabbatical remains, just about, in place. Without relief from my teaching duties between January and August 2019 it would have been impossible to write this. For facilitating that, I must thank Neil Humphrey, Juup Stelma and Susan Brown of the Manchester Institute of Education at the University of Manchester, UK.

The research projects described in Chapters 5 and 6 were collaborations with colleagues. While what is in these pages is my own interpretation, I am drawing on data that could not have been generated and initially analysed without their help, and on prior publications (these references have been cited properly where they occur). For the 'Changing Libraries' project, covered in Chapter 5, thanks to Maria-Carme Torras i Calvo, Bodil Moss, Nazareth Amlesom Kifle and Terje Blåsternes, and at the end, Chris Hewson. Also, the Norwegian National Library (Norsk Nasjonalbiblioteket) for funding this project. For 'SPIDER', discussed in Chapter 6, thanks most of all to Lee Webster and also Helen Gunter, Camille Dickson-Deane and Linda Corrin for additional work with the dataset. Jose Guerrero helped with the archaeological investigation of information literacy and practice that features in Chapters 1 and 3.

My writing was done in an itinerant fashion and several more people are due thanks for inspiring and supporting this journey. Martin Greenwood inspired Chapter 4 in the first place and was kind enough to share his dissertation with me after its completion. Gillian and Richard Bowerman put me up in their very fine house in Crowborough, Sussex. Roger Hillman of Hereford Cathedral patiently talked me through the magnificent Mappa Mundi while I was ravaged by sinusitis. Mariam Tebourbi took me to the National Gallery of Victoria where I became aware of the rich mapping tradition manifested in Australian Aboriginal art.

Many thanks to Stéphane Goldstein, whose shared interest in maps pointed me in interesting directions. He also read and gave useful feedback on a draft version of the manuscript. Fred Garnett helped start all this off by helping organise a workshop on 'Mapping Information Landscapes' in March 2014 at the University of Manchester, and credit should also go to him and the attendees at that event.

Finally, without Mum and Dad generally, and their allegiance to Alfred Wainwright's *Pictorial Guide to the Lakeland Fells* particularly (see the opening passage of Chapter 7), my life – and interest in maps – would have been quite different. And then there are Clare and Joe, whose love and support for me has never wavered. Thanks to all. And thanks to you, for reading this.

Chapter 1

Information literacy and information practice

Introduction

A full history of IL remains to be written. A commonly-stated position – so frequently presented that it has become a fundamental trope of the field – is that the concept was created in a 1974 report by Paul Zurkowski, presented to the US National Commission on Libraries and Information Science and entitled *The Information Service Environment: Relationships and Priorities*. In Kelly's eulogy to this work and its author, he writes (2014, 1): 'The power of Information Literacy was unleashed in 1974 when Paul G. Zurkowski, Esq., founded the IL movement at the dawn of the Information Age.' The statement is, at best, an exaggeration. Yet, many other writers (Rader, 2002; Eisenberg, Lowe and Spitzer, 2004; Markless and Streatfield, 2007) consider Zurkowski (1974) as such a seminal piece that their histories pay no attention to relevant work that comes before it.

Computerisation may have brought about significant changes to how we work with and learn about information landscapes, but the value of information per se has been recognised for millennia. Socrates recognised 'that knowledge ought to be applied to conduct in the same way as it was already applied with such success to carpentry, shoemaking or medicine' (Lindsay, 1906, xii). Plato would 'persuade those who are to share in the highest affairs of the city to take to calculation, and embrace it in no amateur spirit… until they arrive by the help of sheer intelligence at a vision of the nature of numbers' (Lindsay, 1906, 219). In other words, he affirms the importance of information, an ability to handle it effectively and an objective, dispassionate viewpoint, when it comes to taking effective decisions and planning (military) strategy.

Information, and by extension those trained in its effective use and application, has always been valuable to power holders. The history of espionage, propaganda and surveillance acknowledges this, whether in wartime and/or in asserting political strength at home. Control over information gathering and dispersal is a key element in how consent to dominant political orders is secured less through overt force and more through the manufacturing of consent, or what Gramsci (1971) called *hegemony*. Hegemonic processes include control over culture, education and the media. Dahl (1961) included 'control over information' in his analysis of key political resources.

The library and, more broadly, what Zurkowski calls the 'Information Services Environment' have not been separate from the accumulation of capital and the reinforcement of state power. Salvatore describes how the American Library Association, founded in 1876, promoted 'three defining aspects of industrial capitalism in the progressive era: democratic access, rational order, and mass production' (Salvatore, 2005, 420). Allowing the 'common man' the chance to enter any library and find what was needed required 'uniformity in classification rules and an orderly arrangement of collections' (Salvatore, 2005, 420); '...it was the work of the "practical librarian" to transform this chaotic mass into useful products (bibliographical lists) according to the demands of users' (422). Libraries structured and organised their collections via rigorous, generic cognitive schema (e.g. classification systems).

The 'scholars and businessmen' who were perceived as being those with information needs were thereby not defined as in need of 'user education', that is, the development of their own skills as users of the library collections, able to shape an enquiry and make their own judgements as to relevance and importance. But as the stock of relevant data, information and knowledge grew, even learned readers struggled to keep up. Hence Bush's (1945) speculation about the memex, his proposed (but unbuilt) mechanical information retrieval device in which some have seen a precursor of the internet. It was around this time, with the emergence of computing, that library and information science (LIS) began applying scientific techniques to the problem of archiving and classifying the record of human endeavour in ways that, as far as possible, kept it accessible. Saracevic (1975) in his review of how LIS developed the concept of relevance vis-à-vis information, reports on studies conducted from 1950 onwards. He summarises the definition of an *information system* as follows (1975, 326):

> An information system selects from existing subject knowledge, subject literature and/or any of its representations, organises the selections in some manner in its files, and disseminates the selections in some manner to given destinations.

It is worth keeping this model in mind. In the first place, it hints at the importance of information as *flowing* through a system. Information *moves* from place to place and from the past into the present and future. As a result of this movement, pieces of information may gain value or lose it. Value and relevance are therefore not innate properties of the information itself, applicable at all places and times, but are factors of the chronotope at which these judgements are made. Saracevic's review also highlights that an information system is a *sociotechnical* system – as are all human-built systems, really, but here the human involvement is more than just concerned with the design and construction of the system. The librarian or other information specialist, and users, are actively involved in the workings of the system. At each stage described by Saracevic – *selection*, *organisation* and *dissemination* – techniques can be *taught* and *learned* that optimise the system as a whole. Education in each area could help users:

- Make better selections – that is, describe their needs more precisely, filter out lower-quality sources in advance of the search to streamline it.
- Better organise the found information, placing it with respect to pre-existing cognitive schema (Bartlett, 1932; Blaug, 2007) and reviewing these schema if necessary.
- More effectively communicate and disseminate the results of an enquiry, being aware of the audience and optimum choice of medium for this utterance.

These principles outline a basic agenda for programmes of digital and information literacy education, the importance of which was recognised relatively early on by educational policy makers: 'In 1963 the [US] President's Science Advisory Committee recommended that schools and colleges should develop programs to teach students how to retrieve and use published information' (Lancaster, 1970, 56).

(That it took decades more for such recommendations to be properly enacted, whether in the US or elsewhere, is a story related in Whitworth (2009, 77–81). The development of the BASIC computer language at Dartmouth College in the 1970s and the consequent spread of what would now be termed 'digital literacy' through that institution (Nevison, 1976), remains an interesting exception, but its overall impact on the field was minimal and it is now only a historical curiosity.)

Whatever the claims made by precursors and contemporaries, the significance of Zurkowski's report is undoubted. Although he places it firmly in a neoliberal and uncritical context (compare it with Hamelink (1976)), Zurkowski recognises and defines IL as an *epistemic* practice, that is, as knowledge-creating and knowledge-validating (Knorr Cetina, 2001, 185). The importance of these practices, and the solutions suggested for increasing IL in the US population, are argued for at the macro-level of economy and government. At the micro-level – that is, individual engagement with information and attending to how each person could be taught to work at each of the three stages of the system (selection, organisation, communication) – LIS and the emergent discussions of 'IL education' were leading the response. But the problem of the *meso*-level – collective or group judgements of relevance – had been recognised early on as causing difficulties (Saracevic, 2007): this issue is returned to below.

Library-led IL education

IL education, as a field, began to coalesce in the 1980s, due in no small part to Patricia Senn Breivik's evangelising of IL in the US (e.g. Breivik, 1986; 1991) as the 'added value' that both academic and public libraries brought to education and society as a whole, in response to the *A Nation at Risk* report (Gardner, 1983). But the form that IL took here was a functional one, codified by the ALA and Association of College and Research Libraries (ACRL) through the 1990s, culminating in the ACRL's *Information Literacy Competency Standards for Higher Education* (2000) and similar frameworks such as those of ANZIIL in Australia/New Zealand and SCONUL in the UK. Andretta (2005) compares these frameworks and notes that, in general, their ethos was the production of 'competent information consumers' (Andretta, 2005, 5) and that this would take place in a specifically academic, HE setting. Enacting programmes of education in response to the Standards – usually run from within the institution's library and often 'one-shot' or short series of classes held at the beginning of a student's time at university – took forms epitomised by essays and articles focused on the design of appropriate syllabi and/or testing rubrics, and were gathered in collections like Rockman's (2004) and journals such as *Communications in Information Literacy*.

The ACRL standards had a global impact, with countries as diverse as Taiwan, Iran and Botswana enacting IL programmes based on them (see Whitworth, 2014, 65). However, Pilerot and Lindberg (2011) note how the core idea of IL has therefore been shaped by discursive moves made by powerful organisations like the ALA and the International Federation of Library Associations (IFLA); IL being one element of the export of a 'Western' model of education overseas, and a library-based one, as well. The notion of 'standards' is a move towards creating a generic model of IL and, despite the updating of the ACRL guidance into a 'framework' (ACRL, 2015), Critten (2016, 27) shows how this new framework retains the sensibility of a set of standards even though it was purposefully written not to be a set of standards.

More broadly, the ACRL's dominant presence in this dialogue highlights how the discourse of IL education, and the perception of responsibility for it, have been captured by the academic library to the relative exclusion of other educational settings, such as the HE classroom, schools, public libraries and the workplace. Even Lloyd (2010a, 55ff) assigns the educational role to the librarian. Zurkowski's keynote at the 2013 European Conference on Information Literacy (ECIL) calls for nothing less than the renewal of direct democratic process worldwide and the development of an 'Action Literacy Coalition', but says this is to be based around networks of libraries (Zurkowski and Kelly, 2014, 32–4, 55–7 and elsewhere). Badke (2012), discussing how students must learn research processes, does not locate this programme in the library but emphatically in the disciplinary setting – yet still suggests that effective teaching for research processes cannot happen without the librarian's active involvement in a setting they are not typically integrated with (cf. Secker and Coonan, 2012).

Certainly, librarians and the academic library are significant elements of the information landscape of students in HE, and learning to select, organise and disseminate information in terms of the norms and needs of particular academic disciplines is clearly something that both undergraduates and postgraduates need to learn as part of their education (see Chapter 6). The library plays a similarly important role in the research infrastructure. But IL takes many forms beyond HE. Many people who would benefit from greater awareness of how information systems work and how information landscapes can be most effectively navigated will either never go to university, or have already been and do not intend to (or cannot afford to) return: and even if they are in HE, the disciplinary knowledge and 'softer', more transferable skills that they must acquire there will be developed in many more locations than the library. While acknowledging the importance of the university library, therefore, we must consider what IL looks like beyond it.

Workplace IL and critical IL

Zurkowski expressed concern about the low IL of the US population not because he was worried about students getting low grades at college, but because of its broader impact on the economy and the democratic process. Calculations of the economic impact of low IL have continued to be made (e.g. de Saulles, 2007). Goldstein and Whitworth (2017) considered the question at the level of the organisation, noting that their case study firms used various means to promote the effective gathering, organising and disseminating of information in employees beyond just formal 'training', which was relatively rare (particularly for the smaller organisations). Skills learned in HE have some application in these workplaces, but problems that arose in these settings did so with respect to information landscapes that are quite different from those relevant in HE. The problems thereby take different forms. The 'rhythms' of learning are different in the workplace, with problems needing solving as they come up, rather than being deferred until nearer the next assignment deadline. Problems are also 'fuzzier' and usually not written out in explicit form. But nor do many employees in organisations have to establish their own information needs; more typically, needs are declared or assigned to them (Lloyd, 2010a, 88). And while problem specifications may be fuzzier, processes for handling information may at times be rigorous, whether to protect client confidentiality, commercial sensitivities or to follow legal procedure and so on (Goldstein and Whitworth, 2017, 77). All in all:

> … information need, search, critique and application are given context and relationship, performed as they are under impulses derived from a discourse community (such as a particular profession) whose knowledge structures are to be acquired, interpreted, developed and employed.
>
> (Forster, 2017, 15)

The evident differences between how information, and the processes of its selection, organisation and communication, are conceived of in HE and in the workplace demonstrate how IL can play out in profoundly different ways in these contexts. On top of this, universities are themselves workplaces. The information landscapes students must learn to navigate have been, in large part, defined as the result of workplace processes, which may have little to do with 'academia' per se. For example, virtual learning environments (VLEs, or course management systems) are key elements of the information landscape as far as students are concerned, but Benson and Whitworth (2014) show how their design is only infrequently the outcome of deliberations that are concerned with information literacy and/or scholarship. Such systems, and the regimes of assessment and surveillance with which they are fully integrated, may well act as a barrier to the effective selection, organisation and dissemination of information from the learners' perspective.

For the school of IL educators that espouse a more *critical* approach, the processes involved (whether in the university or society more broadly) in producing and validating certain forms of information must themselves be open to scrutiny and critique, aware that 'all texts are constructed and serve particular interests' (McNicol, 2016, xi). There is no 'correct' way to respond to a text. Various stances can be adopted, a process which itself is partly context dependent. For example, 'a reader may read a novel in one way for pleasure reading and in a very different way if they are being examined … as part of a literature course' (McNicol, 2016, 5). A critical literacy involves awareness of these different stances and perspectives, the role that any text plays in sustaining a particular view of the world. IL must incorporate attention to 'the social construction and cultural authority of knowledge, the political economies of knowledge and control, and the development of local communities and cultures' capacities to critique and construct knowledge' (Holschuh Simmons, 2005, 300).

What *cognitive authorities* (Wilson, 1983) are giving weight to some utterances rather than others? Are these authorities legal, scientific, persuasive, propagandist? What is the *position* of the reader as an active participant in constructing meaning, vis-à-vis these authorities (McNicol, 2016, xii)? If an authority is deferred to, is this based on its weight now or in the past? Has the authority in question become reified, accepted as authoritative because 'that's the way we do things here' and/or because those who wield authority over practice in a given setting cannot be challenged without risk? Or is the basis for this authority more open to scrutiny and possible review (Blaug, 2007)?

Awareness of authority is not just passive, but, ideally, transformational (McNicol, 2016, 7). That is, as originally identified by Freire (1970) and then, with specific reference to IL, Hamelink (1976), it should help learners, in whatever social setting, not just to more effectively use the 'information banks' created by others, but to *develop their own* that are relevant to their own problems and concerns. My description of a framework for *radical information literacy* (Whitworth, 2014) was an attempt to bring Hamelink's neglected view of IL back into the forefront of the field and consider how IL could be the basis for a more directly democratic and, in Habermas's sense (1984/7), decolonising approach to problem-solving, distributing authority over information practices and judgements across members of groups. This approach pays homage to the work of democratic theorists such as Blaug (2007), who recognised how organisations 'push' cognitive schema, ways of thinking and organising information, at their members. In many cases, individual information needs become subordinate to those of the organisation itself and their leaders, a process Blaug calls 'battery cognition'. Are individuals, even whole communities of practice (Wenger, 1999), making judgements about information, organising it and communicating it in their own interests (even as employees), or only in line with the interests of their employer? Or, for students in HE, the interests of the university?

Critical and radical approaches to IL are dialogic (Whitworth, 2014, 1; Linell, 2009) – interested in 'the conversations that arise when information literacy attempts to de-centre authorial intent and turn the lens back on the reader, or learner, as the constructor of meaning' (Critten 2016, 19). Various examples of critical IL programmes are described in McNicol's collection (e.g. Cherry, 2016; Crowley, 2016; and others). Other writers such as Downey (2016) and Elmborg (2006) have done valuable work in exploring how critical pedagogies can be used in IL. Yet these latter authors remain wedded to the library as the principal, even the only possible, source of IL education. Downey in particular invokes a model of a classroom in which power and authority are ideally annulled, with the critical librarian (as IL educator) exhorted to define themselves as 'authority-free'. But why should a librarian be any less a product of their own professional context, and thus able to take a genuinely neutral stance, than an academic? Or, indeed, a friend or family member? Neither Downey nor Elmborg really address these questions.

An IL that is rooted in place and time compels the observation that one's *position* on a discourse cannot be annulled and, arguably, the idea of true neutrality cannot exist (except in the irrelevant instance of where someone is completely ignorant of a discourse). Whether the authorities in a given social site should be accepted or critiqued is something that cannot be determined from outside, but only from within, and that means adopting a position vis-à-vis the practices and landscapes that shape the site.

Practice theory

It is the model that defines IL as a *social practice* that has the most to offer the concerns of the present book. Epitomised by the work of Annemaree Lloyd (particularly 2010a, 2010b), this view is based on the recognition that to function in any social setting we must engage in, and with, a wide range of practices. Within a university, for example, practices such as teaching, learning, grading, conducting experiments, searching for information and so on constitute its core activities. These activities, in turn, take place within an infrastructure which forms, and is formed by, many other practices, including, to name just a few, engineering (of the campus and associated information systems), cooking (everyone needs feeding at lunchtime) and accounting (staff need paying).

In this model, 'practice' is more than just a euphemism for 'activity' or 'form of work'. The practice of teaching, for example, is not just 'something that happens' in a university: rather, it is a fundamental means by which understandings of what a university *is* are communicated and agreed upon; it sets up expectations in learners as to how they can, and should, respond; it is wholly enmeshed with other practices such as the setting of assessments, the giving of feedback and the design of teaching space and virtual learning environments. In short, practice is a locus of authority, and shapes judgements about what is considered relevant in a chronotope and what is not. Teaching as a practice is thereby central to the very constitution of the university as an institution, as are the other practices listed above, simultaneously. Without the engineering practices that constructed the classrooms, offices and laboratories in ways that leave them safe to use and that have embedded resources into these spaces, teaching – at least, most accepted and understood forms of this practice – could not take place. Without the accounting systems that paid these engineers and builders, the construction would not have taken place. And so on. Any university, and any other organisation, is therefore a 'nexus' (Hui et al., 2017) of many different practices. It is through this nexus that the institution is formed and constantly re-formed: practices are the medium by which the tacit and explicit knowledge that flows around the institution are manifested in the activities that make that organisation *intelligible* to all within it and outside it: that allow a university to be identified as a place where many different practices (teaching, researching, working, socialising, playing sports, and so on) occur in certain ways. Because of this nexus, not only particular universities, but the whole idea of 'a university', gain coherence and definition. The same is true for other types of organisation.

Practices are what co-ordinate the diverse work of individuals in social settings; sites 'where understanding is structured and intelligibility articulated' (Schatzki, 1996, 12). Practices, therefore, are what we should examine in order to understand how meaning is made, in concrete and tangible ways, through social activity. Thus, practices have an ontological character; they are the 'stuff' from which the social world is built. Lloyd (2010b, 247) uses practice theory to suggest a more rigorous base for information literacy research, drawing on Schatzki's notion of a *site ontology*:

> … site ontologies … analyse social life as constituted through a site, which is understood as a type of context or social field – a place where coexistence transpires through an ongoing web of interwoven practices and arrangements.
>
> (Schatzki, 2000, 26).

This ontology advances the idea that the world around us is not uniform and smooth, but neither is it chaos, in constant flux and lacking shape. Instead the world is 'lumpy', its fabric constituted by innumerable social sites that achieve some level of permanence. Practices carry meaning between and within these sites. In practice theory, practices are not only a form of communication, they are what make communication possible by making it intelligible and by providing multiple, interlocking frameworks which act as an armature for communication and dialogue.

But practices cannot be easily transferred from site to site as if they were objective constructs. Practices intelligible in one setting may be an awkward fit, or even incongruous, somewhere else. In different settings, different *arrangements* exist; different values come into play, physical settings for practice (like office buildings, say) are organised in spatially different ways; different people, with different subjective preferences, occupy key roles. Practices are enmeshed with these site-specific arrangements and so what exists at social sites, and what we can find out about (epistemology), are 'practice-arrangement bundles' (Schatzki, 2017). These bundles have also been called *practice architectures* (Kemmis and Grootenboer, 2008) and encompass the design of space, systems and procedures, all of which channel information flows and govern what practices are possible and/or sanctioned within a setting. Architectures are not as inflexible as machines, good for only one task: their intention can be creatively adapted, subverted at times, although this often happens 'under the radar' (see Wenger (1999) and his case study of how information claims processors worked both within, and outside of, the practice architectures of their company). Nevertheless, they assert a powerful influence over what practices take place within them.

Practice architectures are partly linguistic in form and character. Wittgenstein introduced the idea of a 'language game' (1953) and Bakhtin the similar notion of *genres* of communication (1986). Both are practice architectures of a sort. Genre is how the 'enunciator's position … is revealed' (Hollway and Knowle, 2000, 77) in the multiplicity of available forms of discourse. Within a given game, or genre, we learn what to say and how, where and when to say it most appropriately or effectively (Curry, 2000, 100). For example, military commands are a genre: the command is expected to be obeyed unquestioningly. Teaching, too, is a genre, with both utterances and responses governed by certain social rules, expectations and preconceptions.

However, Schatzki (2017, 131) criticises Bakhtin for being overly concerned with language and dialogue. While Schatzki agrees that genres are phenomena which shape discourse in broad ways, and for individuals at specific places and times (or chronotopes), he notes that architectures are not only linguistic, they encompass and shape the organisation of practical activity ('doings'), as well as just 'sayings'. It is the context as a whole, its linguistic and non-linguistic elements, its past, present and future, that makes the practice intelligible. An observer of teaching practice who does not speak the language of the teacher may not understand the content of the class but they would almost certainly recognise the practice *as* teaching, by drawing on other contextual factors in the environment, their memory of past practices at school or university, and so on.

Being an effective practitioner involves more than just the application of learned rules, and it means more than just knowing the terminology and other linguistic devices in play in a given setting. It means dealing with what is happening in the *here and now*, perhaps having to respond to something that is only a second or two ago 'in the past', but to which if any judgement is to be an *informed* and *intelligible* one, needs also to be judged with references to norms, architectures and linguistic forms that may have been formed a very long time in the past and in different places. For instance, in most universities' teaching practice, the division of roles, into 'lecturer' and 'students', is reinforced by the layout of many teaching spaces. The very term 'lecture *theatre*' implies that here we have an audience whose role it is to observe the 'performance', learn something, but not interfere with it (note also the original notion of 'operating theatre', where surgery was conducted in public as a learning exercise). The content of the teaching is formed of not just what the teacher is saying, but, for example, how they move around a room, how their utterance is embodied in their physical movement and how the students respond to the performance both verbally and physically. Observer(s), performer(s) and the spatial configuration itself are therefore enfolded into the practice-arrangement bundle that makes the practice intelligible.

These doings and sayings are linked in three main ways:

> (1) through understandings, for example, of what to say and do; (2) through explicit rules, principles, precepts and instructions; (3) through … 'teleoaffective' structures embracing ends, projects, tasks, purposes, beliefs, emotions and moods.
>
> (Schatzki, 1996, 89)

Consider how all of these may come into play in the practice of teaching and learning. A student may understand that, generally, he is expected to pay attention to his professor, and explicit instructions may have been uttered by her to this end, for instance, that this class covers topics that will appear in the forthcoming exam. But he finds this topic impenetrable and it's 4 p.m. on a warm and sunny afternoon. The professor is 'lecturing' even though she knows this is a sub-optimal communicative practice because her administrators booked her class into this theatre when the timetable was set six months ago, a decision that still annoys her.

Shifts in space and time may lead to discontinuities where a point of view, or *personal construct* (Kelly, 1963), formed in the past and/or elsewhere, is challenged by new information or is shown to be less relevant to the present situation. We do not let go of our personal constructs lightly and Kuhlthau's study (1993) of student information seeking showed how doing so can cause 'information anxiety'. Rather than challenge the construct, we may simply reject, or not even notice, information that cannot be reconciled with it. This can lead not only to problems with academic study (Kuhlthau, 1993), but potentially life-threatening failures of information processing: a construct such as 'I am healthy' may be maintained in the face of clear evidence (such as a lump or persistent cough) suggesting a visit to the doctor may be in order.

In his essay on practice, Reckwitz (2017) notes the importance of *affects* such as boredom, anxiety or dissatisfaction. Functional analyses of social systems either do not address affect at all or see it as a problem to be engineered out of the situation where possible. But practice theory's more holistic approach recognises how affect is integral to behaviour within a social site. For example, the 'atmosphere' of a setting and the texts, images and artefacts like clothing that permeate it, are all a factor of how people experience the setting (Reckwitz, 2017, 123–4) and, thus, are part of its practice architecture. In many cases (for example, a courtroom), these spaces have been explicitly designed to produce such reactions and relations, through imposing spatial and professional separations between participants and strict procedural rules that define the roles each group must play and how and when they must make their (effective) utterances. What information is considered relevant in this setting is strictly controlled by the ultimate authority (the judge), an authority invested in not only that individual but the whole judicial landscape and how it is configured.

But affect covers more than just emotional reactions. Schatzki uses the term '*teleo*affective', extending the notion to encompass longer-term factors such as purpose and endpoint. The relevance of information and the effectiveness of practice must be judged not only in the present place and time but with reference to possible futures. What goals are implicit in the design of a given practice architecture? What rewards exist for actors who successfully engage with the practices in this setting? What sanctions may be brought to bear against those who deviate from 'acceptable' practice? And how do projections forward in time, perceptions of possible future rewards or penalties, affect how individuals make judgements here and now?

Architectures legitimate certain practices while making others more difficult to undertake. We learn how we are expected to operate in a situation, becoming socialised into practices that are simultaneously ways of thinking, even feeling. Practices multiply us, we exist at many nexuses, expressing ourselves in different ways. Andretta reports how one of the students on her course, which was aimed at helping information professionals develop communication skills, said: 'Although I am still working on my "academic" style I do feel that I am more aware of what is expected and appropriate for certain scenarios' (Andretta, 2005, 127). Andretta concludes (ibid., emphasis added): 'Self-evaluation was … linked to a better understanding of applying a communication style *that was appropriate to specific situations.*' In other words, her students felt more satisfaction (an affective outcome of learning) when they felt they were better able to adopt and respond to what they perceived as the 'academic' genre of communication and selected, organised and communicated information accordingly. This supports the observation of Tuominen et al. (2005, 337), who note that literacy (and this includes information literacy) essentially means 'being able to enact in practice the rules of argumentation and reasoning that an affinity group in a specific knowledge domain considers good or eloquent'.

Another important element of practice theory is the observation that despite the increasing 'virtualisation' and mobility of our relationship with our information landscapes, thanks to the rise of the internet and communications devices such as mobile phones and Wi-Fi, practices nevertheless retain a specifically *material* element. They do not exist in the abstract, but are embodied in the real, physical world. Harvey (1996, 45) is adamant that we cannot understand theory without appreciating how its consequences – that is, practice(s) – become embedded in 'the materialities of place, space and environment'. In some cases, as with the lecture theatre or courtroom examples given earlier, the spatial configuration of a setting is essential to understanding the practices taking place within it. Goldstein and Whitworth (2017, 77) reported how in two of their three case studies, the spatial configuration of the organisation's office had been specifically arranged to facilitate information sharing between employees residing at different levels of the hierarchy. The senior executives of these organisations recognised the value of this configuration in both a financial and cultural sense.

And as well as space and other people:

> … objects (and events) as well acquire meaning within practices. This occurs, most importantly, whenever objects are used in the performance of constituent actions. Teaching, for instance, encompasses writing on blackboards and other surfaces with certain entities, which therewith receive the meaning: things with which to write…. These meanings are 'practical' meanings, and the entities possessing them can be called, following Heidegger, 'equipment' (*Zeug*). Like understanding generally, the understanding of equipment is expressed not only in doings, (i.e., uses) but also in sayings.
>
> (Schatzki, 1996, 113)

Thus, even if one's relationship with information is increasingly mediated through the mobile devices we carry around with us, these devices are still material objects 'used in the performance of constituent actions' and thus 'equipment' in this Heideggerian sense. Equipment is what roots practices in particular places and times. Without these material objects, practice can still be conceived in general terms and this level of awareness is called, by Schatzki (1996, 96ff), *dispersed practice*. An example is the practice of accounting. Most people could probably offer a broad definition of what 'accounting' encompasses in a general sense, that is, it helps individuals or companies control their finances, record income and expenditure and make calculations of profit and loss. They may also have a sense that there are legal and moral imperatives behind the need to account for these flows, such as taxation or the detection of fraud or theft. But to *embody* the dispersed practice of accounting and thereby *integrate* it into a setting, at least some basic equipment is required, even if just pencil and paper; more commonly these days, a spreadsheet and a device on which this spreadsheet can be stored and interacted with. And whatever is accounted for, its summation as a quantity, a debit or credit, represents another material process, such as the movement of goods, the use of energy, and so on. How these are represented on the spreadsheet, how relations are established thereon in ways that most effectively serve the needs of the accounting practitioner, these are aspects of the practice that have to be learned in a particular context: based on a broad, generic understanding of what 'accounting' means as a (dispersed) practice, but encompassing 'interwoven understandings of interrelated equipment' (Schatzki, 1996, 114) and of the informational flows in that context.

In summary then, 'Social space… consists of the organisation of interrelated artefacts, interpreted by both participants and observers' (Reckwitz, 2017, 115). And:

> When a practice, as is usually the case, is carried out in specific settings, the settings are set up to facilitate the efficient and coordinated performance of its constituent actions. The layouts of the settings, as a result, reflect the interwoven meanings that the entities used in those actions possess by virtue of being so used (and talked about) …. their setups derive from the understandings, rules and teleoaffective structure organising the practice …. things are usually so arranged that they can be easily used in the correct and acceptable ways.
>
> (Schatzki, 1996, 114)

Practice as a collective property

Some philosophical arguments about practice theory are worth investigating. First, the question of whether practices are so fundamental as to be ontological, or whether they are just an outward expression of something further, lying within practitioners, whether this be knowledge, thoughts or moods. But neither forms of knowledge, nor emotions, are 'unobservable internal events inside the heads of human agents' (Schmidt, 2017, 141), only manifested after a subsequent internal calculation of how to express these events in practice. Schatzki (1996, 73) states that: 'How things stand and are going is essentially articulated in what people do and say. It is not an already formed thing that they try to describe in words' and notes Wittgenstein's teaching 'that meaning lies in use and not in something that at the time of speaking or writing either takes place or comes before the mind' (ibid., 95). Thus, these 'internal' deliberations are negotiable and observable elements of practice and practice a fundamental characteristic of the extant, built world, rather than the mere representation of something immaterial.

Are people the helpless pawns of practice? Fated to do no more, nor less, than is expected of them by the social setting? This position too can be refuted. As stated by Barnes (2001, 34): 'Rules can never be sufficiently informative or well exemplified to keep instances of rule-following behaviour relevantly identical in all the diverse situations wherein rules are followed.' Practice is unfinalisable, which means that within it there is scope for many creative reactions to a situation. Schatzki (1996, 86) notes that: 'As practices evolve, so do possibilities; and it is never possible even in principle to draw up a complete inventory of a field's contents.' Hui (2017) notes the 'natural' variation in practices. Even where all other things seem equal (e.g. context, membership of groups, material arrangements), people will decide to do things in different ways just because that's what they do; for example, not everyone makes a sandwich in the same way, even with the same ingredients to hand (see also Schatzki, 1996, 53). Like variation in utterances, the richness and multiplicity of possible interpretations is a source of creativity, an encounter from which new ideas emerge and are enacted (Bakhtin, 1984, 166).

Thus, even though practices are transmitted between individuals and groups and are organised into practice-arrangement bundles in ways that give them permanence in the flux, they do not become automated. Individuals must not be seen as 'prisoners' of the socialising process, for all that this process can have very strong influence (Harvey, 1996, 96). Barnes notes how practices:

> … have to be generated on every occasion, by agents concerned all the time to retain coordination and alignment with each other in order to bring them about. Although they are routine at the collective level, they are not routine at the individual level. This is why there is point in referring to a practice as the shared possession of a collective.
>
> (2001, 33)

This axiom makes it necessary to return to the question of how groups make judgements of relevance and whether there can be such a thing as a *collective* information literacy (cf. Harris, 2008). Philosophers such as List and Pettitt (2011) have explored how individual decisions can be aggregated and whether groups can be said to have agency independently of the agency of the members: List and Pettitt, at least, conclude that they can. But in LIS, the problem has then been how to instantiate these collective judgements in information systems. Saracevic (2007, 2135) notes a central 'conundrum', one that sheds doubt on whether more than a 'weak' view of relevance can inform the technological design of information systems. How can relevance be evaluated, and instantiated in a system supporting effective information retrieval, when the human judgements that must be captured are unstable and inconsistent? A 'Pandora's box' (ibid., 2134) was opened through a study by Gull (1956), which investigated group judgements and found that different people rated the relevance of the same information quite differently from each other and would not change their impressions *even after being shown the judgements of others*. From that point on, a central trope of LIS was 'never to use more than a single judge per query' (Saracevic, 2007, 2135).

Saracevic's conundrum stems, in part, from the laboratory-style methods typically used to capture judgements of relevance and which idealise and simplify the messy reality of information behaviour and of IL more broadly. Test subjects, invariably HE students or academics, conduct set-piece information searches and report on the criteria they use to judge whether retrieved texts are relevant or not. Yet this 'does not take into account a host of situational and cognitive factors that enter into relevance assessments and that, in turn, produce significant individual and group disagreements' (Saracevic, 2007, 2132). Judgements about relevance are not always conscious, often being made against the background of practice architectures, judgements of the cognitive authority of others (Wilson, 1983) and tacit knowledge that 'cannot be articulated through text' (Lloyd, 2010a, 21), including 'cues, embodied understandings, sensitivities, perceptions, tricks of the trade' (ibid., 17). All such understandings will vary from person to person even in the same chronotope, being based on decisions that have been made in the past and in other places: histories that cannot be the same for everyone.

Yet nor are people atoms, uninterested in the opinions and understandings of others. There needs to be a basis for this understanding that lies in the teleoaffective goals of the group itself. While studies like Gull's may use multiple subjects, there is no evidence that the groups described are *communities*, groups that identify as collectives with shared learning needs (Wenger, 1999). The notion of a 'community' is a complex one, with the term being applied in the modern world to many collectives, including those based around not only a geographic setting but also religion, sexuality, sports or music fandom, even sufferers of the same disease. In each, the members of a community *share* something (this is implied in the Latin root of the word, *communis*, meaning to have in common: evident also in words like commune, Communism and, most significantly, communication). As Harris points out in his critique of the dominant, and individualised, model of IL:

> ... all communities – in or outside of the academy – offer opportunities to learn and may require displays of information and knowledge. Physical and virtual constructions of social communities, civic groups, religious organizations, professional associations, as well as communities of work are all learning communities. These 'communities of practice' include members that are chosen or self-selected who share specific goals and topics of interest. Information is often created, disseminated, and utilized by members to support the goals of the group.

> Collaboration and experiential development are necessary activities in communities of practice, and specific or unique uses of language may develop between members.
>
> (Harris, 2008, 248)

In such social and collaborative settings, the reality of intersubjective, community-based judgements of relevance is apparent. In the work of authors like Wenger and Lloyd, the idea that individuals can be socialised into the literacy practices and judgements that are made in an organisational setting depends on the notion that somehow, whether tacitly or explicitly, agglomerations of individual judgements coalesce into relevance criteria that are then applied by community members. These judgements may not always be *conscious*, but they are nevertheless *performed*. And through these accumulated performances, practice emerges as an intersubjective agreement through which the information landscape of the group or community is continuously negotiated. Wenger, White and Smith (2009) describe how members of communities, whom they term 'stewards', make judgements about the technologies and communicative spaces (such as e-mail lists or discussion boards) that the community configures around itself to fulfil its shared learning needs: Wenger et al. call this the *digital habitat*. The ideal stewards are continuously assessing the learning needs of the group and configuring this habitat (a form of practice architecture) accordingly. They are also working to distribute stewarding capacity across the group, educating other community members to become stewards (Wenger, White and Smith, 2009, 27).

'Saracevic's conundrum' is therefore not a refutation of the existence of these intersubjective processes, but a statement of an epistemological problem. The problem is how to raise the group's awareness of these processes, then capture them in ways that do not reify or institutionalise the judgements but allow the community to scrutinise them, review them if necessary, and thus distribute authority over information (and for Wenger et al,, stewarding) practice across the group (Whitworth, 2014). But as Harvey (1996, 426) says: 'communities, while not without significance, cannot be understood independent of the social processes that generate, sustain and also dissolve them… it is these socio-spatial processes that are fundamental to social change.' Thus, the judgements that individuals and groups make *in practice* can only be revealed and evaluated with reference to the properties of the social settings in which these judgements are made, and the broader currents of discourse and activity that govern practices at the macro-scale, including laws, public policy, technological change and the processes of capital accumulation.

Information literacy as a practice

What are the consequences of practice theory for the study of IL? Lloyd builds directly on Schatzki's ideas, stating that:

It is through the ontological notion of site and the theoretical framing of practice developed by Schatzki that information literacy can be understood as a critical information practice which is organised and arranged through the site of the social, rather than as a reified and decontexualised set of skills, cast adrift and remote from the discourses and practices that influence and drive human activity and interaction.

(Lloyd, 2010b, 252)

More specifically:

… the process of becoming information literate and developing information literacy practice is constructed and nuanced according to practical understandings (knowing how to do things like searching for information), rules (explicit formulations that direct how a thing is done or what counts) and teleoaffective structures (the overarching purpose, mood or feelings that are linked to tasks) which characterise the social site through which it emerges. Consequently, information literacy should be viewed as a practice that occurs inside other practices, and as such, the unit of analysis for researchers should not be on information skills, but on the sociocultural affordances furnished within a site that lead to the development of information skills.

(Lloyd, 2010b, 247)

And finally, noting the integration of various concepts – the importance of equipment, language use, the collective, meso-level and the operations of authority – into this understanding:

In the process of learning, people interact with the tools of practice (objects, signs, technologies and language) and the activities that define group practices and signify membership. Through these interactions they engage and are introduced to the information modalities and information activities that are sanctioned and legitimised by the community. This experience of information is managed and directed by experienced members of the group and has a twofold purpose. First, it enables new members to engage with the coded information that will enable the formation of a recognisable and acceptable identity that reflects knowledge about practice as it is understood by the community. Secondly, by introducing new members to sanctioned ways of knowing, the community ensures the maintenance of group culture and tradition, enabling new members to develop a sense of place.

(Lloyd, 2010a, 20)

The last word in that quote is highly significant. Much of the foregoing discussion about practice theory, and Lloyd's subsequent work, has drawn not only on the material specificity of the social setting – all information landscapes are engaged with in specific chronotopes, they are not purely 'virtual' – but also on less tangible concepts that are nevertheless couched in terms of 'positionality' or 'relations', such as the notion that one's positionality with regard to dominant discourses is a factor in how comfortably one's practice is served by a given practice architecture. All come together in developing the 'sense of place' that Lloyd mentions.

Does one *feel* in place, or out of place, in a social site? If knowledge and skills have been developed in one particular place, like a university, with its accumulated practice architectures of long standing and great influence over both students and teachers alike, how well can they transfer into the 'outside world' and its many other places in which the programme of study can pay off, whether for the benefit of the student (as an employable individual) or for society as a whole, benefiting from their disciplinary knowledge and their information literacy?

Transferability of knowledge from place to place *must* be more than just replicating a learned process, because in different places, different practice architectures *inevitably* exist. But being a more effective user of diverse information systems, knowing how to navigate a landscape, making effective use of communications media to disseminate insights – all the basic characteristics of information systems (Saracevic, 1975) – these are reflexive capacities that help learners (Alkemeyer and Buschmann, 2016, 11, emphasis added) 'become able to adjust and improve their participation in the context of not just one practice but many similar practices in a process of *learning self-structuration*'. This is an *educational* process that requires attending to different modalities of information outlined by Lloyd (2010, 161ff):

> Epistemic modalities act as knowing locations for know-why or know-that information, which has been codified into written rules and regulations for practice, which can be clearly articulated and evaluated against a set of sanctioned criteria. Information within this modality is used to enact the institutional identity that enables members to be recognised. Universities, schools and training organisations are centralised around epistemic modalities and their information practice, activities and skills are shaped by epistemic forms of knowing, through disciplinary knowledge often seen as fixed and invariable in time and space. From an organisational perspective, this modality reflects the public face of the institution or organisation, for both employees and the general public. It will be highlighted through the rules, regulations and guidelines for internal and external practice. (161)
>
>   The social modality … is sources from the situated experience of collective participation, practice and reflection on action. Social information is drawn from an individual's personal biography as well as collective histories of people in shared practice. Foundational to this modality is experiential information, and information that represents the real and ongoing values and beliefs of participants in practice…

Social modalities are closely associated with reflection and reflexivity about professional practice and professional identity. (163–4)

The corporeal modality is formed through experience and manifests in information that is embodied and situated… This type of information is tacit, or contingent, and it is disseminated through demonstration and observation of practice or accessed through the tactile and kinaesthetic activity associated with actual practice. (164–5)

None of these three modalities – epistemic, social and corporeal – can stand alone: all interplay in practical settings where individuals or group must make judgements about information. Typically, however, as Lloyd notes, the HE institution and the practice architectures (most pertinently, regimes of assessment) around which it is built, tend to reinforce the epistemic modality over other types (Lloyd, 2010a, 161). But learning 'self-structuration' is not just a matter of positioning oneself with respect to disciplinary texts and information. It also involves attending to where one is located within a social network, how well one can engage in dialogue with others that accords with each party's teleoaffective needs at this particular place and time, and how well these judgements can become embodied in material practices that externalise them, constituting an utterance or performance of some kind to which other members of the collective can respond.

The social modality contributes to the *becoming* of the practitioner, the development of an identity and teleoaffective goals ('I *can* do this!') (Lloyd, 2010a, 162). All combine into the ability to understand both one's own personal objectives and those of the community; to make informed judgements about the relevance of both information and technology to fulfil consequent individual and collective learning needs; to organise and configure these habitats (or landscapes) accordingly; and to effectively communicate and disseminate these understandings both within and outside the group. These characteristics combine into what Wenger et al. (2009) call the 'stewarding' role and what Lloyd and other adherents to the practice-based model would define as information literacy. These capacities will therefore be used as the fundamental model of IL that will be used in the remainder of this book.

In summary then:

… understanding the nature of information literacy requires us to explore how people experience information in context and how this experience is afforded in relation to the:

- discourse (the social actions, including language) of the context, which position a person in particular ways towards modalities of information that characterise in situ (site-specific) knowledge …;

- affordances or opportunities furnished within the context, which enable or constrain access to information …;
- discursive practices (actions that are valued and sanctioned) related to information practice that are socially and discursively sanctioned and played out in context.

(Lloyd, 2010a, 158)

And the IL *educator* must in turn ask: how can these understandings be gained? Where are appropriate interventions possible and where will they be most effectively made? One thing that the discussion of practice theory has suggested is that these interventions cannot be made only in the library, academic, public or otherwise. Even Lloyd (e.g. 2010a, Chapter 3) falls back into talking about the library as the 'place' for IL. Even where studies have been done of the vocational education sector, there is, often, still a focus on the librarian as the locus of IL (e.g. Gasteen and O'Sullivan, 2000). Yet this boundary, as well as those that exist around given academic disciplines, must be crossed. Badke says, bemoaning the failure of IL to make noticeable inroads into improving students' research skills, that whatever is done to improve matters:

… educators are going to need to move from teaching about their disciplines to enabling their students to become disciplinarians. The expression, 'welcome to my world', encapsulates the goal … We must invite students into our world and there reproduce ourselves in them, turning our students into active practitioners in our disciplines.

(Badke, 2012, 93)

Thus, Badke suggests learners must be introduced to the practices in play in these settings and develop the capacity to critique these practices and the authority invested within them when necessary to do so. Welcoming learners into a given information landscape means attending to not only their knowledge of the discipline, how it is structured and configured and the terms and concepts in use, but also the social and corporeal modalities in play in that setting, the way that practice is performed and the ways that groups and communities form around spatial, technological and informational practice architectures. What cognitive schema, or ways of thinking, are prevalent among practitioners in the setting? What genres, technologies and practice architectures must be handled to develop knowledge in this setting? What authorities exist and, after scrutiny, should this authority be accepted or challenged and on what grounds?

These are all epistemological problems. As Haraway says, with particular reference to the last of these questions, epistemology 'is about knowing the difference' (1990, 203)· not a collapse into relativism, a nihilistic challenge to *all* authority even when knowledge claims are based on legitimate expertise and objective, scientific procedure (cf. Thompson, 2008), but on *informed learning* (Bruce, 2008), which can take place in formal education (schools or HE), the workplace, public life and inside communities of practice. Harvey asks, 'What is this 'epistemology' which permits us to know the difference? How should we pursue it? And to what politics does it give rise?' (1996, 358). His answer is that, at least, it is an epistemology 'which can understand the social processes of construction of situatedness, places, otherness, difference, political identity and the like' (1996, 363).

This sounds like an agenda for IL as an epistemology. It is therefore time to move on, to talk about how mapping could be part of this agenda, and whether it can add the 'robustness' to IL that writers like Badke demand.

Chapter 2

Maps and mapping

Introduction

This chapter explores how mapping has been used over the last two millennia as a technique for documenting, representing and communicating understandings of the world around us, and how it has consequently impacted on our perception of place and time and our ability to navigate the landscapes (mapped and unmapped) that we encounter. It examines mapping as a genre of communication, a methodology, and a social, material knowledge-forming practice. Starting here, but continuing more explicitly in Chapter 3, it also investigates mapping as a source of power: maps can empower their users, but also disempower them (and others), particularly if one is left 'off the map' for any reason (Bonnett, 2015).

This is not a story written by a cartographer or geographer. Scholars in these fields have documented the rich history of mapping both by examining the documents that it has produced (that is, the maps themselves) and by analysing mapping as a *practice* that helps us both produce the world and consume it (Kitchin et al., 2009, 4; Cosgrove, 1999). I am not making any substantial additions to these histories. But as my goal is to establish the educational value of mapping and how it can help learners make informed judgements about information, I must explore mapping as an *epistemological* and *methodological* practice; a way of developing, and validating, knowledge about information landscapes and the social sites with which they are integrated. Put simply, what can we learn about our information landscapes through mapping them? How can mapping help learners engage with the different modalities of information (epistemic, social and corporeal), and the different stages of information processing (selection, organisation and communication)?

Lloyd mentions this possibility on several occasions. Early on in *Information Literacy Landscapes* she says:

Information landscapes are the communicative spaces that are created by people who co-participate in a field of practice. As people journey into and through these landscapes they engage with site-specific information. *This engagement allows them to map the landscape, constructing an understanding of how it is shaped.* It is through this engagement that people situate themselves within the landscape.

(Lloyd, 2010a, 2, emphasis added)

In a study of the IL practices of refugees, it is noted that:

… they begin to identify the activities and refine the skills that will provide them with opportunities to *develop a map of the information landscape* and which will furnish them with chances to *engage with information that orients them within their new community.*

(Lloyd et al., 2013, 11, emphases added)

Lloyd also suggests mapping's value for IL researchers and practitioners, paying particular attention to transferability:

… in information literacy research, understanding how the features and characteristics of a given context shape, form and influence the participant's experience with information becomes an important task for the researcher. Viewing this experience through its context allows us to see what activities and processes influence the nature and manifestation of information literacy. It also allows us to understand which of these are transferable and which have specific temporal and spatial dimensions. Therefore, the first task for researchers and practitioners becomes the *mapping of the context or setting.*

(Lloyd, 2010a, 157, emphasis added)

All in all, for Lloyd, the notion of mapping seems more than just a metaphor encouraged by the term 'information landscape' and, based on the discussion of her work and practice theory given in Chapter 1, so it should be. The 'site-specific information' she mentions, which will include definitions of place, time, equipment, social relations, authority and so on, exists in complex configurations, and how one is 'situated' or positioned relative to these configurations is a significant factor in evaluating whether particular practices are to be rewarded or penalised in this social setting. Having access to a good map of this landscape will help greatly in determining this positioning. Yet at no point in these works is much greater detail offered that might help either researcher or practitioners move beyond the metaphor. What does 'mapping an information landscape' actually involve – practically, discursively, educationally? Can one only learn to do this in context-specific ways or are the skills transferable to other social sites? How does mapping impact on the 'experience of information in context' (Lloyd, 2010a, 158) and the discourses, affordances and practices that shape that experience?

The practice of mapping

Answering these questions requires an understanding of mapping as a practice. How can the word, the concept, be slotted into phrases that Schatzki uses, like '… something's making sense to someone as Z [where Z might equate to "a map"] regularly presupposes her participation in or familiarity with practices in which things are correctly or acceptably understood as Z' (1996, 114). Thus, whatever the practice of mapping is, it needs first to be *intelligible* as such, even if the product of this intelligible practice, a map developed in a particular chronotope, will not have a single meaning. All maps, and people's understanding of them, are complex, open to different understandings acquired in different practice architectures (Schatzki, 1996, 116). A map might be something to draw, to use in navigation, to admire as art, to guide a choice, to have examined and graded. And yet within these various applications, is there a set of underlying principles that can be used to define and recognise mapping when it is taking place?

Fundamentally, mapping is a process by which the world, and relations within it, are represented. Cosgrove states that a map is a 'register of correspondence between two spaces, whose explicit outcome is a space of representation' (1999, 1). A map makes propositions (Kitchin et al., 2009, 13–14). With geographical maps, or cartographs, the central proposition is 'this is there', followed by 'you are here' – and by being 'here' the user of the map is positioned in a certain relation to whatever is 'there'. The propositions made by the cartograph can then be explored in the world. Other informational devices and tools display objects and their relations; a spreadsheet, for example, displays and calculates relations between values and one can define temporal and spatial locations on a spreadsheet (for example, business accounts displayed by month and department). Maps of non-geographical spaces and places are commonly found, with organisational charts and concept maps just two types (see Chapter 5). But cartographs are more naturalistic than these other forms of map. Elements upon them are depicted in ways that correspond to relations and pathways we can potentially explore using bodily activity and experience (Morton, 2002, 50): that is, in practice.

Beyond this, cartographs function as informational devices that extend the capacity of the human body, allowing it to 'see' (acquire information) at scales not otherwise possible (Cosgrove, 2008, 168). A world map, and the shapes and relations of the continents that it displays, is an image of great familiarity, but it would take a considerable amount of time and effort to confirm all the propositions it makes. And as Corner notes: 'some phenomena … can *only* achieve visibility through representation rather than through direct experience' (1999, 229). A seminal moment in the use of mapping as a device for representing information (and difference) was Snow's study of a cholera outbreak in London in 1854, which led to his identifying the source of the outbreak as a contaminated water pump; previously, cholera had been believed to be an airborne infection. Once the locations of cases – the difference between two states, infected and uninfected – was plotted on Snow's map, the pattern was made visible and better preventive methods resulted. Without this informational device, the correlation between cases of cholera and proximity to this particular pump went unidentified. (However, see Brody et al. (2000) for a more critical assessment of Snow's work.)

Maps extend our perception at the temporal scale, allowing us to perceive the past. Most obviously, a map is a historical 'snapshot' (albeit, not always an accurate one) of the configuration of a landscape in the past. From such records, change can be inferred. I own a map of the Netherlands from c.1850 and around one-sixth of the present land area of that country was absent at that time, having not yet been reclaimed from the Zuider Zee. Past processes can be judged from contemporary maps, as well. It does not take an expert knowledge of geography to know that U-shaped valleys, finger lakes and steep-sided mountains indicate that glaciers once covered a landscape, and such evidence of the past is as clear from a map of, say, northern England or Norway, as much as from observation of the landscape itself. Geological maps, showing rock strata, make the different *layering* processes that have created a landscape even more apparent.

Onto these layers of rock and soil, human activity has deposited further historical and social layers, processes which can also be deduced from examining a map. Harvey (1996, 417) notes that the modern city is a multi-layered *palimpsest*, layers superimposed on each other with the passing of time, with earlier layers often concealed by later ones, yet still profoundly influencing their form: Hommels (2005) terms this phenomenon 'obduracy'. A medieval gathering place may well still be a city's main square, arterial roads having long been directing flows of traffic (and capital) towards it, and centuries of everyday activity having imbued it with status:

> What has gone before is important precisely because it is the locus of collective
> memory, of political identity, and of powerful symbolic meanings at the same time
> as it constitutes a bundle of resources constituting possibilities as well as barriers ...
> (Harvey, 1996, 417)

Lloyd, in turn, observes how layering and obduracy also apply to information landscapes, integrated with the geographical:

> Information landscapes are intersubjectively created spaces that have resulted from
> human interaction, in which information is created and shared and eventually
> sediments as knowledge. Consequently as an information landscape (just like a

physical landscape) evolves, its social, historical, political and economic layers are deposited to form the foundations of the intersubjective space.

(Lloyd, 2010a, 9–10)

Maps are not just documents of the past history of landscapes but are tools that shape this process into the future. Maps both create and record the world. Some cities (for example, St Petersburg and Brasilia) were maps before they existed on the ground (Cosgrove, 2008, 171). Maps are used to govern discourse and suggest future directions for practice: 'mapping is particularly instrumental in the construing and constructing of lived space…. the function of mapping is less to mirror reality than to engender the reshaping of the worlds in which people live' (Corner, 1999, 213). Who has authored a map and why, and what they have selected for inclusion or emphasis on the map – these are important questions when it comes to understanding a map in the fullest sense. Cosgrove makes a crucial point:

… position and context are centrally and inescapably implicated in all constructions of knowledge…. Not only is all mapping 'cognitive' in the broadest sense, inescapably bound within discursive frameworks that are historically and culturally specific, but all mapping involves sets of choices, omissions, uncertainties and intentions – authorship – at once critical to, yet obscured within, its final product, the map itself.

(Cosgrove, 1999, 7)

Authoring of a map is underpinned by a 'complex accretion of cultural engagements with the world' (Cosgrove, 1999, 9) and, in turn, the map is inserted into 'various circuits of use, exchange and meaning' (ibid.). Maps therefore '*make* reality as much as they represent it …. [they] inscribe power and support the dominant political structures' (Crampton and Krygier, 2006, 15). All in all, mapping is a medium with discursive power (Kitchin et al., 2009, 3).

This power could not emerge were mapping not an intelligible practice, identifiable *as* mapping and built around shared expectations and discourses, particular practice architectures and equipment, as is the case with other integrated practices, such as teaching:

Maps are impossible without a shared belief about the materiality and the reality of the world they display, about the claim of the drawing to stand as a substitute for this world, more accessible to study than the reality itself.

(Jacob, 1999, 25)

How, then, do maps work? How do they represent the world in ways that make their mappings intelligible, even to those users who may never have visited the landscape being depicted?

Mapping space and place

Mapping can be a scientific, objective practice, a personal, subjective practice, and a social, intersubjective one. Each realm of knowledge is integrated into any map and its use. Understanding the difference between them is important for establishing the distinction between *place* and *space* that is essential to an understanding of how mapping plays different and sometimes contradictory roles in representing and shaping the world.

Cartography as a technical practice depends on the development of systems of representation. For example, modern 'Western' cartography was significantly defined by Mercator's projection, first published in 1569. With some adjustments to correct distortions in the sizes of polar lands, it is still familiar today. Lines of latitude and longitude, and other co-ordinate systems like the UK's National Grid, are widespread and familiar ways of creating a data 'net' into which observations about the world can be slotted and thereby made quantitative and generalisable. Conventions are employed, for example the typical placing of north at the top of the map. These levels of abstraction and informational transformation mean that a map of somewhere one has never been remains intelligible and useful in navigation. A map is thus 'more than an imaginative picture' (Cosgrove, 2008, 168). Rather:

> Numbers, lines, colours and key coding reinforce the thematic map's scientific status as an 'immutable mobile', to borrow the philosopher of science Bruno Latour's term for an instrument that preserves the meaning and truth claims of scientific observations as they circulate across space and time.
>
> (Cosgrove, 2005, 37)

However, while these functions and representations work well to depict the world as *space,* abstractions like these are, alone, less effective at depicting *place*. Bonnett (2015, 4) quotes the famous line from *Moby Dick*: 'It is not down on any map; true places never are'. And he states how we need to reassert the centrality of place rather than the abstraction of space, even if:

> … modern intellectuals and scientists have hardly any interest in place for they consider their theories to be applicable everywhere …. Space sounds modern in a way place doesn't: it evokes mobility and the absence of restrictions … empty landscapes filled with promise.
>
> (Bonnett, 2015, 3)

A place is, in part, defined by its geographic location, its co-ordinates on the globe. At this location there will be infrastructure: a 'material setting for social relations' (Withers, 2009, 640). Overlaid on this infrastructure over time, however, is the 'experiential essence of a setting, interpreted and imbued with values and meanings' (Gibson and Kaplan, 2017, 132). It is place, not space, that is the 'locus of collective memory' (Harvey, 1996, 304) and the landscape of that place an 'ever-vigilant ally in the efforts of individuals and whole communities to put into practice a set of standards for social living that are uniquely and distinctively their own' (Basso, 1984, cited in Harvey, 1996, 305). Thus, it is against the construct of place that judgements are made about information. Information landscapes are outcomes of not space, but place, and the material, cognitive and affective basis of practice in a given social site.

For example, capital is fixed in places, but differentially, resulting in difference and otherness being '*produced* in space through the simple logic of uneven capital investment' (Harvey, 1996, 295). Such uneven investments impact on poverty and disadvantage in various ways, including informationally. Gibson and Kaplan studied the information horizons of parents in five US states who all had children with Down's syndrome. For these parents, the physical proximity of certain information services to their home was a central factor in their evaluation of the relevance and usefulness of these services (Gibson and Kaplan, 2017, 135). While the internet was accessible at home for most participants and thus 'does not represent additional effort or travel time to resolve an information need' (ibid.), there remained barriers to exploiting it, including poor language skills and poor connectivity, particularly in rural places. There were also information needs that these parents could not meet at home, including those related to childcare, therapy, special schools and recreational activities. Rural parents were once again disadvantaged compared to urban families, with services located further away and many Down's-specialising therapists less willing to travel out to their homes (ibid., 136). As these rural families were also more likely to be African-American, race and place are both determining factors in relative information poverty (Thompson, 2007).

Mapping *can* depict place and the relations between places, but when it does so it must adopt techniques that are less generalisable and more place- and community-specific. The rooting of mapping in a deep understanding of a given place, one that is material and symbolic, geographical and informational, is evident with the mapping practices developed by Aboriginal populations of Australia. Any worthwhile discussion of the depth and richness of the geographical and cultural information embedded in Australian Aboriginal art requires a more intimate knowledge of those landscapes and traditions than I possess (see Belk and Groves, 1999; Morphy, 2001; Coleman, 2005). However, to offer a subjective example, see the work of the artist Donkeyman Lee Tjupurrula, which can be viewed at https://www.ngv.vic.gov.au/explore/collection/work/2496/.

The work shown at this URL is entitled *Tingarri Dreaming at Walawala*, and was displayed in the National Gallery of Victoria, in Melbourne, Australia, on 7 April 2019. At that time it was shown along with an explanatory card that stated the following information about the artist and artwork, and which made it clear that what is seen in the gallery is a map:

Donkeyman Lee Tjupurrula: Kukatja [people], c.1921–94
Tingarri Dreaming at Walawala
1989 Balgo, Western Australia. Synthetic polymer on canvas …
The artist maps water sources and major landforms of his Country, Walawala near Kiwirrkura in the Gibson Desert. The three large roundels depict major water sources of Pilginya, Tingarijara and Porurunya, from which patches of vegetation spring. The parallel contour lines represent sandhills, which dominate this terrain. The smaller concentric circles are waterholes, the green and white lines indicate grasses coming up after rains, and the red curving line is a creek. Above the grassy area is a cluster of sacred caves and a small billabong; below is a medicine place for men of high degree marked by black lines.

This is more than just the contextual information that art galleries typically provide about location; for example, where a picture was painted or, if a landscape or urban panorama, an explanation of why the artist felt moved to paint it (that is, the context). Here, the artwork, the mapping and the landscape itself are presented as entirely integrated. We are clearly informed that we are looking at a map and are given guidance on how to read it. The map is not necessarily recognisable as such to those who do not share the artist's cultural traditions, but there is no reason why one would expect an Ordnance Survey map of northern England, say, to be instantly intelligible to someone from the Gibson Desert who was unfamiliar with its systems of representation either. With any map, one must be taught to read and interpret the symbols, assisted by a collective matrix of interpretation that permits the relating of the symbolism to one's understanding of the places being represented. But armed with this guide, one can indeed 'read' this map. For example, it is clear what resources are important – both symbolically and in practice – in this place with its harsh climate: water most of all, fertile land, but also, we can deduce, ritual and the social structures (possibly, patriarchal) it sustains. I, or others, could now use this map in practice. Although I would have to visit Walawala to test the map's representation against my own embodied experience of the place, armed with the information I cite above I can deduce, for instance, that to get from the 'sacred caves' to the 'medicine place for men of high degree', one must cross the creek. Some level of effective navigation of this place would therefore be possible using this map.

The moral question of whether I *should* make this journey, or whether I would be permitted to, is also unavoidable. Such issues have recently become news in Australia after the decision by the Anangu people to bar climbing on the sacred site of Uluru (formerly known as Ayers Rock) from October 2019, which caused controversy in Australia (see https://theconversation.com/why-we-are-banning-tourists-from-climbing-uluru-86755). Bearing this in mind, it is possible that even the display of this map, making this information public, is a violation of rights over landscape and that my interpretation of this map is not now being directed by its Aboriginal creators, but by the museum and its curators. Tjupurrula's map is now *out of place*, displayed and interpreted in ways that change the context and, thus, the text itself. The *authority* to define and display this map as 'Aboriginal art' is that of the curator. Aboriginal art has *cachet* (Morphy, 2001), value to collectors regardless of its meaning to the artist or to the peoples that live in the landscape being depicted.

The ability to define a sense of place, to take away the places of an indigenous people and replace them with definitions from outside: these are exercises in power, assisted by maps which impose a particular perspective on the world. Space is neutral and unbounded, but that makes it mutable. Even the basic organisational task of overlaying a mathematical construct on space (for example, latitude and longitude) is imposing upon it a structure and form that, layered and layered again with narratives, observations, dialogues, actions and practices, give places perceptibility, persistence and obduracy. When particular practice architectures, and the investments in infrastructure and social relations that they represent, become dominant, a sense of place itself becomes a locus of power:

> Many traditional institutions, such as those of church and nation, depend crucially on the existence of a whole network of symbolic places to secure their power and express their social meaning. Places, as permanences, become symbolic and redolent of those values (such as fame, authority, identity and power) constructed through spatio-temporal practices.
>
> (Harvey, 1996, 306)

And:

> ... those who have invested in the physical qualities of place have to ensure that activities arise which render their investments profitable by ensuring the permanence of place.
>
> (ibid., 296)

Nevertheless, no place is identified merely by a single dominant voice: 'popular understandings of places are organised through the elaboration of often heterogeneous mental maps of the world each of which can be invested with all manner of collective hopes and fears' (ibid., 321). Places are 'an intense focus of discursive activity, filled with symbolic and representational meanings, and they are a distinctive product of institutionalised social and political-economic power' (ibid., 316). Mapping has played, and continues to play, a significant role in helping form a sense of place: thus, to be a focus for this discursive activity.

The history of mapping practice

To support the above point, a brief history of mapping practice follows. I focus here on the history as it has emerged in the British Isles, simply because of the availability of historical documentation and empirical examples of mapping practice. Other European countries, particularly Portugal with maritime navigation and France with terrestrial mapping, at times both challenged and co-operated with British mapping expertise over the rough period 1300–1900 CE. The brief discussion of Aboriginal Australian art above shows that other civilisations have independently developed mapping techniques of great value and subtlety. But my aim is to highlight key themes including: relevant technological developments; how maps are a social site; and how maps and mapping integrate with other societal trends, the broad philosophy of the Enlightenment and finally with power and authority. Mapping in the UK serves as a useful illustration of each.

Medieval mapmakers would rarely have surveyed the land directly. Whether or not they had the opportunity to do so, surveying equipment was primitive and relied largely on 'ready reckoning' – that is, the judgements and estimations made by those who had been 'on the spot' and made some kind of visual survey. In lieu of modern surveying techniques, the role of the mapmaker was one of collecting and gathering this information. Jacob describes the practice of early cartographers:

> Drawing a new map – of the whole earth or of a part of it – demanded some basic conditions: first, being settled in a place where a large amount of information was available, such as a royal court, a library or a commercial crossroads; second, a precise working method. Geographers had to read and interpret texts, to extract and classify bits of information, to order them, to translate them according to a common unity of measure. The basic operations were selecting data, cross-checking them, coordinating them and then translating them into orientations and distances in order to project them into the graphic space of the map itself.
>
> (Jacob, 1999, 36)

The first of these conditions, existing at a nexus, or collection point, for information, shows how these mapmakers worked through *discourse* with either other travellers who had been there or previous surveys and the maps that had been produced by them. Examples of such surveys included that reputedly commissioned by the Roman emperor, Augustus, in 5–6 BCE (see below) and rutters, or *portolani*, textual navigation logs from medieval ships. Lister (1965, 19–20) has an example of the kind of written instructions which would be found in a rutter. These predate nautical charts, with the earliest known examples dating from the tenth century:

From Sallo to Barcelona is 60 miles E.N.E. 1/4 E. Barcelona is a city with a beach facing east and has a roadstead with a depth of 22 paces in front of the city. To the S. E. to S. from Barcelona is a low place called Lobregato. On going out sail eastwards from the shore and watch for a castle which rises up out of a valley which leads to Sallo. The inward mark for Barcelona is a high steep and solitary hill called Monserrat. When you are N. E. of this, continue in the same direction and you will sight a low hill with a tower on it, which is called Montguich. Here is Barcelona.

Rutters and accurate charts were extremely valuable. Possession of the information recorded in these logs was a source of military and economic power. The Portuguese treated all rutters as top secret and smugglers who 'leaked' any of the information within them faced the death penalty (see Milton, 2002, Chapter 1, for example).

Note also the order from the Privy Council given on behalf of Christopher Saxton, who between 1574 and 1579 compiled the first atlas of England and Wales, the most complete survey of the country until the Ordnance Survey (OS) began work in 1791. As well as the importance of local knowledge – and 'honesty' – in map production, this extract (from Lister, 1965, 35) indicates the significance of particular locations within landscapes (those with extensive views) as 'anchors' for observation: key points around which, in effect, a data net could be constructed. The order read that, in Wales, Saxton was (all spelling as in the original):

to be assisted in all places where he shall come for the view of such places to describe certein counties in cartes [maps]… [authorities were] to see him conducted unto any towre, castle, highe place or hill, to view that countrey, and that he may be accompanied with ij or iij [2 or 3] honest men, such as do best know the countrey, for the better accomplishment of that service; and that at his departure from any towne or place that he hath taken the view of, the said towne do set forth a horseman that can speke both Welshe and Englishe, to safe-conduct him to the next market-towne.

Techniques like these, though time-consuming and prone to what more modern map makers would consider inaccuracies, could still produce comprehensive, useful and beautiful maps. Saxton's atlas is discussed further below.

The Hereford Mappa Mundi

The largest remaining medieval world map, the Hereford Mappa Mundi (hereafter, HMM), is a map of Europe, Asia and Africa created around 1300 CE. It is the most detailed map of its kind to survive into the modern era, now exhibited in a purpose-built annex of Hereford Cathedral, which I visited on 12 March 2019. I will describe first my impressions of the map as a *material* object and then, with the help of other scholars' work, its significance as a *representation of an information landscape* and, therefore, *a product of discourse*, created in line with specific discursive and knowledge frameworks and promulgated for particular purposes.

Many photographs of the HMM exist, the earliest extant one taken in 1868 (see Harvey, 2010, 26), but neither these nor textual descriptions (even the substantial Westrem, 2001) can fully evoke its qualities as a material object. It is of great beauty and inspires deep fascination; like all the best works of art, to experience it is to truly become lost in it. Almost everything that could be said about the world at the time of its creation is on it somewhere, scale allowing. It is as much a visual encyclopedia as a map. On the other hand, it is bounded, material, social, representational and relational: a map in every sense of the definition used in this book and an utterance that still remains relevant today, as this discussion, one response to it, indicates.

Originally, the HMM was mounted on an oak frame at the centre of a triptych, the outer wings of which could be folded back over it to protect it from the light. The vellum (calfskin) on which it was written has warped a little over the centuries and been the subject of some preservation work but the art itself has never been retouched or reworked. Apart from at a very few points, the drawings and inscriptions remain sharp and readable. For something around 720 years old, it is in extremely good condition. There is evidence of the embodied and material practice of the map's

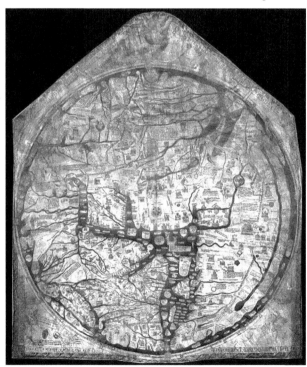

Figure 2.1 The Hereford Mappa Mundi (public domain image)

creators. For example, there is a tiny hole in the vellum, in the very middle of Jerusalem, where the compass point was inserted to draw the large circle that bounds the whole map. Jerusalem is therefore not just the symbolic but the real and absolute centre of the world depicted. Another compass point has left a hole at the centre of the labyrinth on Knossos, where 12 concentric circles form the maze.

The HMM intermingles geographical fact and myth. The largest building drawn on the map is the Tower of Babel, annotated with a substantial block of text that recounts the story of the Tower. Noah's Ark is shown resting atop Mount Ararat. The walled Garden of Eden is at the top, just below the figure of Christ sat in judgement outside the circle, in the map's apex. Bible story and geography interweave completely with the depiction of the book of Exodus as a geographical pathway on the map, like a modern GPS track. A line depicts the Jews being led by Moses out of Egypt and across the Red Sea. They pause at Mount Sinai, wander in the wilderness for 40 years (a series of loops and squiggles), then reach Jericho. Largely in Asia and Africa, fantastic creatures such as mandrake roots and manticores are depicted. Then there is the 'bonnacon' with accompanying inscription that reads:

> Native to Phrygia is an animal called bonnacon, with the head of a bull, the mane of a horse, horns intricately twisted. With vehement voiding of its bowels, it sprays excrement the length of three acres, the heat of which is such that it burns everything it hits.

Look closely at the bonnacon on the map and see that the artist depicts this 'vehement voiding' in gleeful detail.

But there is much information of practical use as well. A huge number of cities and islands are depicted (Westrem, 2001, catalogues over 1,100 separate locations or items on the HMM), more or less in their correct geographical relation to each other, once one absorbs the Jerusalem-centric projection of north to the left, east at the top. China is shown, and India, too, including a picture of a war elephant – perhaps, to many in 14th century England, considered a fantastical beast like the bonnacon, but clearly based on an eye-witness account recorded somewhere in the nexus of information and practice that generated the HMM. In Europe, cities cluster around rivers, with major basins like the Danube's depicted in detail. Cities like Regensburg and Salzburg are shown in their correct relation to tributaries (here, the Salzach and Inn) that join the Danube (although Crone notes mistakes in France in this regard: 1965, 455). Straight lines through north Africa represent trade routes. Crone (1965, 452) suggests that proximity to major trade routes and the itineraries of pilgrims governed the selection of towns plotted on the map. The map can be dated quite accurately due to the appearance, in Wales, of Conwy Castle, not built until 1289: the mapping of that and nearby Caernarfon Castle was a form of commentary on current political affairs (Harvey, 2010, 19).

Thus, the representation of the world on the HMM is not just bound by the past, but is sensitive to the chronotope in which it was created and to the expertise and authorial intent, and thus *authority*, of those who compiled it. Moreland and Bannister (1986, 20) attribute the HMM to one man, Richard of Haldingham, largely while he was at Lincoln Cathedral (he moved to Hereford later). As they note, '[t]he creation of such a map in the late thirteenth century must have called for a quite remarkable and exceptional study of classical manuscripts'.

But the story is more complicated than that, in terms of how we can understand the HMM as an *information landscape* and as a *product of discourse*. In the first place it is unclear whether Richard was one man, or two, probably relatives of one another (Denholm-Young, 1957). Richard – if there were two, the younger man – may have been one of the scribes who actually drew the map. Up to three may have done so, probably one doing the basic shapes and cities, one the creatures and a third the lettering, which has been shown to all be by the same hand (Roger Hillman, personal communication). These scribes were working from instructions, hence there are some mistakes, particularly the immense one (Flint says, 'a mistake whose dimensions inspire a certain awe' (1998, 23)) of getting the labels for Europe and Africa on the wrong continents.

(Gross errors are not confined to medieval maps. Bonnett (2015, 11–16) tells the story of 'Sandy Island', purportedly located near New Caledonia in the south Pacific Ocean. Despite appearing on maps and charts since around 1908, in 2012 the island was found not only to not exist, but, with the seabed at that point being 1400m below the surface, it could never have existed. Yet the fiction was durable enough for Sandy Island to appear on early versions of Google Earth. Bonnett concludes: 'The sudden deletion of Sandy Island forces us to realise that our view of the world still occasionally relies on unverified reports from far away' (ibid., 13).)

The authority of the mapmakers, however, depends very much on the architecture from which the HMM emerged. The HMM is not, per se, valuable because it is unique or original. Other extant maps (for example, one known as the Cotton Map, drawn in England in the 11th century, and one drawn in France in the 12th century and now in Munich) predate it, and are clearly based on the same basic configuration. This is the so-called 'T-O' (Denholm-Young, 1957), which Wogan-Browne (1991, 123) calls 'a well-known and long-established tradition of representation'. Apparent from Figure 2.1, its way of configuring the three known continents, with Asia (and east) at the top, Europe bottom left and Africa bottom right, would have been as familiar to scholars at the time as the Mercator projection is today.

Although the HMM is much larger and more detailed than these other surviving T-O maps, it is clearly based on the same dataset. (Its only known contemporary rival in scale and detail, the Ebstorf map of c.1240, was destroyed in World War 2, although a reconstruction exists.) However, the Cotton Map is 'better' when it comes to depicting the shape of lands (notably around the North Sea – the British Isles,

Netherlands and Jutland) as we would now expect to see them on a map: that is, as more closely corresponding to their actual geographies. Harvey (2010, 63) notes how the Cotton Map was drawn from piecing together the textual descriptions in rutters; that fact also serves to illustrate the depth of information available in these textual sources at the time. But this does not necessarily mean the HMM's creators were ignorant of this information and, as a result, drew the British Isles inaccurately. Harvey (ibid., 48) suggests the outlines around the North Sea are distorted for aesthetic reasons and to fit it in the circular field with the minimum of wasted space. This demonstrates that 'accuracy' was not a factor they considered as relevant as others: or as relevant as it became in later, Enlightenment cartography.

However, it was for these reasons that early scholars of the HMM largely dismissed its worth as a map, even if they grudgingly acknowledged its worth as art and/or a historical document. Crone (see also Wogan-Browne, 1991, 117) cites discussions at the Royal Geographical Society in 1830 (emphasis added):

> ... the general impression ... is one of inaccuracy, carelessness and ignorance .... places [are] more or less in correct relation to their neighbours, but entirely out of scale, and no attempt at correct outline even in the Mediterranean, where *the portolans are so accurate.*
>
> (Crone, 1965, 447)

Yet the conventions and representations on which the HMM are based are evidently 'the product of an intellectual schema, rather than the *faute de mieux* results of geographical ignorance' (Wogan-Browne, 1991, 123). The basis for this 'intellectual schema' was the aforementioned survey prompted by Caesar Augustus, depicted in the bottom left of the HMM, where is also placed a quotation from Luke 2:1; *A decree went out from Caesar Augustus that the whole world should be described*. This survey contributed to the world map of Vipsanius Agrippa, displayed in Rome at the time of the Caesars (Crone, 1965, 448). This, the HMM, Cotton Map, Ebstorf Map and others are all based on this original survey, which is why they look broadly similar. The identity of other texts that have contributed to this schema can also be determined. For example, some descriptions of fantastic creatures on the HMM are drawn from *De imagine mundi* of the 12th century, attributed to either Henry of Mainz or Honorius of Autun (Crone, 1965, 453). These textual descriptions are reproduced then illustrated on the HMM, for example the manticore.

At the same time, there is much variation between the members of this family of maps and not only with regard to the accuracy of coastlines. Information changes depending on time and place, or chronotope. Towns and cities which were non-existent in Roman times but important in 1300, like Venice and Dublin, are depicted in their correct location on the HMM. Local knowledge is also displayed, such as the prominence given to Clee Hill, an insignificant summit that happens to be near to Hereford. Thus, the HMM is a product of both its past and present: 'the world map was not simply copied repeatedly, with differences mainly due to mistakes or misinterpretations. Within the limits possible, the content of the map was expanded from time to time…' (Crone, 1965, 455).

Nevertheless, the commonalities between these various world maps shows how there was a corpus or 'fund' of data that was (relatively) widely accessible in this era. Hence the development of this popular *genre* of communication. Harvey uses this term, as does Wogan-Browne (1991, 117) – *mappa mundi* provided an explicitly Christian reading of the world and one that did not have to embrace geographical accuracy:

> The map had a more elevated purpose than merely copying geographical outlines; it sets before us the harmony of time and space, a statement of divine order in the world, to be sought in its physical form, its geography, as much as in its history, the sequence of events … Certainly we miss the whole point of the Hereford map and of other medieval world maps if we see them as offering no more than distorted geographical outlines.
>
> (Harvey, 2010, 48–9)

Knowing that the HMM is a Christian artefact is essential to a full reading of it. The map played several roles in the life of Hereford as a cathedral, a significant locus of power in the medieval world. It was not just a document but a status symbol, a tourist attraction that generated revenue for the diocese (Flint, 1998). Flint makes the case, at length, that the HMM was embroiled in the ecclesiastical politics of not just Hereford but Lincoln cathedral. Haldingham – creator Richard's birthplace – is in the Lincoln diocese, so how did the map end up being the *Hereford* MM? Flint says, the 'purpose and place' of Richard's map were 'intimately connected' with tensions around patronage, financing, taxation and struggles over the succession to bishoprics (Flint, 1998): she finds allegories to this in the decorations and inscriptions around the borders of the map.

Finally, the HMM was a teaching tool. Note how Richard signs his name to the map:

> … all those who possess this work – or hear, read or see it – pray to Jesus in his godhead to have pity on Richard of Haldingham or Sleaford, who made it or set it out, that he may be granted bliss in heaven.

Users did not just read the textual annotations on the map, as so many were illiterate. They could see it, as an image, without having to understand the annotations (indeed, this sense of 'reading a map' is still the one largely employed). And they could also 'hear' it, by having it explained to them. Thus, the HMM had a 'didactic purpose of some kind' (Flint, 1998, 24). It defined the viewer's 'place in the world', not just with reference to geographical location but as part of a broader discourse:

> … we have become unfamiliar with how central geography once was to morality and religion. Heaven, Hell and all the other destinations and journeys of salvation and damnation were understood as permanent places and geographic realities. They offered a moral map that helped people situate themselves in an ethical landscape. It seems that people need morality to be tied down and rooted to particular places and specific journeys. If our moral categories float free from the earth they float away.
>
> (Bonnett, 2015, 123)

The Ordnance Survey

The HMM is an informational artefact of great depth and complexity. It is a social site in its own right, a locus of power and authority, and an extremely effective record of knowledge as it stood, and could be represented, at the time and place (chronotope) of its creation. It is a representation that has abstracted and simplified and there are errors on it, large and small; but these characteristics give it ongoing value as a teaching and learning tool, a window onto the practice architectures and teleoaffective motivations which drove its creators and users.

For all this value, however, the HMM is rather useless as a tool for navigation at smaller scales, in the same way as is a modern globe. The accolade of the British Isles' first published *atlas*, a collection of cartographs in book form that show not just the world as a whole but more specific regions of it, is accredited to Christopher Saxton's atlas of England and Wales, first published in 1579: the royal order which accompanied him on his survey was quoted above. (The first world atlas was published by Abraham Ortelius in 1570.) Saxton would have been using much the same 'ready reckoning' techniques as his predecessors. This is evident from the book itself: an original copy of the atlas survives in Chetham's Library in Manchester and I consulted this on 19 June 2019. Its maps have a rather casual attitude to what we now consider geographic accuracy. Towns and villages are placed more or less in their correct relationships to each other, but coastlines, and the shapes of features like the lakes of Cumberland are clearly inaccurate. Rivers and forests are marked, but no roads, though Hadrian's Wall appears (as 'The Wall of the Picts'). Nevertheless, Saxton's atlas remains a significant achievement. The maps were drawn over five years, with improvements taking place in technique and artistry. There are no biblical or mythological stories, no pictures of beasts (bar some fish in the sea) nor local inhabitants. The atlas is a documentary record of a landscape, not a teaching tool like the HMM.

Before telescopes were employed in mapmaking, around 1670, surveyors like Saxton were limited to what they could determine with the naked eye (Hewitt, 2010, xxii). But once this technology was employed, mapmaking became a science. The telescope became wedded to ever more precise instrumentation, culminating in Jesse Ramsden's 'Great Theodolite', first used in 1792, which could record the direction of bearings to triangulation stations dozens of miles away to within a second or two of arc (ibid., 127). Triangulation itself was a geometric technique that allowed the calculation of bearings and altitudes to great precision, first employed in Cassini's National Survey of France in the late 17th century (ibid., 67) and in Britain shortly afterwards.

From this point, however, the idea of mapmaking as a personal enterprise, based on dialogue with those who possessed the necessary local knowledge, began to change. Scientific methods, like theodolites and triangulation, inherently surpass the capacities of an individual, even one as dedicated as Saxton, and require the work of a team. The new instrumentation was expensive, and changed the values of mapping. As modern mapmaking developed around these technologies and it became an *organisational* endeavour, the telos of mapping became *precision* and this was achieved to an impressive degree quite early on. When William Roy and his team measured Britain's first cartographic baseline at Hounslow Heath in 1784 (Hewitt, 2010, 73ff), he reported it as being 27,404.7 feet long (8,352.95m): modern GPS technology calculates it as 27,376.8 feet, so he was out by only around 0.1% in the first place and this original measurement was soon refined further. This focus on accuracy shows how cartography became defined as a structural element of the 'language of reason' (ibid., 3) that drove the Enlightenment enterprise.

But cartography was not just a technical exercise in measurement. In the UK (which at that time still incorporated what is now the Republic of Ireland), mapping contributed substantially to the building and defining of the emerging United Kingdom as a single nation. Poor quality maps of Scotland had hampered state efforts to put down the Jacobite rebellion in 1745 (Hewitt, 2010, xvii–xix) and it is from William Roy's subsequent Military Survey of Scotland, completed in 1755, that the Ordnance Survey (OS) eventually grew (ibid., 17). The very name of that organisation, the 'Ordnance' Survey, indicates its origins in military concerns. Yet Hewitt's history of the organisation shows how the OS project led to cultural change. Crucial to this was the decision taken by William Mudge, Director of the OS, to publish the maps for public consumption and not to restrict their access to the military. As Hewitt writes:

> The Ordnance Survey had originated from a mixture of motivations, some martial, some scientific, some ideological. And because the project was not purely military in nature, the resulting maps were not as jealously guarded as other pieces of intelligence. The public utility of the endeavour was on the minds of its progenitors from the start, and on his appointment Mudge argued that the maps themselves should be made available to the general public. In the first volume of the Ordnance

Survey's *Accounts*, he ... was adamant that 'it has been very justly expected by the Public, that from the present undertaking, they should derive the advantage of an improvement in the geography of their country.'

(Hewitt, 2010, 153–4)

Except for a brief period of prohibition soon afterwards, during the Napoleonic Wars – and Mudge objected strenuously to this withdrawal of the maps from public sale (ibid., 214) – the results of the OS's meticulous data collection have been available ever since. Expensive at first, by the mid-19th century maps were cheap enough to be everyday acquisitions. Maps became cultural items, their forms and depictions contributing to other media as diverse as art and board games (the first jigsaw puzzles were based around maps), and adopted by adherents of the emerging pastime of rambling or hiking, allowing the exploration of landscape in one's leisure time and engaging with it at an aesthetic, spiritual level.

The work of the OS has not always been perceived as benign, however. In Wales and, even more so, Ireland, OS surveyors were seen as imperialist agents, and with some justification bearing in mind that Irish people were at first specifically excluded from the OS's work there (Hewitt, 2010, 242ff). And there were philosophical objections, alluding to the power and authority vested not so much in the maps but in the uses to which they were subsequently put:

The presence of a map-maker in an area often indicated changes in taxes, a new Enclosure Act or 'improvement' to the disproportionately large estates of the nobility. As the nineteenth century progressed, map-makers would also become associated with the unstoppable progress of industrialisation and the sacrifice of the landscape to the pursuit of profit .... Above all, map-makers suffered from British citizens' fierce protection of their personal privacy. A map-maker was often seen as a busybody, poking his nose and theodolite into other people's business ....

(ibid., 155)

But the work of the OS was also a media event, with surveyors objects of curiosity, even celebrity. The conflict with Napoleon reduced the chance for the rich and educated intelligentsia to take Grand Tours in Europe, and improvements to road conditions as well as the Romantic poets' lauding of natural landscapes meant the new maps were in great demand as guides to the British Isles. This demand has never really lessened. Despite the rise of Google Maps, which can overlay much more real-time information about *urban* space than a static OS map will ever do, there are still no better tools to guide an exploration of a *rural or mountain* landscape for a UK hiker.

Digital and participatory mapping

Mention of Google Maps brings this history into the present time. The application of the power of information technologies to store, analyse and manage data has brought mapping into the digital era with initiatives such as the GPS (Global Positioning System) and GIS (Geographical Information Systems), as well as 'Big Data' more generally. The datasets which are used to compile maps are now global in scale. The changes these bring to how we can map the world is evident with the publication of works such as Cheshire and Uberti's *London: The Information Capital* (2014). This book bills itself as '100 Maps and Graphics that will change how you view the city [of London]'. Its pages show maps that cover topics common to infographics down the years – for example, relative deprivation (ibid., 164–5) or property prices (ibid., 64–7) – but also quirkier ones such as how to travel through all 270 tube stations in a day (ibid., 134–5) or locations from which the most tweets are sent about the capital's various football teams (ibid., 202–3). This last map, and others based on data drawn from datasets accumulated through technologies such as Twitter and London's 'Oyster' public transport card, reflect how: 'this book could not have been made ten years ago. Computers weren't powerful enough. Data weren't as detailed or freely available' (ibid., 20).

Maps like these can still be viewed as art and still offer narratives about place that can be used as the basis for subsequent judgements about information. The modern mapmaker, like the medieval one, is still positioned at a crucial point in the flows of information, even if the pathways and patterns are now revealed through algorithms and data mining. And despite the emphasis on digital technology, 21st century maps remain *material*, tactile objects (Dodge et al., 2009, 229). This is clearly true even for online maps like those of Google, where we use our fingers – digits – to manipulate it, zooming in and out (changing the scale to whatever we find most relevant) and using it to find some location or resource in the physical world. Digital copies of OS maps replicate the representational schema of the paper versions and even if they can potentially be carried around within one's mobile device, are still used in much the same ways. In these respects, mapping in the 21st century is a practice rooted in architectures that are many centuries old.

On the other hand, technology has made maps ever more *unfinalisable*; the digital map allows greater interactivity, people placing themselves on the map, interacting 'with a set of tools, sharing results and negotiating with other stakeholders in an ongoing process that is never really complete …' (Perkins, 2009, 174). New technologies provide opportunities for a democratisation of the process, a distribution of the authority inherent in maps. Crampton and Krygier (2006), in their review of critical cartography, observe that the spread of powerful mapping technologies (and related ones such as digital photography) challenges the dominance of cartographic elites:

… the increasingly ubiquitous and mobile mapping capabilities are changing the structure of map production and labor. Maps are no longer imparted to us by a trained cadre of experts, but along with most other information we create them as needed ourselves.

(Crampton and Krygier, 2006, 15)

However, while new technologies have been used to promote more participatory approaches to mapping, they also add to the power one can secure by being placed at the centre of new, digital information flows. When Google Maps shows me the nearest pub to my present location and accompanies this annotation with a 'star rating' based on n number of 'reviews', I am positioning myself at the tip of a complex series of judgements that I am encouraged to feel is that of my peers, who share my interests at this given place and time. To some extent this is the case, but just because the information has been gathered from 'the general public', the representational schema that is in play in this case remains that of Google (and its close collaborator, TripAdvisor).

Technology like GIS was implicated in events like the Gulf War, while simultaneously also offering opportunities to more socially aware projects (Crampton and Krygier, 2006, 16). Crampton's discussion of the political potential of mapping describes 'Q-Tool', which can mine census data and be used to find voters that are, say, African-American in a given district, even their previous voting history. This is seen as a positive step, employed by the 'Get Out The Vote' operation that helped raise the African-American vote and elect Barack Obama (Crampton, 2009, 844). Much the same techniques were then used by Republican interests to engineer votes in key states in the 2016 election of Donald Trump. (See the documentary 'The Great Hack' released in 2019, amongst others.) Political uses for maps do not depend on the form of the maps (Crampton, 2009, 845).

The *theirwork* project (Williamson and Connolly, 2009), is an example of a more socially-aware mapping project, one which aimed to distribute authority over mapping practice and make it more inclusive. *theirwork* is:

… a participatory online 'open' mapping project put together by project participants' local knowledge and direct experiences of their lived environment with the aim of creating a democratic and first-hand, local definition of place …. [the project] opens up the possibility of creating an emancipatory, continuously evolving mapping that is situated in a given space and addresses its creators' – which are simultaneously also its potential end-users – main concerns. Thus, the map becomes rooted in local identity, fulfilling the needs and reflecting the interests of the community.

(For other examples, see the Humanitarian Open Street Map Team (https://www.hotosm.org/) and Healthsites (https://www.healthsites.io/#).)

Essentially, *theirwork* aims to map a local landscape in ways that combine multiple perspectives and include not just technical information about where things stand in relation to each other in physical *space*, but to accommodate experience, memory, affect and other constituents of *place*. It builds on the idea, discussed on pages 29–32, with reference to Australian Aboriginal art but applicable anywhere, that indigenous populations have 'tacit maps' of their landscape which can be articulated as a counterpoint to maps developed from positions outside the community. The UK's OS maps are technically superb and work well as a guide to the physical location of things, but the regularity of the representative devices, symbols, colours and so on homogenise the landscape and make it seem the same everywhere. Maps like these cannot, therefore, distinguish between one building and another in terms of their aesthetic qualities, roads on the basis of their propensity to get snarled up with traffic, beauty spots vis-à-vis tranquillity and lack of litter. This knowledge is acquired only through experience and frequent proximity to the landscape.

Using mapping to represent this fund of knowledge has become a common mode of summarising information relevant to environmental issues (Salovaara, 2016). In the late 1990s, Friends of the Earth UK added a section to their website where visitors could enter their postcode (a pre-existing schema for organising information) and download information on the worst local polluters (Whitworth, 2001). The aim of projects like this, shared by Williamson and Connolly's work, is not simply to summarise information but to mobilise action to attempt to resolve local environmental issues, action informed by the knowledge the community has about the landscape around it (Williamson and Connolly, 2009, 100). They note (ibid., 101) that environmental management problems (including information landscape management: see Furlong and Tippett, 2013, and Chapter 5 of this book) may arise because of conflicts over naming, scaling and valuing between different groups who consider different timescales, use the same words but in different ways, and so on.

The *theirwork* methodology combines multiple perspectives in the mapping process:

> … multiple voices and autonomous experiences are documented via first person sensory experience and through a community's felt experience of landscape ….
> *theirwork* adopts three cognate disciplines: psychophysical geography; phenomenology; and ethnography. These complementary approaches have created a methodological framework, through which open data are sourced and collected. Ethnographic methodology ensures multiple voices construct the map: the phenomenological approach ensures autonomous experiences are documented via first person sensory experience, and through a community's felt experience of landscape. Last, a psychophysical geographic approach ensures the map is emotive and deeply personal. All three approaches ensure the map is grounded in locality, subjectivity and a lived experience of place.
>
> (Williamson and Connolly, 2009, 99–100)

The project was centred on the 'psychophysical' mapping of a lake, Loe Pool in Cornwall, UK. Around this location:

> … the relationship of emotion, memory, and sensory engagement with the landscape was mapped. First, data was sourced while walking, talking and recording with participants on the landscape. After an initial recruitment period and focus session, each co-developer chose a location for a 'one-to- one' walk that in some way was connected to the lake. Co-developers chose the date and time – some brought their binoculars or dog along … The co-developers were helped in tracking the walk; sites of interest, objects, plants and animals, favourite places, memory spots and stories connected to the place.
>
> (ibid., 106)

Through using this 'tracking' and amalgamating the data from these many participants (or 'co-developers'), the community, in collaboration with the researchers, is 'collectively finding a way to share knowledge about a place' (ibid., 108). This method is embodied in physical experience within the landscape, as well as reflection on its affective qualities. Technological developments permit the rich data gathered by *theirwork* to be structured around, and layered over, the physical configuration of Loe Pool. Generally, technological developments like GIS are provoking more widespread use of collaborative mapping (see also Hacıgüzeller, 2017, Salovaara, 2016). The digital nature of the map gives it dynamism, making it editable, provisional, when compared to the printed map or atlas. For Williamson and Connolly, the methodology in general and the application within it of technologies like folksonomy (tagging), allow the map to be emergent and community-driven – a map creation process 'that coherently represents the combined impressions of an unrelated group of self-interested actors, and conveys a truly distributed simulation of a geographic space' (Williamson and Connolly, 2009, 106).

Mapping Mars

The development of new mapping technologies has extended our perception of reality into ever more distant realms. This extension provides an interesting opportunity to explore how mapping helps develop a sense of place, even in the modern era. Although it is not the only such place (Antarctica is at least one other example), there is a landscape of great scale which has *first* come into being, in human terms, as a map; that has been observed and documented in detail by various methods (scientific, photographic, artistic, and more), despite never having been inhabited. That is the planet Mars.

Mars is a fine case study of how an information landscape has come into existence largely independent of politics and power, but how it has nevertheless enfolded into its geographical 'reality' various information and communication technologies and social interactions. This section will argue that despite the lack of habitation, Mars is more than just space, it is becoming a *place*: but this sense of place and the social constructs that this implies have been, and must have been, created only by mapping. The mapping of much of the world by colonial powers took place *as if* 'native' populations were not there: but for this, see Chapter 3. It is acknowledged that the motivations for space exploration, and how it is funded and justified, are driven by a range of socio- and geo-political considerations. But these do not change the fact that *at present*, and in the mappings discussed here, the surface of Mars remains innocent of politics and power.

Martian place has been emerging since remote viewing technology – telescopes, in the first instance – became powerful enough to begin to pick out details on the planet's surface. These viewing technologies, and the technologies of space travel, have improved over the centuries and allowed finer and finer details to emerge. The Mariner orbiters of the early 1970s, through photographic methods, discovered the planet's colossal volcanoes (the highest mountains ever mapped) and other impressive surface features. The MOLA (Mars Orbiting Laser Altimeter) map (https://attic.gsfc.nasa.gov/mola/images.html) was created by bouncing innumerable pulses of laser light off the surface of the planet and measuring the time taken for these pulses to return to the orbiter, thus measuring altitude. Despite the complexity of the infrastructure required to get this device in place, the mapping technique is ultimately a simple one and yet it has created a map of great depth on which surface features as small as a few kilometres across can be discerned. The latest generation of images are even more finely detailed, to the extent that the visioning of channels a few hundred metres wide provide persuasive evidence that water (or, at least, some form of liquid) has been flowing on Mars very recently in geological terms (Heldmann et al., 2005).

The mapping of Mars, as with any other landscape, is more than just a matter of accumulating imagery. The nuggets of information gathered must be triangulated, placed in correct relation to each other via a cognitive schema that has come into being elsewhere (viz., on Earth). The Martian 'control net' – the mathematical construct into which can be slotted data from these observations (beginning with photos taken by the Mariner missions) – was the work of one man, Merton Davies of NASA (Morton, 2002, 16ff). The data collected are more than just visual. For example, Mars has been mapped geochemically: Taylor et al. (2010) used information collected by the Mars Odyssey gamma ray spectrometer to identify six distinct geochemical 'provinces' on the planet.

These maps will go on to shape activity in the future. The maps are not just a summation of the landscape of Mars as it stands now, but part of an iterative process of understanding and the basis for further judgements. Olson et al. (2007) explore how maps of the terrain can be generated by combining observations from a variety of sources, including Mars rovers as they descend to the surface. They observe how if a rover depends only on data sent from Earth and there are errors in those data, valuable time will be lost as rovers are typically in direct communication with mission control only once per day. But a rover that can generate and store its own maps – in other words, one that can learn about the terrain around it and is programmed to make future judgements against this new map – is more robust. This can be done by identifying data points evident across these different maps and incorporating observations of how these change as the rover moves across the surface. The aim is to make the rovers more 'autonomous' (Olson et al., 2007, 73); this is a learning process of a kind.

What is more significant to the purposes of this book is how these scientific maps and practices have subsequently become 'imbued with symbolic value' (Lloyd, 2010a, 9). For a start, we on Earth have projected elements from our own landscapes onto those of Mars. Names, first from mythology and then the names of scientists and astronomers, have been layered over Martian surface features (Morton, 2002, xi): such as Olympus Mons (Mount Olympus) or the giant canyon of Valles Marineris, named for the Mariner probe that discovered it. In these features, early astronomers such as Schiaparelli – creator of some of the first maps of the planet in the late 19th century – saw cognates of terrestrial forms, even of culture. Most famously, this led to the notion that the planet was irrigated by a series of canals and thus the common science fiction trope of Mars as an arid, but inhabited world.

The impact of these representations has been significant. The search for life on Mars was a fundamental aim of the 1976 Viking missions. When these observations proved that Mars was lifeless (at least, in the present epoch), science fiction largely lost interest in the planet, as lifelessness was something the genre found difficult to articulate. Nevertheless:

> … the same science had brought into being an extraordinarily documented, well-mapped planet, a setting whose coherence could be guaranteed by something more objective than whatever discipline the author might bring to imagining it.
>
> (Morton, 2002, 170)

Once the disappointment of Mars's sterility had been overcome, novelists found inspiration in the maps that NASA had created and articulated. The best example of this is the *Mars Trilogy* by Kim Stanley Robinson (1992). This epic novel spans two hundred years of future Martian history, from the arrival of the first hundred colonists in 2027, entwining this narrative with speculations about the political, economic and scientific development of humanity as a whole over this period. It is no exaggeration to say that Robinson's work develops as rich a sense of place as does Tolkien with Middle-earth in *The Lord of the Rings*. The maps of Mars are not just a source of inspiration but validate Robinson's own representations of this landscape: they are the 'material which would shape the protagonists' world' (Morton, 2002, 171). Characters' travel itineraries and the locations of key scenes in the novel can be traced and pinpointed on the MOLA map. The novel depicts Mars as somewhere to be inhabited and changed, not as an inert space, a stage set that houses activity but has no other impact upon it. Mars has no native life, but Robinson's characters give it life, and thus a sense of place, both within the book and for the readers of his detailed descriptions. For Robinson, the NASA maps of Mars and the scientific understandings of the planet's geology and geography that have been informed by them, are an information landscape of great richness. And in turn, so are his novels (and so is Morton's book).

The relevance of Mars, and its various mappings, to the discussion here is that it is *not* an 'imaginary' world (as is Middle-earth), yet it is, nevertheless, a construct of multiple human imaginations and representations: we can see it, understand it, analyse it, though we cannot yet inhabit it. But so pervasive are these 'pre-imaginings' that if people eventually do reach the planet and stay there, these colonists will not be creating the world from scratch. Expectations and hopes – teleoaffective goals – which will drive them are already being created on Earth today (Morton, 2002, xiv).

Consequently, Mars is a place that has begun to influence terrestrial technology, communications and culture. The exploration of Mars by the Pathfinder rover in 1997 was a defining moment in the development of the World Wide Web as a significant medium. As Morton writes:

> The mission's website got something like half a billion hits in July 1997, which was the most any single event, or thing, or place had ever seen ... The fact that Pathfinder's main achievement – landing on Mars – was a reprise of something done decades earlier could have made the mission seem old hat, but the web dimension made it seem utterly contemporary. At a time when people were discovering they could see all sorts of distant parts of the Earth through little webcams, the ability to see somewhere beyond the Earth in just the same way was at once compellingly different and excitingly the same; it made that world part of this one.
>
> (ibid., 232)

He goes on to observe that:

> ... [t]he lesson of Pathfinder is that the more accessible small parts of the surface of Mars become in cyberspace, the more placelike they will come to feel. Places need space to exist in, and time to change, and communities to give them meaning.
>
> (ibid., 236)

The principal block on this kind of mass engagement with Mars as a *dynamic* information landscape is the difficulty of transmitting data back to Earth, as at the moment, each lander must perform this task separately and (as Olson et al.'s paper noted) is limited by when it is in contact with mission control. Better would be a ring of satellites around Mars, in communication with devices on the surface and then in more-or-less permanent communication with Earth. Bandwidth and accessibility would increase enormously, and:

> … [i]n the long run, this infrastructure may come to be as important in transforming the human experience of Mars as the data which come back through it …. An Internet that extended to Mars would be an important statement in and of itself. And its product – an increasingly rich corpus of data from which ever more powerful computers could produce ever better Martian virtual realities – could bring Mars into the everyday lives of those with an interest.
>
> (ibid., 236)

There is one final aspect of the mapping of Mars which Morton describes and which is worth mentioning here, these being the social experiments that have taken place at Haughton Crater on Devon Island in the Canadian arctic. This is one of Earth's most desolate places and therefore also one of its most Mars-like. There, NASA set up the Haughton Mars project. In the first instance this was a scientific study of the crater (an astrobleme, the site of a meteorite impact). But the point was also 'studying how you go about studying somewhere like Haughton' (ibid., 269) – and 'studying the people studying Haughton', seeing how they share information and develop knowledge about this place. What is required to understand these interactions between people and landscape is 'not just a bunch of people and supplies' but 'the researchers' world in all its complexity…'. This is what 'a Mars mission must try to transplant to another planet'. It is a form of *meta*-mapping: mapping an *information* landscape, in relation to its specific geography, to ascertain the impact of that geography on the formation of knowledge in that setting.

Such studies, and the detailed understanding of Mars that we have developed through the last few decades of scientific attention to the planet, mean that while the people involved in future missions to Mars will be more physically isolated than any humans have ever been, they will be considerably less *informationally* isolated than, say, Scott's expedition to the South Pole: they 'will be immersed in a world of human data. They will know where they are and where their companions are' (ibid., 274). And as they make use of these maps to explore further, they will change the landscape and adapt it – and the maps themselves will have to change, both in what they depict, and symbolically.

Conclusion

The history and case studies presented in this chapter show how mapping as a practice has always been related to how the mapmaker is positioned at a nexus of practice; the conjunction of information flowing from different places and times. A mapmaker like Richard of Haldingham or Christopher Saxton was exploiting a privileged position within these information flows just as much as is NASA or Google in the present. All the maps discussed herein are ways to select information and bound, or frame, its presentation; they are tools for organising that information and for communicating one's understanding of a landscape to audiences in the present and into the future.

But as the communication device, the map, spreads itself and its representations into different places and times, so the nature of its message changes. In many ways an old map may still be very accurate, meaningful and relevant, but these will be for reasons that are not those its creators intended. Then again, the same is true of any utterance, even those made very recently (Bakhtin, 1986).

Nevertheless, this discussion of maps cannot yet be complete, for while the chapter has touched on it briefly, I have not yet attended to the discursive *power* evident in maps and the practice of mapping. That is the subject of the next chapter.

Chapter 3

Mapping and power

Introduction

Mapping as a practice is wholly intertwined with conceptions of *power*, the ability to impose one's practices and perspectives on the world and on others. An argument in favour of this stance is constructed, in detail, by David Harvey in his book *Justice, Nature and the Geography of Difference* (1996), and this chapter's argument is significantly based on that work. In addition, Harvey offers the important notion of *discursive mapping*, an essential foundation for the chapters to follow. The discussion in Chapter 2 hinted at the idea that mapping *processes* can be occurring without an image, or cartograph, actually being produced (as with, for example, the rutter). Understanding this distinction is essential for appreciating how mapping – not just maps as a product, but the processes of dialogue, abstraction, organisation, representation and communication that create them – fundamentally shapes the information practices within social settings and is thus a locus of power.

What is being created through such processes are not just maps in the graphic sense – the Hereford Mappa Mundi, MOLA, etc. – but *cognitive schema*. Schema are ways in which we organise the knowledge in our minds and are thus part of the background against which we make judgements about information selection and the media of dissemination; they are learned, stored ways of thinking and:

> … function to pick out relevant, 'schema-consistent' data from the rush of information we regularly confront. As such, they are pre-existing selection criteria that manage cognitive overload and enhance the capacity to solve problems.
>
> (Blaug, 2007, 30)

In other words, schema are substructures of the collective matrix of interpretation (ibid., passim). Schema – and the mapping processes from which they emerge and which help define their form – act as media through which power can be used to impose information practices on subordinate groups and the information landscapes they steward. But the same processes can also be used by communities to better understand and organise their own landscape, share information about how that landscape can be nurtured for the collective benefit of the community which inhabits it, and ultimately, distribute authority over it, and the associated information practices, among members of the group. These ideas were explored in an initial way in Chapter 1, but it is Harvey's work that allows them to be specifically connected to the notion of discursive mapping and, through that, the way that *place* is nurtured in discourse and used as a locus of difference.

Discursive mapping

Harvey seeks to 'define a set of workable foundational concepts for understanding space-time, place and environment (nature)' (1996, 2). To this task, difference is key – or rather *'the just production of just geographical differences'* (ibid., 5, emphasis in original). Difference and diversity are vital to the health of environments and social practices, but are also often the source of injustice, domination and inequality. How can the 'positive' value of differences be exploited for the benefit of all? As Harvey puts it:

> What is it that constitutes a privileged claim to knowledge and how can we judge, understand, adjudicate, and perhaps negotiate through different knowledges constructed at very different levels of abstraction under radically different material conditions?
>
> (ibid., 23)

Enlightenment rationality, and the scientific culture that developed around it, promotes the view that universality and the generalisability of claims are the hallmarks of informational validity. This does not make place irrelevant as the basis of understanding but does reduce its significance to that of one variable among others. Using this kind of objectively validated information as the basis for judgements and the development of practice and practice architectures would be considered a 'rational' approach. But Harvey (ibid., 37) quotes Ingold (1993, 41) in stating that:

> … the local is not a more limited or narrowly focused apprehension than the global, it is one that rests on an altogether different mode of apprehension – one based on an active, perceptual engagement with components of the dwelt-in world, in the practical business of life, rather than on the detached, disinterested observation of a world apart.

Haraway (1991, 195) also propounds the view that rather than impartiality, it is *partiality* (specificity to place) that is 'the condition of being heard to make rational knowledge claims'. Generic knowledge must be *applied* by a body, acting *some*where (not *any*where). Through that action, the knowledge claim can be tested (cf. Carr and Kemmis, 1986).

Yet we cannot make every judgement through referring to practices and information evident in our chronotope. We must at times confront processes not accessible to direct local experience. And this requires moving to a different level of abstraction, one 'capable of reaching out across space'. Mapping, at least in its scientific, Enlightenment guise (the map as 'immutable mobile'), is such an abstractive process, but there are ineluctable tensions 'between distinctively understood particularities of places and the necessary abstractions required to take those understandings into a wider realm' (Harvey, 1996, 34). The abstractions and subsequent representations on the map form connections between what is on the map and what is in the world, but these connections may be interpreted in different ways from different perspectives and this is exactly why maps have discursive force. Being able to define particular representations, or interpretations, as having 'meaning' or 'value' while alternative representations are effaced or concealed is a locus of power.

As a result, Harvey is quite critical of maps, calling them:

> … typically totalising, usually two-dimensional, Cartesian and very undialectical devices … This is not to say that maps are useless – far from it … But the mapping metaphor subsumes (and sometimes obscures) the problematics of representation within an often unquestioned choice to employ one particular projection (and I deliberately use the term in both its mathematical and psychological sense) rather than some other.
>
> (1996, 4–5)

The overt connection between maps and military and economic power has been evident since at least 1400 CE (ibid., 240). The value placed on rutters is one example. The work of Mercator, Saxton, Cassini and other mapmakers who appeared in the narrative above can be defined as an 'exercise in western domination. The "imperial gaze" mapped the world according to its own needs, wants and desires, imposing a map of the world in such a way as to suppress difference' (ibid., 284). This process continues. More recent examples of where maps have been used to assert naked power include the constant bulldozing of the Bedouin village of Twayil Abu Jarwal by Israeli forces:

> Ilan Yeshurun, a local director of the Israeli Land Authority, explained the ceaseless round of demolition by simply stating, 'this is not a village'. Without irony, he added, 'It doesn't exist on any map or in any legal registration. It's only a village in

the eyes of the Bedouin.' In other words, it is because Twayil Abu Jarwal doesn't exist that it both can be and has to be bulldozed again and again.

(Bonnett, 2015, 104)

Even where the uses of maps are not so nakedly dominating, they still collapse variation into a single representation, perhaps forcing the appearance of consensus where none exists. Hewitt describes how the work of the OS in both Wales and Ireland in the 19th century was complicated by differences between the toponymies of these locations – that is, their place-naming practices – and those of the mostly English surveyors. On top of difficulties with settling on spelling and, for instance, differentiating between the Welsh place terms *lan* ('an eminence') and *llan* ('a church'), distinctions not universally recognised even among Welsh-speakers (Hewitt, 2010, 194), surveyors found that inhabitants of localities did not always agree on what places were called. The creation of the OS maps was, in effect, a declaration that one particular place name, and its orthography, were authoritative. Whatever a place had been called before, it was henceforth 'officially' known as whatever appeared on the map. (Place names are durable but can change for various reasons. See the example of 'Pooh Bridge' in Chapter 4.)

Harvey then steps back from cartography and discusses the power evident in mapping in a more discursive sense. It is worth here restating some of the basic features of maps as presented in Chapter 2: they are 'a register of correspondence between two spaces, whose explicit outcome is a space of representation' (Cosgrove, 1999, 1); that a map makes propositions; and that these propositions can then be explored in the world, that is, the place represented upon the map.

As an example of discursive mapping, Harvey notes (1996, 291ff) a case in Baltimore, US, where an affluent, and mainly white, district, Guilford, stands alongside much poorer areas inhabited mainly by other ethnic groups. Through discussing reports of a murder committed in Guilford, Harvey shows how the border between this district and its neighbours is not just a 'line on a map' but represents deep-rooted divisions between competing schema that drive a range of other information practices including those of urban planners and the media. The border around Guilford represents, for Harvey, a *discontinuity*, a spatial boundary that is difficult to cross – physically, but also economically, culturally and informationally – without provoking emotional reactions of varying kinds (affect). Matters arising from how this boundary is represented in local discourse, and how certain propositions then flow from these representations, are brought into focus for Harvey in how local newspaper reports on the murder were unanimous at first in blaming the crime on (non-white) 'invaders' into Guilford, motivated by burglary; it was only later on that the perpetrator was revealed to be the (white) grandson of the victims. But this was a harder story to fit with the dominant representations – that is, the discursive maps – that shaped information dissemination via the Baltimore media at this time.

Harvey's critical, discursive and place-based analytical lens brings out detail in the ways that dominating representations crystallise into discursive maps that subsequently serve as *reified* cognitive schema; permanences within the flux of social and dialogic interaction that shape informational judgements and, as a result, practice architectures and subsequent social and dialogic interactions. A key passage from Harvey reads as follows:

> The discursive activity of 'mapping space' is a fundamental prerequisite to the structuring of any kind of knowledge. All talk about 'situatedness', 'location' and 'positionality' is meaningless without a mapping of the space in which those situations, locations and positions occur. And this is equally true whether the space being mapped is metaphorical or real ....
>
> Mapping is a discursive activity that incorporates power. The power to map the world in one way rather than another is a crucial tool in political struggles. Power struggles over mapping (again, no matter whether these are maps of so-called 'real' or metaphorical spaces) are therefore fundamental moments in the production of discourses.
>
> Social relations are always spatial and exist within a certain produced framework of spatialities. Put another way, social relations are, in all respects, mappings of some sort, be they symbolic, figurative, or material. The organisation of social relations demands a mapping so that people know their place ...
>
> Material practices transform the spaces of experience from which all knowledge of spatiality is derived. These transformative material practices in part accord with discursive maps and plans (and are therefore expressing of both social relations and power) but they are also manifestations of symbolic meanings, mythologies, desires ...
>
> Institutions are produced spaces of a more or less durable sort... [they] entail the organisation of symbolic spaces (monuments, shrines, walls, gates, interior spaces of the house) and the spatial orchestration of symbolic systems that support and guide all manner of institutional practices and allegiances. Insertion into the symbolic spatial order and learning to read the semiotics of institutionalised landscapes is an effect of power on the individual ...
>
> (1996, 111–12)

Harvey thus firmly links mapping as a *discursive* activity to the production of social relations, institutions and material practices that subsequently transmit and sustain power. The spaces being mapped may be real, but they may also be conceptual (for example, a field of study, an organisational hierarchy), and the subsequent mapped representation of space, and place, does not have to be graphical in form. This is clear from the section in Harvey headed 'Cartographies' (ibid., 282–5) though clearly not discussing the graphic map as it is understood in the everyday. What Harvey does in these passages is highlight how multiple perspectives can, and indeed must, exist on information landscapes:

> Different perspectives on the same world can be constructed from different positions …. all cartographies of the world are representations of the same world but each monad (body) necessarily has its own perspective depending on its position in that world. Different things dominate, loom large or look remote and irrelevant according to the perspective embedded in a different position …

> (ibid., 283)

Always, we see the world from a particular chronotope. Everybody (and every body) occupies a unique time and space and Bakhtin sees the person (the body) as a 'means… of particularising the otherwise infinitely general aspects of time/space, I become the instrument for assigning specific value to abstract time and space' (Holquist, 1990, xxv, in Harvey, 1996, 270). Yet a body is not a singular thing, either (ibid., 274). The learner is never entirely a learner, even in a classroom during a class, just as I am never entirely 'a teacher' in the same setting. We both bring in past experiences, present concerns and future goals that have manifested or will manifest themselves in a range of other places and times. Multiple contexts, from the past, present and future, coexist in the same practice architecture, which is formed not as a 'flat' entity but a palimpsest, with many layers.

Yet rather than producing an unruly relativist chaos in which judgements about validity and relevance are made purely with reference to one's own subjective concerns – the phenomenon of 'counterknowledge' about which authors such as Thompson (2008) are so rightly concerned – Harvey notes that:

> …multiple windows on a same reality, like the multiple theorisations available to us, can constitute a way of triangulating in on this same reality from multiple perspectives. Learning to see the world from multiple positions – if such an exercise is possible – then becomes a means to better understand how the world as a totality works …. This technique of conjoining information from different positionalities is a basic principle of all cartographic construction: to make an accurate map (representation) of the world we require at the very minimum a procedure of triangulation that moves across multiple points.

> (1996, 283–4)

This view of how knowledge – and a map – of an information landscape might be constructed is reflected in the work of those authors such as Christine Bruce who invoke the value of 'experiencing variation' (Bruce et al., 2006; Bruce, 2008) in teaching IL. Those working in the 'relational frame' of IL are exhorted to employ methods that give learners this experience of variation in making informational judgements. Bruce suggests that this helps learners develop cognitive schema more akin to those of professionals in a given discipline (2008). Yet as I have argued before (Whitworth, 2014, 179ff), this approach is not innately critical. It needs to be sensitive to how differing perspectives may not have equal status in the architectures that shape practice in these social settings. A consensus may not have been reached, or even be reachable, and the perspectives emerging on a landscape from different chronotopes may be incommensurable, or at least construed as such by those who hold them. In that case:

> We cannot transform one map into another. To produce one dominant cartographic image out of all this multiplicity is a power-laden act of domination. It is to force a singular discursive representational exercise upon multiple cartographies, to suppress difference and to establish homogeneity of representation.
>
> (Harvey, 1996, 284)

A 'singular discursive representational exercise' imposed on a social site constitutes a *reification* of 'free-flowing processes' (ibid., 81). Representations are constantly being produced and each 'freezes' the moment of its production: whenever we base a future judgement on these maps, we are bringing the past, and other places, into the present chronotope to some extent. Things may have changed in the meantime, the representation may not be as useful or as accurate as it once was. At the same time, we could not function cognitively in the world without such reifications: otherwise we would become like the protagonist in the movie *Memento* (2000; dir: Christopher Nolan) who cannot make new short-term memories and thus never has any sense of where he is or what he is doing there. (An alternative informational technique that the character, Leonard Shelby, uses to function in the world is to tattoo key facts on his body. These are intended to help him reach his teleoaffective goals: to find the man responsible for both his injury and the death of his wife.)

The creation and communication of discursive maps – whether overtly (e.g. the publication of a 'mission statement' for an organisation, the listing of procedures that must be followed when organising information within a practice architecture) or more covertly (e.g. the design of an information system or a VLE) – is a way to create some kind of permanence within the flux, a 'freezing' of the dynamic processes taking place in that landscape at a particular point in time. To identify the emergence of such discursive maps, we should pay close attention to 'shifts in language from free flowing processes to a crystallised causal schema' (Harvey, 1996, 82). Wenger also warns that reification of this kind may be a barrier to learning within a community of practice (Binder, 1996). The discursive maps become embedded into architectures, the assumptions and judgements they represent taken as a given in future judgements.

But Wenger then contrasts this with more *participatory* moments at which these discursive maps can be lifted up into awareness and scrutinised. Mapping is more nuanced than simply being a way for dominant interests to impose cognitive schema on subordinates. To say *some* maps and mapping perpetuate power is not to say that mapping cannot, at times, be empowering, epistemologically useful for individuals and communities, enfolded into different discourses. Everyday mappings can be performative, ludic, affective: maps can be seen as a form of resistance to power, participatory (Crampton and Krygier, 2006, 25; Crampton, 2009). Corner observes that:

> … mapping differs from 'planning' in that it entails searching, finding and unfolding complex and latent forces in the existing milieu rather than imposing a more-or-less idealised project from on high. Moreover, the synoptic imposition of the 'plan' implies a consumption (or extinguishing) of contextual potential, wherein all that is available is subsumed into the making of the project. Mapping, by contrast, discloses, stages and even adds potential for later acts and events to unfold. Whereas the plan leads to an end, the map provides a generative means, a suggestive vehicle that 'points' but does not overly determine.
>
> (1999, 228)

From this perspective, planning imposes schema on a social site, whereas mapping reveals difference in more positive ways, helping generate ideas without determining them in advance. While not all objects have the same *transformative potential* as others, it is the task for the critical theorist, the practitioner, to establish which do and can be exploited as such. As noted in the conclusion to Chapter 1, this is an *educational* task (Harvey, 1996, 56), one that explores possibilities, using the map as both a means to demonstrate, but also scrutinise, claims to authority over information practice.

Power and knowledge

The notion that mapping can be a vehicle for both reification and participation alludes to Foucault's view of power as generative as well as oppressive. Foucault notes how 'power is neither given, nor exchanged, nor recovered, but rather exercised' (1980, 89). Power, for Foucault, should not be seen as 'essentially repressive' (Kendall and Wickham, 1999, 50), but more like 'power' defined in a material sense (for example, the supply of energy through the generation of electrical power). In this worldview, power is generated at the micro-moments of discourse. Foucault's work illuminates the relationship between power and knowledge, as he explores how dominant stakeholders exercise the power to define what goals are sought and thus what counts as 'knowledge', or 'valid information', in social settings (Foucault, 1980, 52). Power is also bound up with resistance to that power, providing a means by which people can act, learn, form knowledge and change practice by resisting it, whether in organisational or educational settings (for the latter see Brookfield, 2005, 120).

Nevertheless, power certainly *can* be used oppressively through imposing discursive representations and definitions. These processes are revealed in Foucault's other work, where he turns his archaeological approach (Foucault, 1972) to various historical subjects in turn, including mental health (1973) and the legal/incarceration system (1975). These studies argue that the power to define what counts as, for example, 'sane/insane' or 'innocent/guilty' in these systems is fundamental to them, being the basis for complex and highly structured practice architectures based around this explicit stratification in power and the surveillance of those defined as subordinate within these systems (patients, prisoners). Foucault draws on Bentham's model prison, the *Panopticon*, where all prisoners could be subject to the direct gaze of a single guard, as a metaphor for how discipline is asserted within these architectures. While each inmate is *potentially* the subject of direct surveillance, more likely is that the authoritative gaze is directed elsewhere; yet because we can never be sure about this, we self-discipline ourselves, adopt the behaviour that is expected of us in this setting. And yet if we define 'surveillance' as *monitoring* and distribute the authority and the capacity to engage in it more widely across a population, this kind of scrutiny can also be the basis for the generation of power in previously subordinate populations. This scrutiny 'from below' has been, accordingly, termed '*sous*veillance', for instance, by the cyber-activist Steve Mann (see Whitworth, 2009, 80ff). Webster and Gunter (2018) draw on Foucault's theories as a lens for analysing how learners in an HE setting perceived authority and I will discuss their work further in Chapter 6.

A final case study of the mapping of a geographical landscape will now be offered, one that took place not just through the creation and improvement of cartographs but through a range of discursive and representational media. The case illuminates how these processes are shaped by, and shape, dominant discourses and serve as the basis of 'soft' power, here, at an international scale.

In a number of papers, Salvatore (2003; 2005; 2006) investigates how, particularly in the first three decades of the 20th century, US governmental, industrial, commercial and intellectual interests combined into a 'machine' operating to secure hegemonic domination of Latin America, manufacturing consent (cf. Gramsci, 1971) to this domination as the outcome of 'natural' and/or 'progressive' developments in capital accumulation. Salvatore (2006) focuses on the building of the Panama Canal as a crucial project on which hinged both the economic and the cultural dominance of the US over the rest of the Americas. A construction project, and an environmental alteration, on a scale never before conceived, the Canal fundamentally altered transportation routes and capital flows across the hemisphere and was 'a material expression of the original Monroe Doctrine, and a validation of the wisdom of that doctrine. It was a machine with an ideological purpose' (Salvatore, 2006, 671).

Around this key infrastructural development grew also a series of other representations, less overtly technological in form but still called by Salvatore a 'machine':

The US informal empire in Latin America can be seen as a 'soft machine', intensive in representations – a machine that produced, processed, and disseminated texts and images in order to accommodate older notions of self and other to the new conditions of capitalist accumulation (mass consumer capitalism and its technologies of representation) …. The soft machinery of empire organised practices and technologies of observation and representation (photography, travel writing, statistical handbooks, consumer surveys etc.) to make available to the 'American public' the diversity and difference of 'Spanish America'. Representational machines were fundamental for the construction of new knowledge about South/Latin America. Indeed, the construction of an informal empire in South America was a collective enterprise dependent upon representations.

(Salvatore, 2006, 665)

More substantial, and better organised, knowledge of the region was a predicate for the conquering of Latin American markets by American business interests. There was intense public interest in information about the region thanks to the cultural interest in 'Pan-Americanism', which characterised the 1910s and 1920s and was given a huge popular boost by Hiram Bingham's (re)discovery of Machu Picchu in 1911 (Salvatore, 2003). This caused a sensation, with magazines like the *National Geographic* then keen to sustain the explosion of interest with a series of further articles about this site and Latin America generally. 'Scientific' mappings of the landscape, like Bingham's subsequent expedition, sponsored by Yale from 1911–16, became media events and were 'considered a means to expand the field of visibility of the informal empire. The obstacles they encountered were crucial to the construction of difference within this imagined expanded territory ("the Americas")' (ibid., 69).

Salvatore states that:

An informal empire, in order to build hegemony, requires the production and circulation of truthful representations about the regions that fall under its gaze and influence. Without reliable regional knowledge (geography, resources, production, culture and history), the flows of investment and management that emanate from the centre would have greater difficulty consolidating the centre's presence, 'conquering' the region's markets, or exploiting its resources. Museum collections, photographic exhibits, books and articles, and maps are some of the means through which a center displays knowledge accumulated about peripheral regions. These representations embody the center's will to know and, at the same time, reveal fragments of a larger project of incorporating the Other (the peripheral region) into the dominant field of visibility.

(2003, 67)

This process did not go unchallenged. Bingham's work in Peru was subject to increasingly vociferous objections from local museums, scientific societies and universities. The Yale expedition was seen as an imperial project of knowledge, preventing locals from gaining access to evidence that would help them understand their own prehistory. But the Peruvian universities had nowhere near the budget nor infrastructure to either conduct research of this scale nor – more significantly – get the results out to the hungry public in the form of the sort of representations that were in demand, i.e. photographs and illustrated magazines (ibid., 74). The knowledge they did develop locally about Quechua culture and language and more critical investigations of contemporary interest about the status of native populations in Peru was thereby fragmented and 'not accepted in the great universities of the world until quite recently' (ibid., 76).

Instead, it was the libraries of major US academic institutions, like Yale, who played the most active role in 'making Latin America legible' (Salvatore, 2005, 425). The accumulation of collections in these libraries, the emergence of the discipline of 'Latin American Studies' and the growth of the most prestigious US research universities are all connected. Salvatore directly links this process to US attempts to follow the path of European, particularly German, universities, moving from the classical college to the research university model (ibid., 417), aimed at generating innovations that could be commercially exploited for the US economy as a whole.

Ultimately, this is a similar process to those Foucault recognises with, say, mental health: control over representations of a phenomenon used to attract resources, build infrastructure and install practice architectures based on discursive maps that cement these representations into place. 'Worthwhile' knowledge of Latin America became defined as whatever helped these hegemonic interests flourish in the region. The scale of library acquisitions increased greatly during the time of Pan-Americanism, with 'regional knowledge … predicated upon the possession of printed materials' (Salvatore, 2005, 416). Librarians accumulated huge numbers of manuscripts, reports, journals, newspapers and so on; building the informational base (that is, the landscape) on which further research could be based. But this accumulation implies the physical removal of these archives from their original Latin American context into a very different one, just as Donkeyman Lee Tjupurrula's map of part of the Gibson Desert is now out of place in the National Gallery of Victoria. This spatial move implies 'the relocation of enunciatory authority to the places where books and manuscripts were located' (ibid., 416). Thus, the discourse of 'soft empire' in Latin America intersects with the broader role the US library system has played in capitalist accumulation, as outlined in Chapter 1. Representations of the continent and the potentials of its rich landscapes have been subordinate to the discursive maps developed and then given authority by the process of capital accumulation and technological alterations to the environment that have occurred in the US.

Learning to see

The discussion of the Latin American case might suggest that the processes and practices that structure our engagement with information landscapes are so enormous in scale, and so globally pervasive, that resistance is futile. We exist within systems defined by the powerful and to battle against them is difficult at best and actively dangerous at worst. And yet it is central to Foucault's philosophy – and that of Gramsci, with his notion of the 'counterhegemony' (1971), and Habermas, who believes that colonisation can be countered by decolonising activity (1987), to name but two other influential democratic theorists   that these processes not only *can be* countered, but *are being* countered whenever people get together and try to organise their social arrangements in different ways. Whether these places are termed 'heterotopias' (Foucault, 1966; Johnson, 2006) or 'counterpublics' (Fraser, 1992), places such as co-operatives, institutions offering critical pedagogies, social movement groups: wherever consciousness is raised (Freire, 1970), and/or where scrutiny of practice, of 'taken-for-granted' discursive maps takes place (Blaug, 2007).

Such political activities do not have to be restricted to Situationist-style 'happenings' or isolated communes. Individuals and communities can be empowered to bring their own deliberations to bear when it comes to solving problems that they face; that is, they can *learn* and *be taught* to do this, and there are certain skills, including informational ones, that offer tangible and observable improvements to their ability to do so. We can 'learn to see' things in a different way, reveal relationships between issues and practices that are otherwise obscured, kept fragmented through the operations of the media (Hamelink, 1976; Habermas, 1987, 355). Through such active enquiries, the scrutiny of 'hidden transcripts' (Scott, 1990), communities can use the discontinuities between the validity claims of 'authority' and their practical experiences in specific places (e.g. poverty, environmental damage, injustice) to not only criticise power but to generate it and wield it democratically, to distribute authority, not centralise it: yet still to remain *vigilant* over it.

The notion that IL is something empowering is implicitly based on the view that power is something that can be generated within a community, a setting, a discourse and an educational environment, and that by developing IL in particular ways rather than others, this distributes authority among a group, or out from teachers to students, librarians to users. This is in accordance with the tenets of practice theory, which 'must be in a position to cast distinctive light on, say, how inequality results from uneven distributions of the capacities to act' (Watson, 2017, 173) in given situations, or at least act *effectively*. Sensitivity to these uneven distributions of power, in this sense, is a way of identifying where power and authority lie in these settings and, potentially, of empowering actors to act in ways that scrutinise and validate these sources of authority, remaining vigilant over the practice architectures that structure activity in particular settings (Blaug, 2007). Watson observes that:

… some sites, some organisations and some people are clearly situated in systematically advantageous positions amidst the associations, arrangements and alignments comprising social life, such that they have distinctive capacity to act purposively in ways which shape action over distance and across locales of action. The challenge is to develop concepts and methods that can help grasp how arrangements and associations of practices and the heterogenous flows they are bound with are produced through, and reproduce, systematic inequities in capacities to act, including to act in ways which shape others' capacities to act.

(2017, 179)

Writers on radical democratic practice have noted that directly democratic, decolonising activity is well suited to the small group, due to the increased likelihood that such a group can develop procedures that allow all voices to be heard (e.g. Gastil, 1993) and because social affinities are more likely to be sustainable in a small group (Bookchin, 1986). But this literature, and the lived history of many radical experiments in alternative organisational forms (see Landry et al., 1985), also notes that by no means all such groups are, or remain, ideally structured. A community can become highly dysfunctional; acting to constrain learning, limit possibilities, bind its members tightly to existing, orthodox practice and develop knowledge in ways that turn these practices into habit or even ritual.

Yet, the potential for change is always present, as it is in any social, discursive setting. Groups, and individuals within them, can learn to act more effectively within a given information landscape; one they have the power to populate and structure, bringing to bear the full range of modalities (epistemic, social and corporeal) as they do so. If it is the role of the critical pedagogue or consciousness-raiser (Freire, 1970), in whatever form this role takes, to reveal potentials and allow the scrutiny of claims to authority, then that means somehow revealing the discursive maps that structure information and practice in that setting in the present time and those that lie beneath the present architecture, in earlier layers of the palimpsest. The question is, to repeat – how do we *learn to see* the transformational potentials that exist in a social site and help practitioners bring these potentials into fruition, giving them the cognitive and discursive tools they require in order to make changes to their practice architectures when such changes are needed?

The reasons why these potentials may be obscured is not always because of the operations of power, whether coercive or more subtly hegemonic, though obviously this is true in many cases. There are also cases where the problem is more one of communication; of being inadequately able to express tacit knowledge to those who are not (yet) members of the community. Lloyd notes that when one defines IL, or literacy more broadly, as a social practice:

... within any setting or context, there will be literacies that are authorised and some that are not. For Tuominen et al (2005, 337), literacy essentially means 'being able to enact in practice the rules of argumentation and reasoning that an affinity group in a specific knowledge domain considers good or eloquent.'

(Lloyd, 2010a, 13)

An example of this is related by Badke:

Valentine (2001), in a series of studies, found that the paramount concern of many students doing research papers was discerning 'what the professor wants'. That is, students were writing for the grades they received and believed that meeting professorial expectations was the key to receiving those grades. While they were quite willing to acknowledge their own failings, they blamed the professor if their low grades were seen as resulting from poor instructions or unreasonable restrictions placed upon their projects.

(Badke, 2012, 5)

On the surface this seems to exemplify the 'self-disciplining' nature of academic discourse, à la Foucault, and also the power relation implicit in both the institution of grading and, ultimately, the power to award degrees, with all the direct and indirect impact this has on academia and how it is sustained financially and discursively. Yet this quote hints also at the issue's rooting in difficulties with articulating tacit knowledge. Consider this second passage from Badke:

I received a telephone call from a 52-year-old woman finishing a bachelor's degree ... taking a course for which the professor had asked the class to write an interdisciplinary research paper. In her estimation, while the professor had provided her with some rather broad examples of what could be done in such an assignment, he had made no real attempt to explain how actually to do it. Nor did she have any confidence that *even he knew what the process might be, let alone how to explain it to the class.*

(Badke, 2012, 26, emphasis added)

Therefore, it is by no means always the case that those embedded in a discipline are able to articulate the discursive maps and practices that structure knowledge in that field. Badke notes that those embedded in a discipline, 'might be hard-pressed to teach that epistemology to others' (ibid., 95); that is, how they know what they know and why they value certain sources of information over others. Having copious disciplinary knowledge, or what Lloyd calls the 'epistemic modality', is one thing, but other modalities come into play: 'Accumulated data require sense-making skills on two fronts – determining what is reliable/significant/relevant and organising the data into a structure that is manageable so that it can be used to address the issue at hand' (ibid., 135–6).

Conclusion

Using mapping as a way of developing knowledge about both geographical and information landscapes has rich potential; maps are tools that can help select, organise and disseminate knowledge both tacit and explicit, as subsequent chapters will demonstrate. But this discussion of power shows that we must see all maps in play in particular social (educational) settings as potentially serving both as restrictive *definitions* of cognitive schema and, at the same time, as tools that allow the *scrutiny* of these schema. Harvey's work confirms the need for a more explicitly political view of difference (variation), attention to how authority is distributed between members of a group, and (in formal education) between teacher and student, and how this is linked to the implementation of mapping as an epistemological and methodological practice in a given setting.

It is necessary to problematise the issue of power and difference in information literacy and information practice and to make mapping part of this *problematique*, seeing it as not just a 'solution' to it but as also constitutive of how power has been drawn on in a particular context to create discursive structures that govern practice in the first place. How do groups make judgements of relevance ('Saracevic's conundrum') in ways that allow them to make equally effective, and ideally *better*, judgements in the future (Blaug, 1999)? How can effective, informed and democratic decision-making, and the practices which flow from it, be made sustainable? And how can this happen in higher/adult educational settings, whether in the university or the workplace, in ways that acknowledge the power structures within these settings and the constraints of their extant practice architectures?

In order to address these questions, and others posed thus far, it is now necessary to move on to investigate empirical examples of where mapping has been used in these ways. That is the topic of the next and subsequent chapters.

Chapter 4

Three psychogeographies

Introduction

The aim of the next three chapters is to report on studies of mapping and navigation in terms of how they play out in real landscapes and what can be learned by applying certain mapping techniques, both in a research sense and educationally. Chapters 5 and 6 report on research projects that were conducted in a more traditional way than the investigation presented in this chapter. Here, I engage in a self-reflective and autobiographical exercise in order to generate a rich description of my own navigational practice.

This approach is similar to autoethnography. As a scholar, I am not here trying to view the landscape from a detached point, but (re-)inserting my mind and body into it, 'as the site from which the story is generated' (Spry, 2001, 708). In autoethnography, the researcher 'is the epistemological and ontological nexus upon which the research process turns' (ibid., 711). Spry notes that for many this is 'scholarly treason and heresy' (ibid., 709). But it is also a way of assessing affect in a given setting and accumulating a rich, thick description of practices within a landscape and the chronotopes that comprise it, in a form that would be difficult to replicate experimentally (although not practically impossible, as *theirwork* suggested).

Autoethnography appears periodically in studies of IL. For example, Purdue (2003, 654–5), considers the old ACRL IL standards and self-reflects on his performance as a researcher against each, finding himself wanting when it comes to most of them. A number of published works on IL pedagogy are effectively autoethnographies, the authors self-reflexively exploring their experiences in the IL classroom in depth, to produce rich, thick descriptions of practice. Books by Downey (2016) and Badke (2012) are examples. However, the concept also has a (self-)critical angle that is not present in this chapter. Here, I do not set out to make observations about the sociopolitical contexts in which I exist and am engaging in informational practice. I am not critiquing myself, nor my positioning with respect to these contexts (cf. Spry, 2001, 710).

If this chapter is not a true autoethnography, then what is it? The term 'autotopography' was coined by Gonzalez (1995) and has since been used in different ways. Gonzalez's original reference was to 'personal objects arranged by a subject as physical signs that spatially represent that subject's identity' (Arlander, 2012, 255), thus, using objects such as trophies, photographs, souvenirs, etc., as a form of self-representation. Heddon (2008, cited in ibid.) defines autotopography as 'writing place through self (and simultaneously writing self through place) ... a creative act of seeing, interpretation and invention, all of which depend on where you are standing, when and for what purpose'. In turn, Karjalainen (2006) coins the term 'topobiography' as a way of interpreting biographical experiences with reference to particular places. Arlander notes that both 'autotopography' and 'topobiography' are terms 'relating self, site, temporality and movement' – a way to 'describe practices related to topobiographically meaningful places' (Arlander, 2012, 251). Arlander's topobiography is built around her repeated visits, once a week for a year, to a site from her childhood, and there creating site-specific art (like a film depicting her sat on the same branch of a tree each time). She reflects in the paper on her professional goals, the aim of the artworks being to focus viewers' attention on environmental changes, but also her private aims, with the intention being to revitalise her memory and restore a connection to elements of her youth. Here, however, Arlander reports that the repetitive nature of her visits 'walked myself out of my memories and commitments to that landscape. Old emotional images were replaced by routine observations' (2012, 254).

I choose to define my approach as 'psychogeography' (Debord, 1958; Bassett, 2004). Debord and the Situationists built on Walter Benjamin's promotion of the *flâneur*, a detached observer who would walk randomly, drifting, through the city. Specific means can be employed to destabilise the psyche and raise awareness of the habitual ways in which we navigate place, particularly urban place, and also (as Arlander suggests above and I will reaffirm shortly) navigate time. An example of this is to 'purposely get lost by using a map of one place to navigate oneself around another' (Bonnett, 2015, 5). One could navigate in a set, algorithmic way, sticking to fixed patterns of turn-making (e.g. always second right, first left, repeated regardless of where this leads). These are informational discrepancies, created deliberately, to raise awareness and provoke reflection on the 'psychogeographical contours' of cities: their 'currents, fixed points and vortexes that strongly discourage entry into or exit from certain zones' (Debord, 1958, cited in Bassett, 2004). Bassett adds: 'Psychogeography demand[s] new forms of cartography, capable of representing states of consciousness and feeling' (2004, 402).

Maps produced by authorities such as the OS have no way of recording affect, such as emotional reactions to certain places. Bassett takes his geography students on walks (*dérives*) through areas of Paris, encouraging them to find their own way of 'drifting', e.g. possibly following an algorithmic approach, or using dice to decide on a route, and 'periodically stopping and recording group or individual discussions, decisions, impressions, feelings, attitudes etc… [They are] asked to think about ways of representing the hard and soft phenomena of the city (feelings, senses of calm or dislocation, attractions and repulsions etc.) in cartographic form' (Bassett, 2004, 404–5), and encouraged to collect relevant artefacts en route.

My intention is to provide examples of, and thus support for, key ideas introduced in the book so far. Firstly, the indivisibility of the geographical from the informational landscape and the idea that layered within the flows of both are points of interruption to those flows which have personal and social meaning. It is these points of interruption, these relative permanences, which provide learning opportunities, while at the same time constituting nodes of power, through fixing meanings. Second, the geographies described here all, in one way or another, draw on 'equipment' as Schatzki puts it (1996, 113). The dispersed practice of 'navigating a landscape', by being given specific form in three locations, is thereby integrated with my own informational needs, arising from the writing of this book. As an integrative practice, the information and meaning that can be derived from my navigation of *these* landscapes, three specific places to which I have a different geographical and informational relationship, I try to establish what is learned about these landscapes as I bring to bear in them different mapping and navigational practices, whether using habit, memory or logical reasoning. I show here also that, in accordance with the definitions developed so far, the processes taking place can result in substantive communicative acts and effective utterances, without necessarily having to lead to the production of a cartograph, a map in the popular sense. What I produce here are more akin to rutters, a form of discursive map, and for one of the landscapes used here I refer also to discursive maps created by other authors.

At one level I am taking a similar approach to Williamson and Connolly in the *theirwork* project, described in Chapter 2; tracking journeys through a landscape, not just in the sense of movement through *space*, but through *place*, and all the local understandings and affect/emotion that this adds to the technical aspects of mapping. Sotelo (2010) also uses walking to stimulate dialogue and reflection. He describes a group walk made with a number of participants near Bogotá, Colombia, that brought together indigenous and non-indigenous people in an area once rife with slave labour and now of concern regarding its water resources. The aim of the group walk was to enable 'a series of intercultural and environmental dialogues to take place' within and about this landscape. Sotelo also observes that any environment offers resources to the walker – and challenges. There is an 'interaction between path, environment and being-in-movement (the walker)'; and at least at one level (though not necessarily consciously), walking is a 'decision-making process' (Sotelo, 2010) aimed at maximising the effective use of the resources in this landscape to avoid hazard and meet the walker's instrumental goals. I take this view of walking as the basis for the reflections to come.

For walks two and three, as with Bassett's students in Paris, I used field notes to record observations as I walked. These notes contain practical observations about how I was navigating the landscape at particular points, and my emotional, affective reactions to certain places, moments, or the task as a whole. At the end of the third walk, these field notes were typed up onto my laptop, but have not been revised since. Where the notes are quoted here, then, they represent my thoughts and feelings as at 29 January 2019.

Walk 1: Manchester

My first psychogeography was revealed when I acted as one of eight participants in the research of an MA Sociology student at the University of Manchester, Martin Greenwood. His dissertation (Greenwood, 2018) explored the role pedestrian crossings play in maintaining a sense of public safety and benefit. While crossings are doubtless seen by most these days as just a minor feature of the transport infrastructure, Greenwood recounts how when they were first introduced in the UK in the early 20th century to help combat a rise in pedestrian casualties as automobiles became more prevalent, many objected to this imposition of arbitrary authority (see also Hornsey, 2012). Movement through the city landscape became more controlled, channelled through certain locations (crossings) and times (when the 'green man' shows). Culturally there are different interpretations of this signal: in some countries (such as Germany and the USA) there can be legal sanctions imposed against those who cross at the 'red man', but Britons are more likely to ignore that signal and cross if they judge it is safe. Pedestrian crossings are thus informational, cultural, spatial and part of the practice architecture: they are moments of interruption and thus impose structure on the flows of people and cars through proximal, yet different, routes through the landscape (pavements/sidewalks and roads respectively).

Greenwood sought to investigate how pedestrians made judgements as they moved through the city streets and encountered key crossing points, and how they interacted with traffic and other pedestrians as they walked. His methodology was observational and designed to provoke reflection both in himself and in his participants. He first recorded (in the same way as I will with walks 2 and 3) his self-reflections as he completed a circuit around Manchester city centre that involved three pedestrian crossings that each displayed 'spikes' on accident graphs. He then recruited eight participants and asked us each to walk through the city with a GoPro strapped to our foreheads, simultaneously being recorded from behind. These two movies were spliced together and each participant viewed the 'split-screen' movie with the researcher while he probed our feelings and motivations at particular points in the journey. This method therefore resembles 'Think-Aloud Protocol' (e.g. Fonteyn, Kuipers and Grobe, 1993), a tried-and-tested technique for exploring how people make decisions about route and goals when navigating a virtual landscape (for example, a website), here transferred into the real-world setting with the help of technology.

While Greenwood's research foci – crossings, ideas of 'freedom' and what motivates pedestrians – are interesting, they are not directly relevant to my immediate concerns. But the experience of watching myself take this walk revealed ways in which I *habitually* drew on resources in this landscape to fulfil my instrumental goals on this journey: the walk from my office on campus to Manchester Victoria station, a 35-minute walk that I have done hundreds of times since 2005. (As with the other two walks in this chapter, the full route is outlined in Appendix 1.) I had *motivations*; I had *learned practices* and not only them, but the best places in which to enact them – in Schatzki's terms, where the necessary equipment lies in the landscape.

For example, I was filmed on a hot and sunny afternoon in July 2018. Without consciously articulating it at the time, but quite evidently from observing my performance in the movie afterwards (e.g. when I crossed a road for no reason connected to my route per se), I stuck to the shady side of streets. This judgement had a temporal element, too, for had this been a morning walk, the sun's rays would have fallen differently and to avoid them I would have chosen to have walked on the other side. And had it been a winter's morning I might have chosen to walk in the sun, rather than the shade. Real-time judgements therefore lead to adjustments in how I exploit the resources in the landscape to meet my own subjective needs.

Another example comes with an observation I repeated to Martin in my interview concerning the timing of lights on a pedestrian crossing at the junction of Princess Street and Whitworth Street:

> I know that if I can see the cars are about to go up and down Princess Street, I know I don't have to break my stride and I will just go straight across that crossing 'cause it will be green. And I also know that … if I know that … Princess Street is clear and nothing's … coming up and turning … right, I will again – I will walk before it goes green … it's just something I've learned.
>
> (Greenwood, 2018, 43)

These practices have become part of my *bodily repertoire* (see Schatzki, 1996, 58). I cross the road to the shady side and know how to relate my walking speed to the point that the lights stand in their cycle, and I do these things spontaneously, but not randomly: without *conscious* thought (until Martin's research methodology raised the practice into my awareness), yet not without *knowing*. The behaviour was *nächstliegenden* or 'next-to-hand' (Wittgenstein, 1953, in Schatzki, ibid.).

The pathway itself is also a 'next-to-hand' resource for me in this landscape, one that I use routinely. My walking route through the city is one I have crafted over nearly a decade and a half of working there. It is a *personal* pathway, not necessarily the logical route, nor the shortest, but built around subjective preferences (it is quieter and has only two busy road crossings, for example). It is a landscape I am intimately familiar with, yet it is long and narrow: I know *only* this pathway well – a few hundred metres to either side and I would need a map. I know how long it takes me to walk the whole thing, and sections of it, and this awareness meshes with the more rigorous and inflexible timetable followed by the trains I catch at the far end, Manchester Victoria station. Disruptions to it, for whatever reason, provoke negative emotional reactions. For the last year building works across one street have forced me into a detour and I cannot wait for these works to be completed.

Clearly, the route between my office and the railway station is one I know intimately, a pathway (resource) that I exploit without much conscious thought. My inner cognitive map of this pathway appears fully up-to-date and fit for purpose. How, then, might I navigate:

- A landscape with which I feel intimately familiar, yet have not visited in 30 years – I have clear memories of it, but no up-to-date knowledge;
- A landscape with which I am unfamiliar?

Can I navigate these without technological aid, without a map of any kind? How much cognition is delegated to such equipment and, if I eschew it, how will I handle the information discrepancies that arise in these two situations?

Walk 2: Crowborough, Sussex

To test my knowledge of the first of these landscape types – one with which I was once very familiar, but lack up-to-date knowledge – I took a 'field trip' in January 2019 to the place in which I grew up, the town of Crowborough in Sussex, England. I lived there until 1988, but since leaving I have spent only a few more days there, and none since a brief visit in 2013. Nevertheless, before the trip I self-reflected and concluded that the navigational and informational practices I learned in my first 19 years left me with an indelible map of this landscape inscribed in memory. The walk described here (actually two, undertaken on consecutive days) was an attempt to test the accuracy and contemporary relevance of this mental map and my ability to exploit it, and to reflect on whether I would, in the end, need other equipment to successfully undertake this task and how I would draw on this information, digital or otherwise.

Some notes on the geography help put my task into context (further observations, drawn from historical and literary sources, follow later). Crowborough is a town of about 20,000 inhabitants located in the northern part of the county of Sussex, roughly halfway between London and the south coast of Britain, on the edge of a heathland area known as Ashdown Forest. Apart from a few scattered dwellings it did not exist until the railway came past in 1868. Since then it has grown in a series of developmental bursts, including the Warren, a prestigious residential district from the 1930s, and a large estate built in the 1980s. There has been no major development since, although some small areas have been 'filled in' with new housing. On many streets, houses are named, but not numbered. In terms of its physical configuration it is, for an English settlement, unusual in that it is built on top of a hill. The highest points are nearly 800 feet (243m) above sea level and these are quite close to the centre of town. (This summit, incidentally, was one of the key triangulation points used in the original Ordnance Survey in the 1790s (Hewitt, 2010, 131) and was also the site of one of a network of signal beacons, hence the name of the town's, and my old, high school, Beacon Community College.)

These geographical and historical facts mean that: (a) there is no good vantage point from which one can survey the town prior to its exploration (compare this to the case of Seaford, discussed below, and to the practices of medieval mapmakers outlined in Chapter 2); and (b) while two main roads (the A26 and B2100) run roughly at right angles through the whole town, with the obvious 'town centre' being at their junction, there is no prominent landmark building, like a castle, tall church or significant river crossing, to orient the visitor. All in all, I surmise that without a map and with no prior knowledge of the landscape, Crowborough would be a relatively challenging place to navigate, particularly to any locations away from those main roads. The psychogeographical task I set myself is therefore not one principally of navigation, but of testing the durability and continued relevance of memories that are at least 30 years old and have hardly been drawn upon in that time.

I spent two full days walking in Crowborough on the weekend of 26 and 27 January 2019. On these walks I set myself the task of making the following journey without carrying a paper map or accessing an online map at any point (I did not, however, ignore maps or signposts I came across during my walk: reflecting on the availability of such information was an important aspect of this psychogeography):

1   Get from Crowborough railway station to the Limekiln football ground (to watch a match taking place there);
2   Get from the football ground to my bed and breakfast (B&B) accommodation;
3   [The following day] Get from my B&B to my former house;
4   From there to both my former schools [these stand next door to one another, so in effect this was one task];
5   From there to the town centre for lunch;
6   And finally, back to the B&B.

The combined distance of both walks was about 9 miles (14.5 km). In tasks 1 and 2, I had not been to these specific destinations before but I knew their street addresses. This information had been acquired from online sources prior to my visit, but I had not checked their location on a map (paper or online). Incidentally, there seems little benefit to be gained by disguising the identity of places such as my old schools and the names of streets, but I do not compromise anyone's anonymity by, for example, identifying specific houses.

I managed to complete all six sub-tasks with almost complete success: that is, finding each place without referring to Google or any other map. The only exception was when I did reach for Google Maps at the very end of sub-task 2 to confirm the location of my B&B. I was sure that I was in the right location but there was no street lighting and it was cold, dark and raining: in the end Google just confirmed that shelter for the night was some twenty metres further up the road and that I had, indeed, made the correct decision back at the last junction. In daylight, or with street lighting, regardless of the weather, I would not have needed this final validation.

There were points in the walk where I was very conscious of following a specific pathway, particularly with tasks 3–5, as these took place mostly in parts of town that I would once have traversed on a daily basis. I knew exactly where I was, where I was going and how to get from one point to the other. On the other hand, when I was not so familiar with the area – and my B&B was located in one such district – or when, during task 2, I left named streets and instead took footpaths through woodland known as 'the Ghyll', I was not following a pathway laid out in my head (unlike in Manchester). However, I was still conscious of the town's broad configuration and where I currently stood in relation to it and in relation to where I wanted to go. This awareness, plus some key informational resources within the landscape (particularly street signs), helped me reorient and adapt my perspective on the two occasions across the six tasks where I did go slightly off-path, by a few hundred metres in each case. From my notes:

> After the football ... I took a less efficient route than I might have, and came out of the Ghyll nature reserve not quite where I thought I was, but the map board at the entrance helped me reorient myself. This is the only time over the three days that I consulted a map that was embedded as a text in the environment, rather than being online.

And on day two:

> Final walk back from town to the B & B. I deliberately take a more roundabout route. Still, I know where to go; at one point I am dropping down to a junction and I just know that I must turn left here even though it is certain I have not passed this particular road junction since 1988 at the latest. It's not because I have an exact map in my head. It's that I know the configuration of where I've been and where I am going – LOGICALLY this must be a left turn here. It would warp the dimensions if I was to turn right.

I was therefore making assumptions about the topography of the town: albeit safe and justifiable ones. There is no fourth dimension to this landscape, no wormholes, or even a more everyday subterranean pathway like a subway that could have seen me 'leap' across intervening ground. The Warren district, where my B&B was sited, was never 'my' part of this landscape but I still knew enough about its broad configuration and how it was located in relation to other areas of town to be confident that, though I might go temporarily astray, I would not 'get lost' in these particular streets. *Pathways* emerged both from my memory of navigating this landscape in the past and in situ, as I re-familiarised myself with it decades later: an example of the latter being that once I had confirmed the location of the B&B at the end of day one, come day two, on both leaving the house in the morning and returning there in the afternoon, it had been 'slotted in' to my inner cognitive map and the technological aid, Google Maps, was no longer required.

On day one, I exploited what I perceived as a boundary to the landscape. This is a road, Palesgate Lane, that when I was growing up always represented 'the edge of town' to the east. This is a culturally-defined limit, not a natural one (compare it with the example of Seaford to follow), but nevertheless, in my youth, one side of this lane was always 'Crowborough' and the other side not (and this is still the case: no development has subsequently taken place on the east side of this road). Not all boundaries are this clear and when they are fuzzier, different clues need to be sought in terms of how far through a transition or threshold zone one has moved. But with the football ground (destination 1) being located on this lane, I did not have to worry about my precise route: I knew that when I hit Palesgate Lane, I could just follow this boundary: there was nothing *relevant* beyond. I knew that following, but staying within, the boundary would lead to my goal.

The one printed map, embedded in the landscape, was supplemented by the most important equipment, the street signage, labels at key junctions that gave moments of confirmation, particularly in less familiar regions (e.g. the Warren). Minor though these may seem, they provide an identity to particular places that can have significant impact: for example, house prices can shift by going literally around the corner to an otherwise identical property with a more 'desirable' street address. To me, though, the signage provided a continuous drip-feed of orienting moments, embedded checks to my awareness of where I thought I was placed in the landscape. Thus, my technical ability to navigate Crowborough was *mainly* a function of my memory of it, but not *completely*. Signs and other equipment embedded in the landscape were useful checks and helped reorient me when I went slightly off my intended (memorised) route.

What was also apparent from my walk were the *affective* elements, the feelings provoked by certain locations in the landscape. Most powerfully, this occurred on my approach to the house where I lived until I was 13 years old (1983), which prompted this passage in my notes:

Notes written while standing on Old Lane outside my house. And I can still call it that – MY house. The details here, not just the exterior of the house itself but also the hinterland, the fence just outside for example (that obscures the view of the house when you come in from Crowborough Hill), the junction with West Beeches Road – these have been astonishingly well remembered, seen in dreams. There is an elderly gentleman standing in the driveway as I walk past. This feels wrong. The house should be inhabited by a young couple with a baby. Like we were. The name of the house has been changed. The old gent cannot possibly have any idea that the 49-year-old guy in the long coat who just walked past used to live in his house. But the connection is irrevocable.

(On reading an early draft of this manuscript, Stéphane Goldstein asked me why I did not strike up a conversation with this gentleman. I can only answer by saying that at that particular time and place the thought simply did not occur to me. In a wholly unscientific way (hence my relegating it to this parenthesis), this may indicate quite how much I was wandering around a past Crowborough rather than a present one.)

These memories were provoked not only by the presence of things in the landscape, but their absence and other signs of change (like the name of the house). These notes were made at my old schools; bear in mind that I had not set foot in my primary school, Sir Henry Fermor, at all since 1980, and for Beacon Community College I had been back only once since 1985.

Beacon School, seen from the footpath (and no one from Crowborough would need to ask 'which footpath'). Again, perfectly remembered. There are a couple of new buildings. The playing field has now been levelled and turned into 3G pitches surrounded by green fencing. What I remember is as much what is **not** there as what is. Here, in the corner by the sports hall, used to be a prefab with two classrooms in it. Images come to mind of particular lessons I had in that prefab. Just typical ones but I remember them. I remember Mr E_____ with a face like thunder painting over graffiti on the prefab wall. These memories have been provoked by an **absence** not a presence, a **change** from what was to what is. The object (the prefab) that provokes these memories and associations is tangible – but tangible in a **past** setting, not in the current one. The only trace of its presence right at that moment in time is in my mind. Layers of context, not a flat temporality.

Fermor school two minutes later, just the same. Astonishing precision, down to remembering the little concrete garage in the infant playground. But over the main road, the field where the funfairs used to be held is now all housing. Anomalous.

My psychogeographical experiment allowed me to perceive *layers* in the landscape. There were some obvious schisms between Crowborough pre-1988 and now, such as the houses on the field that in 'my time' used to play host to the annual funfairs. But this discrepancy largely exists just for me. Nevertheless, I wrote this in my field notes at the time and with three months' hindsight (I write these words in late April 2019), the final statement has turned out to be correct:

> I'm wholly confident I can get myself to almost any street in this town from memory – *as long as* it's one that was here up until 1988. Perhaps there are a couple of the more obscure ones I'd struggle with. But I won't have a clue with any of the new little closes and gated estates around the place. Even having seen them today, I won't remember them.

This divide between 'my' Crowborough (my internal representations of this place) and what exists in January 2019 is not just a matter of physical, geographical difference. There are differences which have a more temporal character and represent new cultural and informational layers over this landscape. For example, the most famous of Crowborough's former residents is Sir Arthur Conan Doyle, author of the *Sherlock Holmes* stories amongst others, who resided for the latter part of his life in Windlesham Manor on the town's south-western edge (I walked past this early on day two). As I wrote in my field notes:

> Many more references in street and place names to Conan Doyle than when I was here (when I lived largely in ignorance of Sir ACD's connection to Crowborough). New housing developments called Holmes Place and Sherlock Shaw and Watson's Close. Cafe Baskerville in the town centre (a bookshop in my time). The Attention Economy? Capital appropriating heritage to add value – in a way not done (in Crowborough anyway) until at least the 1990s?

What I allude to at the end is Goldhaber's 1997 paper, 'The Attention Economy', and, though this is speculation, how the newer layers of the town are informationally more oriented to the perceived need to attract tourists and/or investors in property, to direct capital to this local economy. Whether I am right or not, it is a manifestation of the town's cultural heritage (albeit a rather indirect one as no Conan Doyle novel uses Crowborough as a location, disguised or otherwise) that was not apparent in the 1988 version of the landscape.

Crowborough then, like all landscapes, is not a unitary field but a *palimpsest*, layers written over other layers. Most of the judgements I made about it, and the affect that it provoked, on those days in January 2019, happened with reference to my knowledge of this landscape *in the past*, not the present. While these cognitive maps have been revised to some extent following my visit – for example, I would now have no difficulty at all re-finding the Limekiln football ground nor my B&B even though I had never been to either place prior to 26 January 2019 – I have not managed to integrate other more recent information, such as the location of some of the new housing developments. These latter places never have been, and are still not, *relevant* to me so there is no reason to put in the cognitive work required to integrate them with my (pre-1988) mental map.

Other discursive maps of the Crowborough area have been created and continue to be written. On a global scale, by far the best known is that provided by A. A. Milne and his illustrator, E. H. Shepard, in the *Winnie-the-Pooh* books. Milne lived in Cotchford Farm near the village of Hartfield, a few miles from Crowborough on the other edge of Ashdown Forest. In his introduction to Barbara Willard's book about Ashdown Forest (1989, and see below), Christopher Robin Milne acknowledges that the forest of Pooh is identical to this physical landscape. Milne and Shepard expropriated and remapped the Forest, imposing their own artistic visions upon it, but even today many geographical features are easily recognisable from Shepard's illustrations. (See https://www.just-pooh.com/ashdown.html. On the same website, https://www.just-pooh.com/map.html has a map aimed at 'Pooh tourists', which integrates the book's locations with the geographical landscape and provides directions to key places; mapping that reinforces the points being made in this section.)

The Pooh connection has in turn led to changes in the landscape – and also the absence of change, such as when C. R. Milne and others actively and successfully campaigned against plans to drill for oil on Ashdown Forest in the 1970s. An obvious example comes with the bridge originally called Posingford Bridge but now officially (that is, on OS maps) known as either 'Pooh Bridge' or 'Poohsticks Bridge', as it is the place in the books where Pooh and Piglet play the game in which they drop sticks into the stream on one side of the bridge and see which comes out first on the other side. The stream that the bridge spans is a very small one and on my last visit there some years ago, the water had stopped flowing properly due to the volume of sticks that had been dropped in by recent visitors, creating a temporary dam. The bridge had to be rebuilt in the 1990s due to the damage caused by the many visitors who came there to see the bridge and play the game. The Disney corporation – which has, in turn, made huge profits from its own appropriation of the narratives (though not the Sussex landscape) – donated funds that permitted this rebuilding and during this renovation the construction of the bridge was altered to better resemble Shepard's illustrations.

Willard's book, *The Forest: Ashdown in East Sussex* (1989), structures a history of this natural landscape chronologically from chapter 2 onwards, but begins with a first chapter that is a personal eulogy to this landscape, an 11-page introspection. This quote provides the flavour:

> Love of place, which seems to develop mostly in later life, may hold less actual anguish than love of person, but it is painfully possessive … At any season I find the Forest best of all on a Monday morning, for the totally unworthy reason that it seems to have been given back [from the weekend visitors]
>
> (Willard, 1989, 3)

Willard's historical narrative cannot but be read in the light of this initial, detailed exploration of her subjective feelings towards the Ashdown Forest landscape (she also wrote a series of novels, *Mantlemass*, set in the Forest in the 15th century (see Helbig, 1982)). The whole book leaves us in no doubt that she sees this as a context, a (loved) place, that has been under threat, whether from expropriation by the military or environmental and social change, for centuries – but her message is: it endures. Her discursive, affective map of the landscape positions its geography, nature and history relative to the external world, locating it for the reader. Note also the *authority* given to this work (this utterance) by the inclusion of the preface written by Christopher Milne, prominently advertised on the book cover to attract potential readers.

In his *Observations on the Topography and Climate of Crowborough Hill, Sussex* (1898), C. Leeson Prince presents a different kind of map from an earlier era – the late 19th century, the opening stages in Crowborough's relatively short history. His book begins like Willard's, with a preface written from a personal viewpoint. Only now, the message is not one of a threatened environment but one very much 'emerging', 'open for business', including tourism (the local environment is said to be health-enhancing), but more significantly, new residents. In the preface, Leeson Prince laments that a recent run of dry summers – an observation confirmed by the data he presents in the book – shows why this hilltop town needs to sort out its water supply. He calls for local authorities to develop housing of 'a more suitable type'. After this preface, the book is then an exhaustive, meticulous series of observations of the physical characteristics of the town, its flora and fauna, geology, topography and, most of all, climate, with weather data presented month by month over a period of several years.

While Willard is a novelist and offers her *perspective* on the area in a lyrical fashion, Leeson Prince is a Victorian gentleman scientist (obvious from his list of memberships on the book's title page, e.g. 'Member of the Royal College of Surgeons; Fellow of the Royal Astronomical and Meteorological Societies …', plus several others) and presents a different, but no less valid view. In both cases the use of discursive mapping is quite apparent, as Willard and Leeson Prince present their views on this landscape as the basis for future judgements and a way of justifying practices. There is a correspondence between the representations and the reality and both works make propositions that can be tested in that reality.

In the present time, few towns or villages lack their own page on Wikipedia and at the time of writing Crowborough's page (https://en.wikipedia.org/wiki/Crowborough) provides pertinent information about the town, organised into categories. Though, like all Wikipedia pages, it has the appearance of objectivity, as a collaborative production it is in fact a record of a series of selections, judgements and representations. It is certainly a valuable informational resource in one way and is undoubtedly the easiest way that any visitor, prior to coming to the town, could discover certain facts about it, such as that it retains a maternity unit or has two non-league football clubs. But the page is of no help to the embodied practice of navigating the town and actually getting to these services. As with the other sources mentioned here (Leeson Prince, Willard, Milne), none could *singularly* suffice to help someone navigate the landscape of Crowborough and its vicinity; each has omissions and is somehow partial – as is my own account in the last few pages. Yet for all its seeming ubiquity, Google Maps would not uniquely serve this purpose either. But together, knitting into the many other unfolding understandings of this landscape, such as the data gathered from weather stations, air quality monitoring sites, taxes collected by Wealden district council, looking at hashtags (#Crowborough) on Twitter, Instagram or other social media … the layers accumulate, cross-references can be made and the landscape develops its empirical richness.

In summary, my psychogeographical work on Walk 2 has demonstrated more than the fact that I have a reliable and effective memory of the configuration of this place (though that is itself notable, bearing in mind the long span of time since these mental maps were last properly used). It has helped reveal the form of this inner map, that it is based more on an understanding of the broad configuration and boundaries of the landscape than precise details; that I make judgements as much against what was the case in the past, as in the present; and that affect and emotion help with the recall of landscape features and justify and give form to the subsequent moves in dialogue (utterances) that emerge from this practice. These points are illuminated further by Walk 3.

Walk 3: Seaford, Sussex

The last of these three psychogeographic explorations takes place in a landscape of which I had very limited prior knowledge. This is the town of Seaford, also in Sussex, on the English Channel coast. Of a similar size to Crowborough (23,000 inhabitants) and with a similar history (thus, it also lacks a landmark historical building like a castle) it is quite different in configuration. Most obviously, it is a seaside town, giving it a definite boundary to (more-or-less) the south. It is mostly located at sea level but overlooked by a substantial headland, Seaford Head, which provides the high vantage point that is missing around Crowborough (once again, recall the medieval mapmaking practice recounted in Chapter 2).

I had visited Seaford maybe three times before and not at all since 1987: I had no memory of any specifics about its landscape except the existence of the Head and the fact that from atop it there is a classic view of the Seven Sisters chalk cliffs. In advance, I thus knew the configuration of this landscape only in the broadest sense. I knew there would be an obvious limit to it (the sea); and I *assumed* Seaford would be laid out in more-or-less the fashion of other English towns of similar size, that is, *comparable* landscapes with which I was already familiar.

I set myself the following tasks in Seaford and committed, once again, to not consulting a map beforehand nor at any point during the walk (which took place on 28 January 2019):

1   Get from the railway station to the best viewpoint for the Seven Sisters (and engage in the practice of photographing the view);
2   Get from there to a pub for lunch. The name of this pub – The Old Boot – was given to me by my wife Clare, by phone, on the morning of the task, but she provided no other information about its location. (See below, however, as to what I deduce about how she went about this task and drew on technologies – her own information and digital landscape – and also her affect towards me when undertaking this task and thus nominating my second destination);
3   Get back from the pub to the railway station.

My assumptions were that task 1 would be fairly straightforward, and so it proved. I decided in advance that the simplest way to proceed was to get from the station to the sea front as quickly as I could. Although I had no advance information about how to do this, I was prepared to navigate by means of the sun (knowing that the sea lay roughly to the south). But as it turned out – that is, in practice – I was immediately helped by the existence of a signpost just outside the station, reading, unambiguously, 'To The Sea'. Once I duly reached the sea a few minutes later, I merely had the simple task of identifying Seaford Head, which lay to the left. From there, I stuck to the edge of the land until the viewpoint came ahead. Limited as my prior knowledge of Seaford was, it was nevertheless enough to exploit the very helpful *boundary* of this landscape as a navigational aid. The sea was, like Palesgate Lane in Crowborough, a clear boundary between areas of the landscape that were relevant to my task and those that were not. This boundary is physical but it is also informational. Beyond it, the configuration of the landscape remains, but is obscured (by the waters of the Channel) and irrelevant to my informational needs. Task 1 was therefore completed to my satisfaction less than an hour after leaving the station (having covered around 2.5 miles in that time). To provide further context, Figure 4.1 on the next page is the photograph of the Seven Sisters that I took at this point.

That January day was a bright and sunny one: the task would have been more difficult (and less pleasant) in poor visibility. In clear weather, the high vantage point of the Head gave me an excellent opportunity to survey the town below. Yet despite this opportunity, task 2 was more complex as, unlike the Head, the Old Boot pub could not possibly have been identified from afar. Again, I therefore drew on assumptions. These were partly related to the configuration of Seaford, but also I was drawing on assumptions regarding how Clare would have set up the parameters of the task. It is worth citing my reflective notes in full at this point:

Figure 4.1 The Seven Sisters (photo by the author)

Once back down off the Head and to Seaford's housing, I am forced to make more conscious decisions. These are based on the survey I have been able to do from the high vantage points on the Head. On this basis is made most of my judgement when it comes to what road to take, that I know I have to turn left at first, but then bear right. (All of this is based on the <u>assumption</u> that the Old Boot is indeed in the town centre.)

[but Clare has my interests at heart, she's not going to set me an overly difficult puzzle, like a pub on the edge of town]

Little things confirm my choices. The cyclist, seen clearly leaving his house, starting a journey. The direction he was going in was more likely to be productive for me. The people coming with shopping bags in the other direction, then the mini-horde of schoolgirls returning to the school I'd passed earlier, after their lunch break. These promise me that I am heading in the right direction for the town centre.

Things start to just look that little bit more urban, the buildings ahead looking more dense than before.

[I'm looking for certain qualities in my environment ... I also want to complete the task as set, and not cop out by simply going in the first pub I pass]

Once in the town centre, I head in the same general direction. If it looks like the buildings are thinning out, I will pick another route until satisfied I have covered the centre. If the pub cannot be found and I get too hungry/thirsty then my plan is to go into a different pub and ask directions.

In the end I find the Old Boot by chance – but the point is, I was always going to.

An initial cognitive map of Seaford had been established by my survey from the Head and on my walk into the town from there I used, but also continuously checked and enhanced, this map. The 'qualities' I was looking for – a sense that the buildings were becoming more closely packed, for example – served as fresh information that confirmed I was on more-or-less the right pathway. I also acquired information from observing the behaviour of other people. I did not need to do this in Crowborough: in other words, it was not an informational practice that provided relevant information in that landscape. But the schoolgirls and shoppers I saw in Seaford were very useful to me, serving as sources of information and points of orientation. However, I was still making assumptions about the practices they were engaged in and that these were intelligible. I could not be certain about the point of origin of the two people with shopping bags, for example, but that there were two different people helped reinforce the observation. It was, in any case, just one extra test, a check to my understanding of the broad configuration of this landscape that I had established from the survey.

The third sub-task, to return to the railway station, turned out to be simple. The Old Boot was quite close to the station, and I could filter out certain directions to take on leaving the pub as I had not passed the station on the way to it. I also remembered from the first part of the day roughly how the station was located with reference to the compass points (confirmable by the sun) and the key informational boundary in this landscape, that is, the sea.

One final point is worth noting. Although I received no locational information from Clare when she gave me the name of the pub, she did let slip some other information when we spoke on the phone prior to my arrival in Seaford. Through this I surmised how she had used her own information landscape and her affect (in this case, concern for my interests and well-being) to filter possibilities and make judgements, beyond just my assumption that the pub was most likely to be in the town centre. I made the following notes after we spoke on the phone that morning:

> Clare gives me the pub name. BUT: the way she eventually does so makes it clear that she has used her own criteria for information seeking. I told her I just wanted a pub that would serve lunch – she discounts one (unnamed) because it did not serve food. There was another one where she says 'it has racist fucks' … so I assume she's quoting Trip Advisor. Thus, my destination is not completely random. Filtered by her at first, then behind her the technologies and/or other people's opinions.

Conclusion

These three psychogeographies are rich, thick descriptions of how one person went about finding and using resources in three different landscapes, one very familiar but constrained, the second familiar but only in memory, the third unfamiliar. What can this self-reflective task say about information practice?

Graphical maps did not form part of the equipment I needed to navigate these landscapes, except in a transient way at two points. Nevertheless, I had mental representations, or cognitive schema, against which I was making judgements about information in an ongoing way, checking the landscape around me against these cognitive, internal maps.

In Manchester my map is current, up-to-date: when changes are needed (e.g. where I need presently to follow an alternative route due to the closure of Abingdon Street), I make temporary adjustments. I also make them for practical reasons, such as when I walk in the shade on a hot day. There are temporal elements too. I know not just which way to walk, but how long it takes me. If I need to change my pace in order to meet my instrumental goal (which, in one direction anyway, invariably is to get to Victoria station in time for my train home), I also make this adjustment, absorbing information (the time, from public clocks or my phone) from the environment but also from the schema itself (my knowledge of how long it takes to complete the task as a whole and sub-sections of it). These are 'next-to-hand' changes in practice, but the routine itself is not altered in any meaningful way. The cognitive schema is very accurate and fit for purpose, but it is also narrow. The frame contains just enough information to complete the task regularly.

In Crowborough, my internal cognitive map is old, but the changes in the environment since it was embedded in my memory have not been substantive enough to make it irrelevant, even at the smallest scales. On occasion, where things had been removed or changed since the 1980s, these absences were themselves points of orientation. My map covered the whole town, a larger area than my Manchester map, but not with as much precision. I did not remember every street, but instead the town had become divided into a configuration of districts. Where I needed to make decisions about my route – which I never need to do on Walk 1 – these were conscious and based on memory (as opposed to routine) and my general awareness of the configuration of the town.

Finally, in Seaford, although I lacked a pre-existing cognitive map of the town's geography except in the most basic sense (the existence of the coastline and of the Head), I was able to overlay upon it information drawn from certain general assumptions regarding how English towns are typically configured. I also applied assumptions about the task that I had been set. A series of observations accumulated as I moved through the landscape, including the broad survey that I was able to perform from the key vantage point (the Head), and my noting the movements and behaviour of other people. These observations all intersected with my assumptions about what would be considered typical in that chronotope, that place and time.

In summary, although (except at two brief moments on day one of Walk 2) I did not make use of any graphic map to complete these three walks, whether online or on paper, and whether self-created or created by others, I nevertheless was clearly making judgements, within this landscape, that were based both on observations and memory and which interacted to form my cognitive schema. My information seeking and application of found information were based not on a systematic and exhaustive 'sweep' of every street and pathway (compare this to the techniques applied by the OS or Google), but on a number of cognitive 'short cuts'.

I have also accumulated and communicated (here see Appendix 1) enough information about these landscapes for others to replicate these journeys. The pathways I describe have an objective existence: they have become utterances, potential moves in a dialogue. Others could base future practices on them. They are, in many ways, like the rutters of medieval navigators described in Chapter 2. If it stretches the point to make this observation, and to suggest this chapter is now analogous to the other literary and documentary texts about Crowborough that I mention above, then that discounts the ways in which these texts – discursive maps of a kind – each describe (Willard), promote (Leeson Prince) or indirectly provoke (Milne) the movements of quite substantial amounts of attention and resources to this region, not to mention changes in the landscape and further informational products. Yet, as with my own map of this town, the narratives of Willard and Milne draw on an understanding of place as affect, and even if Leeson Prince's discursive map is structured more around scientific observation, his teleoaffective goals (to promote interest in this landscape as a site for economic development) are clearly stated in his introduction.

One issue relevant to practice theory that I did not *directly* test with these walks was the social aspect of practice: each walk was conducted alone. Had I been accompanied, the journeys may have played out differently depending on various factors such as that companion's prior knowledge of these landscapes, their tolerance for the nature and extent of the task and their ability to make their own observations on the day and integrate these with assumptions about these and comparable landscapes. Nevertheless in order to make Walk 3 work as a useful task, I provoked an utterance from a second party – Clare, who gave me the name of the pub I had to find – and as soon as this was done I was bringing to bear further assumptions about how that person (information source) related to me and how she would introduce this information into my landscape. She in turn drew on the wider 'hive mind' (e.g. via TripAdvisor) to make her own judgements.

In Walk 2, street signage and the map at the entrance to the Ghyll were useful orientation points, despite my familiarity with this landscape, and represent the tip of a long-standing social agreement about toponymy, one that is still ongoing and (thanks in part to the 'attention economy') has taken slightly different forms in the last three decades, hence all the Conan Doyle references in the names of newer Crowborough streets. In Seaford, the movements of other people through the landscape were themselves a useful resource; in Manchester, on the other hand, these can be an irritant or active blockage (see also Greenwood, 2018).

Mental maps can be built quickly. They can also be very durable. But what has been described in this section are processes that are usually intuitive – only rarely are they, or can they, be brought into conscious awareness. Sometimes it will happen because we do not know our way to somewhere and have to stop and think about it. (We have almost entirely delegated our cognition in this regard to technology and, as already noted, some have expressed real concern about the impact of this on our ability to retain our awareness of space and place.) Here it happened because of the reflective nature of the method I was using to gather data about my mental processes, the autoethnography or psychogeography.

In this chapter, I have tried to uncover the deepest roots of the link between mapping and the judgements we make about information. Affect is a part of practice and also essential to how we relate to *place,* not just space; therefore, affect is an essential element of how we learn to make effective judgements about information and build informational and technological environments that help us act within the world (IL).

Just as the techniques and strategies we use to navigate space and place are evidently informational, so our information landscapes have an inherently spatial aspect. Appreciating how we navigate geography, and how we structure the observations we make as we do so, is important for understanding how we can use mapping to navigate information landscapes more broadly. We are also continuously making judgements about, and against, these landscapes as they existed in the past as well as the present. Changes in things, and the absence of things, are as much points of orientation, and thus learning, as is presence in the here and now.

Moving on, this chapter has said nothing directly about IL *education* except in the most informal sense. It may well be that many of the skills I bring to bear on each of these walks, in their different ways, are transferable to other contexts, whether geographical or otherwise, such as in the workplace. But at this level of cognition the specific outcomes of mapping are vague and fuzzy, affective (which matters) and connected with *place* (which also matters). I have not yet discussed *placing* in any real way; that is, the conscious act of mapping and creating a map. Thus, the next two chapters, the first of which (Chapter 5) deals with graphic mapping of information landscapes, and Chapter 6, discursive techniques.

Chapter 5

Maps of cognition

Introduction

So far I have discussed mapping as both a graphic and discursive practice, but the case studies used have been mostly concerned with the mapping and navigation of geographical space. While I hope I have already shown that all mapping is a mapping of information as well as geographical landscapes, what I focus on in this chapter are mappings that, on the surface, have no relation to physical geography: the concept or mind map.

This chapter brings in the notion that the mapping techniques explored so far can be applied to informational space, at least at some level and without losing basic principles: such as maps' boundedness and materiality, the social nature of the mapping process and maps as a reification of agreements made at particular places and times. Through discussing several prior research studies, I investigate how concept mapping has been used in two principal ways vis-à-vis information literacy: first, the generation of data regarding research subjects' information horizons and landscapes; second, as teaching tools to raise learners' awareness of resources and pathways within a landscape.

The educational interventions discussed here are not necessarily exemplars. I agree with Jane Secker (in her foreword to Forster, 2017): given that IL interventions must always be customised to (and within) the context, I should be wary of generalising from these cases and concluding that they will be applicable in different, or all, contexts. Rather, the aim is to use these case studies to ask what we can learn from them vis-à-vis mapping specifically and the development of IL practice more broadly. There are lessons to be learned about not just how these prior studies engaged participants with creating a map (graphical or discursive), but what participants learned about mapping as a practice; how their maps were talked into being, via a discursive and/or dialogic process; and social aspects of mapping, affect and power.

Non-geographical maps

First, though, it is necessary to establish that maps do not have to be geographical. Consider the organisation chart in Figure 5.1: this is an imaginary organisation but it is a prevalent and familiar type of image.

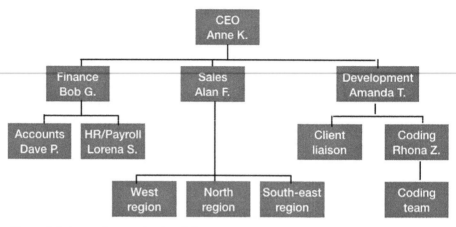

Figure 5.1 A sample organisational chart

A field of interest has been defined and the map is framed around that field: borders have been drawn around what constitutes 'the organisation' and what is outside it. This applies both to what the map *contains* (the departments, jobs and individuals considered 'mappable', contrasted with those – cleaning staff, for example – who, in this case, are 'off the map'), but also what it *depicts*: the way these selected elements are plotted and organised and how the map indicates relationships between them. This starts with the use of conventions of representation; just as we now expect maps to have north at the top, so the typical convention in organisational mapping is 'CEO at the top': if not the top, then invariably at the centre, à la Jerusalem on the Hereford Mappa Mundi.

The detail of the depiction of elements and their interrelations is also promoting a specific perspective on what is valuable in this social site, of what 'an organisation' actually *is*. The lines between the boxes on the chart are not arbitrary, they indicate chains of command and information flows 'up' and 'down' the hierarchy, while communication flows between people in different 'branches' of the hierarchy are excluded. There is a geographical element to the map, with different regions depicted when it comes to the Sales department, but the spatial configuration of the organisation (where offices are located, for example) is not considered *relevant* to the purpose for which the map was created. This was to define a hierarchical power and information structure, whether for those within or external to the organisation. To, as Harvey (1996, 111) puts it, discursively map social relations and ensure people 'know their place'.

More positively, this chart might be a tool for learning, whether in a functional way (say I have a problem with getting paid for consultancy work done for this company, I can use this map to help reach the person in charge of payroll) and even, possibly, in a critical way – as I am doing here. The chart is a space of representation that makes propositions that can be explored in the world. Both the chart as an utterance, and the possible responses to it as an utterance and how these might then impact upon further information practices, indicate that charts like these can most assuredly be treated as maps. I will restrict my use of the term 'cartograph' to maps that depict physical landscapes: maps like these I will henceforth term 'graphical maps'.

Graphical maps can also show relations between mapped elements other than the social. Geographers have begun applying technologies and underlying concepts from their field to the systematic recording and analysis of non-geographical, yet still relational, spaces: see Skupin and Fabrikant (2003), who as one example of this offer maps of the relations between stories in a Reuters news archive. The methodological and mathematical processes involved in mapping social networks (e.g. Scott, 2000) are of long standing and contributed to the classic study by Granovetter (1973) of 'the strength of weak ties'. Granovetter observed how the crucial nodes for information transfer in social networks were people who bridged the gaps between strongly-integrated social groups. The ties between these 'clusters' might have been weaker than the ties which bound them together internally, but without these weak ties, the group would not have access to information that circulated around other groups. People with weak ties thereby served as 'brokers' to help information flow across the boundary. Such insights depend on not only Granovetter and other researchers, but, more crucially, the brokers themselves being aware of their positioning in this network and actively working to maintain these weak ties, recognising them as a valuable resource: what Lloyd calls the 'social modality'.

Mind or concept mapping

Organisational charts and sociograms map relations between people. Moving still further into the virtual space, however, the notion that one can map concepts, and the relations between them, to better understand a field of knowledge (learning to navigate it), should be a familiar notion thanks to the work of writers such as Buzan on mind mapping (2006) and Novak and associates on concept mapping (1990). Visualisations like these – plotting relations between concepts or texts, rather than people or geographic locations – can help people access the tacit dimension of their own and others' knowledge and cognitive structures. This is Buzan's core argument in favour of mind mapping (based in turn on the ideas of Ausubel, 1960) and can also be used by observers to establish the level of sophistication of a learner's knowledge structure. Hay (2007), for example, asks his students to draw mind maps before and after exposure to teaching on a topic, and in the changes between them he sees evidence of either deep learning, surface learning or non-learning. He displays two maps drawn by the same learner at different points (Hay 2007, 45–6). The first map shows what Hay identifies as a 'trivial exposition of the topic' (in this case, a class on research interview techniques), but:

> … [i]n her second map, Asha again used only eight concepts to describe the topic, but overall, the knowledge was much better structured. It was also significantly improved in explanatory content and showed a more comprehensive grasp of meaning. Potential confusion between interview 'processes', 'styles' and 'question types', for example, was resolved by using the collective term 'approaches', and this was linked to 'planning' in a meaningful way. The link between the 'environment' and the interview 'subject' was also explained sensibly, and in a way that it was not in the first map. The second map included three new concepts – 'structured', 'semi-structured' and 'conversational' interview 'approaches'. These concepts were added in ways that suggest deep learning, because they were integrated within the overarching knowledge structure and linked to prior knowledge. Here, Asha was able to show how these 'approaches' were related to the interview 'planning' process, for example.
>
> (Hay, 2007)

Based on the depth of understanding which can be attained, Hay (2007) and, following his work, others such as Gregoriades, Pampaka and Michail (2009) suggest that concept mapping provides an alternative to text-based approaches to research and other types of knowledge sharing. Whether in a classroom or research situation, it is not always easy for people to articulate knowledge through words alone, particularly when this knowledge is tacit and/or when the concepts involve complex relationships between many elements. As the original proponents of concept/mind mapping suggested, it is a way of stimulating thought, finding a different perspective on the relations between concepts that might otherwise be elusive (it was for this reason that I created the concept map of this book, given in Appendix 2). Concept mapping is also useful when participants have literacy deficits of some kind. This last point obviously applies to younger children or populations who are not working in their first language or among whom literacy is generally low (Tippett, Handley and Ravetz, 2007; see below). But it could be an *information* literacy deficit, where knowledge must be shared between groups who are not necessarily familiar with keywords or forms of expression used in certain settings (Tippett et al., 2009). Yet eliciting such knowledge is essential if workplaces are to be understood in a collective way and become a space for social learning (Wenger, 1999). It is also an essential element of learning to become a practitioner, adopting the discourses and genres of a social site. In principle then, concept mapping has much to offer when it comes to learning about and navigating information landscapes.

Concept maps are a way of eliciting and communicating knowledge, just as are other types of mapping. Wandersee calls them 'maps of cognition' and observes that '[t]o map is to construct a bounded graphic representation that corresponds to a perceived reality' (1990, 923). Maps are things that can be *read*: 'the real world yields the raw data of perception which are transformed by the map maker into a map that represents knowledge worth sharing; the map reader then extracts the relevant meaning and uses it for problem solving and decision making' (Wandersee, 1990, 924). Cartographs depict and represent space, and to some extent place, yet one can detach strictly *geographical* location from consideration and still retain a sense of *informational* location within a landscape. This is what the concept map helps to reveal.

The linguistic devices that we use to describe where information 'resides' and how it is positioned relative to other resources invariably draw on spatial metaphors including information horizons, pathways and navigation; concept maps draw on this link, as Hepworth and Walton describe:

> Notions of up, back, front, movement, inside and outside are shaped by our physicality and are used to help conceptualise our interaction with the physical world around us. These physical experiences are associated with and get translated into verbal structures and language, which enables us to develop knowledge and communicate our experience. These experiences can be seen in fundamental metaphors we use to explain, conceptualise and communicate with others about the world around us. Many cultures, Lakoff argues, use these structures to compare, contrast and categorise – to process data, information and knowledge … They provide a frame within which the learner can predict future situations and place new knowledge. For example, considering a line of thought as a path immediately gives the learner a structure and a set of expectations – it has a beginning and an end; there is a likelihood of having to choose between different paths and the expectation of dead ends, short cuts and so on.
>
> (Hepworth and Walton, 2009, 39, via Lakoff, 1999)

There is a crucial difference between concept maps and cartographs, however, in terms of the *reliability* of the observations they make. Although concept maps, like geographic maps, can be stored, retrieved and used repeatedly, as they do not specify geographical locations, there is upon them no 'mathematically definable point from which the visual world … [can] be deduced and represented' (Craine and Aitken, 2009, 163). There is no standardised set of conventions for concept mapping, no overarching data net into which observations can be positioned, as there is for Earthly geography and even for the Martian landscape. In consequence, the benefits that concept maps may bring to navigation of information are not as clearly evident as those brought by even a crude, but reliable, cartograph, if one is lost in a physical landscape. This chapter is therefore an effort to evaluate the methodological contribution of concept mapping to the epistemological task of developing knowledge about information landscapes, via some key research papers and studies.

Mapping information horizons

In a 1999 paper, Sonnenwald suggested the notion of *information horizons*: the subset of the information landscape that an individual is aware of, that they routinely use and of which, subjectively, they are at the centre. This horizon may contain informational resources of various kinds (print, digital, social, etc.), some of which will be used more frequently and thus appear more central within this horizon: others, while relevant, remain more peripheral. As with their geographical equivalents, information horizons are subjective, centred, and dependent on, the individual. However, they are far from inert. Horizons are dynamic and an individual's perception of their horizons can change depending on the extent of their knowledge and on social interaction. A subject may hold an opinion on the relevance and utility of a particular resource, such as a website or app, but interactions with peers and others may change this opinion; friends may recommend a different app, a tutor may suggest a journal article (Sonnenwald et al., 2001, 3). Trust, credibility and prior experiences contribute to *authority* and, according to Sonnenwald, the influence of various authorities should therefore be visible through analysis of how individuals define their information horizons.

In an attempt to capture this dynamism and assess the influences on individuals' information horizons, the subsequent paper by Sonnenwald, Wildemuth and Harmon (2001) builds on Sonnenwald's original proposal and outlines how mapping, integrated with research interviews, can be applied in data collection. In Sonnenwald et al.'s study of the information seeking behaviour of students from lower socio-economic sectors, they note that to understand how someone perceives their information horizons, researchers need to collect data that:

> ... include decisions made and activities undertaken during the information seeking process; when and why information resources, including individuals, are accessed (and not accessed); relationships or interconnectedness among information resources; individual preferences and evaluation of information resources; the proactive nature of information resources; and the impact of contexts and situations on the information seeking process.
>
> (Sonnenwald, Wildemuth and Harmon, 2001, 4)

Their method involves participants drawing a concept map on which they place information resources that they feel are significant. This process of selection, organisation and representation is performed after the participants have engaged in a prior research interview:

> Study participants are asked to describe several recent information seeking situations for a particular context, and to draw a map of their information horizon in this context, graphically representing the information resources (including people) they typically access and their preferences for these resources. The resulting graphical representations of their information horizons are analysed in conjunction with the interview data using a variety of techniques derived from social network analysis and content analysis.
>
> (ibid., 1)

One cannot simply be asked to 'draw a map', whether of information horizons or anything else. If the task is to be meaningful, the map needs to be *of* something: in other words, it needs to be *framed*. The interview is therefore essential to this methodology, as it helps define this frame and prompts participants to extract elements from their information landscape and plot them, and connections between them, on the map.

To analyse the maps, Sonnenwald et al. convert them to matrices, using techniques akin to those applied in social network analysis. The cells of the matrix are populated with numbers that represent student preferences: resources used the most are ranked 1, the next most 2, and so on. These data are amalgamated and conclusions reached regarding the popularity of certain resources across all students engaged in this task and connections between the resources. Sonnenwald et al. represent this with a composite map, showing the amalgamated horizons of the various participants: in other words, the broader landscape.

This composite map is a representation of the content and extent of information horizons and, in concert, the significance of particular resources in the information landscapes of these students. With the study having gathered data in 1999, students are still listing 'the internet' as a single source; all 11 students reported on in the study place it somewhere and it ranks as the most important of all listed resources. University faculty come second in this ranking and, in third, 'information places', which Sonnenwald et al. define as specific geographic locations such as career centres, doctor's offices and so on. The participating students were studying a molecular biology course and among the category of 'experts' identified, sources such as the authors of scientific papers but also sufferers from the particular disease the student was investigating were included.

Sonnenwald et al. then use the individual and summary maps to identify pathways through the landscape. They define five types of resources: *starting* resources (where people go first, but not later); *ending* resources (the end of a chain of links, people don't report going anywhere after this); *recommending* (more links out than in; the resource points to others, but alone it is typically not enough to complete the information seeking task); and *focusing* (more links in than out). Where links in and out are the same, the resource is *balanced*. For example, despite the prominence of the internet, it was not typically the end point of a search. Rather, it served as a recommending resource, helping students find experts, information places, faculty and the university library: the composite map shows this clearly. All four of these, in turn, serve as focusing resources, helping learners narrow the parameters of their search.

There is not a direct link made here to Kuhlthau's work (1993) but it is apparent nonetheless. Kuhlthau remains one of the best sources for exploring the HE student's information searching process. Her exploration of how this process should have two stages – first, exploration of the broader field, and then focusing on the core topic – suggests implicitly that the two stages of the information search process can potentially be addressed by different resources. The composite map of Sonnenwald et al. supports this. (With her description of the phenomenon of *information anxiety*, Kuhlthau also recognises how affect influences, and can sometimes retard, information practice. This connection is obvious in the work of Hultgren (2009), to be discussed shortly.)

Sonnewald et al. draw conclusions from the absence, as well as presence, of certain links on the map. For example, they express surprise at:

> ... the lack of outgoing connections between information places and the internet. One information place mentioned by several students was a career center; the data suggest that the career center either does not recommend the internet, employers, university catalogs and other university libraries as potential resources to students, or else the students have already investigated these resources before coming to the career center and they find no new information to suggest they should access the resources again ...
>
> The data further suggest that the library does not recommend or suggest employers, local libraries, university catalogs, experts, information places, or internet resources to students. These data ... indicate that the university library is not a preferred resource and is not well integrated with other information resources in students' information horizons.
>
> (Sonnenwald et al., 2001, 14)

In summary then, this paper is an interesting and, in some respects, seminal investigation of how mapping can be used as an empirical method to gather and summarise data about an information landscape. It encompasses notions of geographical space and, through investigating flows and pathways, temporality: recognising that judgements about relevance can change from stage to stage. But what does it show regarding mapping as an educational practice?

The *methodological* question asked by Sonnenwald et al. is: 'whether study participants would be able to articulate or describe their information horizons graphically and verbally' (2001, 4). They conclude that in this respect mapping is both a valid and reliable method. They assess its validity by measuring the overlap between resources depicted on the map and resources mentioned by their study participants when answering the semi-structured interview questions. As the measured overlap is 93% (ibid., 17), they conclude that mapping has validity as a way of developing knowledge about information horizons, that the participants can, as noted above, 'articulate … their information horizons graphically and verbally', and that these two modes complement each other. For assessing the method's reliability, Sonnenwald et al. ask whether the technique would work with groups other than students and go on to use the method with scientists in major corporations. Hultgren's and Steinerová's studies, reported on below, also support the point that mapping is applicable beyond just an HE student group.

All in all though, mapping is used in this paper, and discussed, as a research methodology only. The drawing of maps is shown to be a useful, valid and reliable method, but Sonnenwald et al. are not concerned with whether drawing the map was a learning experience for the student, whether consciously or not, nor whether it led to changes in the students' horizons – the interaction with the researcher having as much potential in this respect as interactions with other resources (and, in turn, possibly having the characteristics of a focusing resource, possibly starting, etc.). Beyond the amalgamation of the data that has taken place and an *implication* that this reflects the social, interactive and dynamic nature of how these subjects construct their information horizons and the wider landscape, Sonnenwald et al. do not attend to the notion of how their methodology, including mapping, can be a collective educational practice.

Hultgren's *Approaching the future* study

Hultgren (2009) applies Sonnenwald et al.'s mapping method to a study of the information seeking behaviour of young people in Sweden. The work is her PhD thesis presented in full and this format allows her to go into her findings in depth. The maps of four participants (out of the 21 in her study), and articulations of what they represent, are presented in detail. Hultgren introduces a longitudinal element, asking participants to create two maps six months apart, engaging participants in a dialogue about the changes that have occurred to their information horizons between these dates. This added depth makes it worth discussing the study at length, even if the technique is essentially the same as for Sonnenwald et al.; Hultgren's work is better at highlighting the meaning of maps for the *individual* participants and how the maps represent quite different attitudes towards information and information seeking.

Hultgren positions her investigation of students' information seeking behaviour with respect to broader political and social discourse. The participants in her study are at a significant temporal point (chronotope): they are about to leave high school, entering either the job market or further/higher education. In these circumstances they possess multiple information needs and are being expected to make choices that may have significant short-, medium- and long-term consequences. School leavers are obliged, probably for the first time, to not just decide 'what they want to do' but also the identity, or persona, they present to others regarding whether or not they are 'employable', either at that specific time or as a factor in selecting a course of study. This self-construction also encompasses the information landscape of which these young people are a part. They need not only to find information relevant to their life and career decisions, establishing a pathway through a complex landscape and making decisions about what sources to filter in and out of the landscape, but also to use these resources to present themselves to others. All this requires self-understanding, self-efficacy, self-evaluation and self-structuration (Alkemeyer and Buschmann, 2016).

The school system plays a role in helping learners develop these capacities and orient themselves in this landscape. The Swedish National Curriculum alludes to mapping when it declares that learners should 'be able to keep their bearings in a complex reality involving vast flows of information and a rapid rate of change. Their ability to find, acquire and use new knowledge thus becomes important' (Hultgren, 2009, 21). What schools, and other stakeholders, supply is information aplenty, but not *individual* guidance, nor *support* (ibid., 26–7). What 'guidance' is on offer may just be adding to the feelings of overload felt by many. The information literacy issue these learners face, then, is less that of the (un)availability of information, but more its interpretation and how well it fits their own developing identity:

> The thematic relevance of the information afforded by the careers guidance system to career and study choice may not be in question in an objective sense. However, its *interpretational* relevance – whether or not school leavers can relate it to their own situations and aspirations, the extent to which they *share the assumptions and perspectives which shape its presentation and content*, as well as the extent to which its perspectives are endorsed by the social groups to which the individual belongs, or aspires to belong to, are all issues that are of interest ….
>
> (ibid., 84, emphasis added)

Guidance on offer from careers counsellors may well be very relevant to learners like 'Nora' (one of Hultgren's case studies) who has a clear idea of what she wants to study at university and why; but less so to 'Neil', who has not begun to make these decisions yet and prefers to defer them until after he has had a gap year; or to 'Emily' who feels alienated from the process and is not only deferring her information seeking but avoiding it, for self-protection. She has 'a view of the future blurred by barriers' and is 'inactivated' vis-à-vis the landscape that people like Nora are already productively navigating (ibid., 230).

Many of Hultgren's participants think that people, particularly friends and family, are more useful sources of information than the kinds of generic texts on offer online and in what Sonnenwald et al. called 'information centres', here meaning places like careers offices or school libraries: 'people are more flexible than brochures or search engines when queried' (ibid., 63). Hultgren finds that her participants invested authority and credibility in these people in different ways. When seeking job information, prior studies have noted (e.g. Edwards and Poston-Anderson, 1996, cited by Hultgren, 2009, 63) how perceived authority varied for groups of 12–14-year-old girls who were seeking information on future occupations: mothers first, fathers more seldom and only rarely friends. Such people may be prominent in information landscapes, but not primarily as a source of information per se. Rather, they are important because they are sources of inspiration and support (ibid., 107). In summary, as with the participants in Sonnenwald et al.'s study, the landscape these learners must navigate is complex, multimodal, dynamic, social and structured by a range of forces and influences, few of which are under their control.

To her investigation Hultgren applies the same mapping method as Sonnenwald et al., but conducts interviews twice, six months apart. She uses the maps to support the interview data, not supplant it (ibid., 106), and states that:

> My hopes for the horizons were threefold: one was to confirm what had already been said by the participant in the foregoing interview and to encourage more detail in a kind of pictorial recapitulation, the second was to *support my attempts to explore relations* between the participants, information sources and their future aspirations in the interviews, and finally, given the pictorial character of the exercise, I hoped that other perspectives or details would come to light through the actual drawing of information horizons: that participants would be stimulated to further reflection on *changes that occurred over time and on the relations between sources.*
>
> (ibid., 102, emphasis added)

The longitudinal element is the most significant addition that Hultgren makes to Sonnenwald et al.'s methodology. Changes between a participant's two maps represent changes in the information landscape: sources may be added, removed or repositioned somehow. It is by no means the case that landscapes increase in complexity between the two sessions. In fact, the opposite tends to be true and sources diminish over time, which Hultgren interprets as:

> … indicating that participants had integrated information and were in the process of planning for the future. Several participants exhibited this idea by drawing larger

pictures of themselves or writing their names in very large letters on the second horizon … Others made few or no changes to their horizons which can also be described as a tactic in itself.

(ibid., 107)

What has developed over time is greater focus and recognition – at least, by the more actively engaged learners like Nora – of how establishing *pathways* through the landscape can help learners 'find a way' (the wording is significant) to fulfil their ideals (ibid., 159). For example, participant Andreas establishes a pathway that he thinks will help him attain his goal of becoming a journalist, namely through integrating this kind of work with his forthcoming military service. This connection helps him focus his information seeking, with relevant informational resources drawn into his horizons and, eventually, people that have done this kind of work before whom he could ask for advice (ibid., 149–50). This pathway is, in part, self-constructed, but is also structured by knowledge drawn from other members of Andreas's social network, those with expertise and familiar with the occupation at a cultural level, whom he uses to corroborate more formal, less personal sources.

Place is important to these learners, both in physical and social terms. Hultgren cross-refers to the notion of the 'information ground' (Fisher and Naumer, 2006) when discussing how these places are 'sociophysical locations' (Hultgren, 2009, 140) which both facilitate access to information and make it relevant. For example, one of her participants, Tom, exploits his membership of a social network oriented around playing video games to make contact with students located in a particular town. They invite him to visit to check the place out and advise him about the local landscape (e.g. which residential halls are central and which on the outskirts of town) to help him make judgements about whether or not to apply to that university. Tom is not just seeking information but actively placing himself in a position where he can be identified by others as interested in information (ibid., 141). In short, he is exploiting social and corporeal modalities to good effect.

The maps and interview data of four participants are examined in detail to draw 'portraits' and position each as representative of particular approaches to information seeking. Nora is identified as 'active' when it comes to organising her information landscape to meet her goals. Between the first and second mapping sessions, she has filtered out universities that are not in a particular region. Like Tom, she seeks out a friend who is familiar with a university and visits her to confirm her interest in this pathway. In her second map, brochures, websites and careers counsellors have become more central and relevant (ibid., 192). Hultgren compares Nora with Shirin, who is also actively engaged with planning for the future and holds similar goals, but as the child of Iranian immigrants is an 'outsider' to the contexts and pathways that Nora navigates more easily. Shirin needs to reinterpret information found and 'translate' between two perspectives: her Iranian parents and their culture, and her present position in Sweden and its dominant discourse. In her later map, Shirin places teachers as more significant than they were in the first, whereas resources like brochures disappear. Hultgren uses this, and associated interview data, to conclude that for Shirin, teachers are important because they are seen as 'insiders' to Swedish culture, helping her navigate a local context where she doesn't feel she can rely on her parents' expertise (though she still sees them as important sources of advice and inspiration). Shirin sees the information seeking behaviour of middle-class Swedish native peers as something to aspire to: she seeks to appropriate the methods and pathways she sees such people putting to use (ibid., 218–19).

Not all participants are active information seekers. Hultgren interprets Neil's maps and interview as representative of deferred information seeking. Neil does not see information on careers and future study as particularly relevant at this point in time. His horizons, his maps, do not include it, nor much else that is specific: by the second session his map is stripped down to just himself, 'people around me' and 'society'. On the first of Neil's horizons there is little more, although more specific 'authorities' such as teachers do make an appearance. Sparse as his maps are, Hultgren sees in them more than simply vagueness and imprecise goals (career or otherwise). She suggests that the maps show how Neil is, at the moment, concerned more with higher-level questions:

> Neil's information horizon is, in a sense, a representation of his endeavour to 'decide what is important' in life and he describes how he attempts to balance what was expected of him with who he wanted to become … He describes a tension between a pragmatic view of occupational skills as useful to have and the need to develop personally ….
>
> (ibid., 226)

He is not focused in the way that Nora and Shirin are, but nevertheless sees before him a 'landscape of choice' (ibid., 229). Yet the fact that (fundamental) choices have been deferred means his perception of the landscape lacks pathways and structure.

The fourth of the detailed portraits offered is that of Emily, mentioned earlier as being alienated from the process. The map is, for Emily, itself representative of how people (in this case Hultgren, as a researcher) make demands on her to plan, take decisions and clarify what she wants from the future. Just as she rejects these demands, so she comes to reject the device that is mapping: in her second mapping session Emily declines to draw a new horizon:

> … stating that 'it's the same as it was before'; and although the interviews revealed she had not been entirely inactive, the results of the information seeking she had carried out had not encouraged her to persist.
>
> (ibid., 232)

In her conclusion (ibid., 250–2), Hultgren notes how her study highlights the importance of social and physical places, and mobility between them, in accounts of information seeking. Many of her interviewees speak of 'travel and social and physical mobility as aspects of their strategies or tactics for the future that underlay information seeking activities' (ibid., 250). Judgements about place frame other judgements, becoming the basis for filtering options in or out of the horizon. For instance, some participants identify themselves as preferring to be placed in big city universities in the future or wanting to stay in their local town or region. Others, such as Tom, restructure pathways after making a visit to a particular place (campus). Some interviewees have very fixed views of place, or place is closely linked to family in cases like Shirin. Others see a 'whole world out there' with many opportunities and choices – but still, none see a pathway ahead where they would move to a place where they were a complete stranger and have no previous experience mediated by close friends (that is, a recommendation, information in the form of photographs and stories, etc.). They are confident about travel but remain within these 'socioscapes'.

But for all of the value of Hultgren's work, the role that mapping plays within it is, as in Sonnenwald et al.'s original study, a useful and powerful research device, but not intended directly as a learning tool for the participants. Mapping is being developed as a practice that can help gather and analyse data on their informational practice, but not, in itself, to make them more information literate.

Other studies of information horizons

Several other studies have used the basic technique pioneered by Sonnenwald et al. (2001) and a selection is discussed here. Gibson and Kaplan's report on their study of place and information states that Sonnenwald et al.'s mapping technique was used and:

> … participants were asked to build egocentric social network maps of their support communities, with themselves and immediate families in the centre, and members of the support community as nodes, adding names and addresses of places within the local community where they found information or services.
>
> (Gibson and Kaplan, 2017, 134)

However, no maps are shown in the paper, nor is analysis of the maps discussed. Steinerová (2010) is a more general discussion of an 'ecological' approach to IL but it does refer to Sonnenwald et al. in a way that suggests the developmental, and hence educational, potential of the technique:

> Two stages of information seeking were determined in our research, i.e. the orientation and the analytic stages. In the orientation stage it can be productive to

build an information horizon as part of information literacy development (Savolainen 2008; Sonnenwald et al. 2001). An information horizon is a map of information sources including experts, criteria of source preferences, issues of interest and information pathways. It also uses criteria for relevance assessment, especially credibility and cognitive authority and contexts and situations which make an impact on the added value to information.

By depicting an information horizon we develop information strategies as a special approach to solving an information problem. Information activities then involve orientation (perception of problem, setting the goal, analysis), strategy (choice of procedures, practices) and synthesis and verification (feedback). While building information horizons people often form a hierarchy of information and information sources (most relevant, sources of secondary importance, peripheral). In our memory we have recorded successful strategies and errors which we use as examples of building a new information horizon.

(Steinerová, 2010, no pagination)

The second paragraph, in essence, describes investigations that could take place with reference to a map of information horizons, explicitly or implicitly. These investigations could be undertaken by the learner alone, self-reflecting on their map or in collaboration with a teacher or counsellor of some kind. However, Steinerová provides very little further detail about these aspects of mapping, although concept mapping is used later in the paper to summarise research findings. Nevertheless, these two paragraphs above show the possibility for mapping of one's information landscape as a learning process, in order to better understand, optimise and steward it.

Greyson, O'Brien and Shoveller (2017) refer to 'information world mapping' as a 'participatory arts-based [research] method'. They observe how visual and creative methods are useful for working with populations with low literacy levels. Again, the intention is to 'augment data collection within traditional qualitative interviews' (2017, 149). The authors recognise that mapping draws on 'elements of multiple conceptual geographies of information behaviours: information grounds, information horizons, information ecologies, and information worlds' (ibid., 150). Information grounds are seen as the most 'concretely geographical of these constructs'; the notion of the 'information world' is vaguer, but they do make a link (ibid.) to Habermas's conception of the lifeworld as an equivalent; a collective matrix of interpretation against which judgements are made. Greyson et al. studied young parents' information practices. Like Hultgren's, the study is longitudinal, and they discuss one case, Sofia, in depth, as her maps change form and orientation over time:

… at intake, when Sofia first drew her health information world map, she was a twenty year old mother of one. Her information world was in a state of flux as she had recently aged out of eligibility for various youth programs and transitioned from high school to college. She had many sources on her original map, but several of them were no longer readily available to her.

Two years later, when she drew another map, Sofia was expecting a second baby with her new fiancé. Many of the individuals listed on her intake map (high school teacher, doula from her first birth) were no longer important parts of her information world, although some (family doctor) still were. Sofia's first child had also aged out of services by this time, cutting off additional information sources from the initial map. On her second map, Sofia clearly delineated pathways she would follow for different types of information needs – for example, if a concern might be an emergency, call 911 and then, if needed, go to hospital; if it was minor and not embarrassing, ask a nurse friend; if potentially embarrassing or sex-related, Google. This clarity about information seeking pathways for different types of information needs appeared to have developed over time and through experience, and was striking in its contrast with the more cluttered and less directional intake map. Sofia's follow-up map also contained a substantial portion focused on providing information to others – something touched on as an emerging social role in her intake interview, but stated much more firmly and clearly in the follow-up.

(ibid., 153)

Thus, by the second map, Sofia's information landscape shows evidence of being more effectively stewarded than when she drew the first. Pathways are in evidence and Sofia has begun acting as an information disseminator, a source of help and advice in her own right. She is aware enough of these practices to have depicted them in her map.

Another point of interest in this study comes with Lilah, who instead of a recognisable map drew a picture of a farm with herself depicted in the foreground. The researcher could not use this image as was intended for the maps, that is, to stimulate recall of a critical informational incident, but:

Although the researcher left that interview feeling that the IWM [information world mapping] had failed, upon later reflection it became evident that Lilah was communicating her subscription to a different understanding of information than that which is commonly understood. By drawing her idyllic farmscape as an aspirational information world, Lilah was underscoring her stated beliefs in natural healing and trusting nature over human science and information, and her frustrations that the information she received from the medical system and mass media devalued this belief. Once identified, this theme was addressed in a follow-up interview with Lilah, in which she validated and expanded upon the researcher's understanding of her message.

(ibid., 155)

Thus, the distinctiveness of the 'farmscape' indicated how Lilah rejected the viewpoint – of the value of information – that the researchers assumed. Perhaps this artwork cannot be called a 'map' without stretching the concept too far, but at least this shows that as a research device, the depiction of information horizons can be done in creative ways. On the other hand, this potential diversity, in form and (lack of) structure, of produced maps or other images makes systematic and/or quantitative data analysis more difficult (see Greyson, O'Brien and Shankar, 2019, for a discussion of the analytical issues emerging). No concepts on Lilah's map could have produced values to fill the cells in Sonnenwald et al.'s matrix, for example.

Zimmerman also works with marginalised groups, in this case female refugees and migrants who need health information. She concludes: 'Women who drew more complex maps had survey responses that correlated with higher health literacy and eHealth literacy' (2018, 1). She uses the same 'matrix' analytical method as Sonnenwald et al. and draws a summary map in the same way. But her study is larger (65 women) and seeks to compare sub-groups within this sample using various filters. Correlations are found between the number of sources depicted and years of education (more years, more sources); frequency of internet use (more frequent use, more sources); and whether the women entered the US as refugees (fewer sources) or not. Zimmerman discusses how mapping is useful for its *predictive* value: the more sources on the map, the more likely are her women to be able to access the information needed (2018, 9).

Mapping as a *collective* activity is hinted at by Sonnenwald et al. but is only really evident in their aggregation of the data. The maps were still formed individually, with one-to-one facilitation by the interviewer. One attempt to develop a more collaborative approach is that of Le Louvier and Innocenti (2019). This is a project only emerging at the time of writing and the cited paper provides only a brief overview of the way these authors turned mapping into a collaborative game, again working with marginalised groups (refugees). There are not yet enough details published to fully evaluate this interesting approach. But it does represent a move to using mapping in an explicitly collaborative way. The playful process and the 'talking of the map into being', not only now with the researcher (who remained part of the process as a facilitator), but also with other people, inhabiting similar landscapes, was seen as valuable in its own right, particularly as all the groups were 'outsiders' and could, for example, use the game to practice their English (2019, 5). (See also Walsh's ongoing work on the value of play in IL education (2014; 2015).) They also began to share information with each other regardless of whether the 'rules' of the game required it. The game incorporated a real city map and participants used the game to *physically* direct peers to information grounds:

> They shared tips on where to find free food, courses, leisure activities, and cheap mobile phone companies. Thus, they transformed the game into an information

ground and displaced the competition to who knew the city best and could make the most of their situation. As they became aware of how they had managed to make sense of the system and make the most of it, they seemed to gain confidence. Sharing information thus appeared more important than seeking information, for it meant appropriating the city and showcasing expertise.

(Le Louvier and Innocenti, 2019, 5)

This is moving beyond Sonnenwald et al.'s use of mapping as a research methodology and into an exploration of its educational potential. Appropriated to the learners' own needs, the game has become *equipment* in the sense meant by practice theorists (cf. Schatzki, 1996, 96ff); central to not just 'doings', but 'sayings' and 'relatings'. The game has acquired meaning within the practice of using it. The participants in Le Louvier and Innocenti's project show evidence of having begun to find their own uses for it, autonomously – as a device that can help them with information needs, but also as something they can use to assert and distribute authority and position themselves within social networks, communities of practice and the landscapes within which these exist. Most of the other authors cited in this chapter thus far have only really considered the facilitator's (researcher's) role as a resource in the landscape that can be drawn on to facilitate the practice of mapping. Greyson et al. hint at the importance of incorporating art materials. But here the game is explicitly 'equipment' in the sense meant by Heidegger, and employed by Schatzki, as material objects around which practice can coalesce.

Concept mapping and the teaching of IL

How has mapping been used in IL work, not to gather data for researchers, but to raise learners' awareness of their information landscape and develop navigation skills?

Herring (2009) worked with a class of students of around 12–13 years old who had been given an essay to write in which they were expected to present a balanced argument in relation to a particular topic. These students had been introduced to mind mapping in the previous academic year and the teacher of this year's class was working directly with them on question formulation. At points in the process, the learners were asked to write short reflective pieces on: Brainstorming and doing a mind map; Writing your questions; Finding and evaluating sources and note taking; Writing your essay; and Looking back on your essay. To quote Herring:

Students were asked to write at least 3 sentences under each heading in each section. For example, on the Brainstorming and doing a mind map page, students were asked to:
Please write some notes on:

- What you liked about brainstorming with your group
- What you did not like about brainstorming with your group
- How you think brainstorming will help with your discursive essay
- How you think having a mind map will help with your discursive essay

(ibid., 4)

These reflective pieces built up into a 'diary' recording students' reactions to each stage in the research process. These diaries formed the study's dataset, along with a semi-structured interview with the teacher.

Herring argues that students should not only employ particular information handling techniques, but also reflect on why they did so and what they learned. He says:

> … if there is an emphasis on school students not only applying information literacy skills which they have been taught by teacher librarians and/or teachers, but also on thinking and reflecting on why, where and when they might use these skills, then information literacy may be defined as a way of thinking. This way of thinking would include not only thinking about information literacy skills but also about information literacy as a practice … this practice would involve students: thinking about their own information environment – digital, textual and person-based; thinking about making choices in relation to aspects such as concept mapping (written or mental) or to relevant sources or interpretations of meaning in sources or what to include or exclude in their assignment; and thinking about what skills and/or ways of thinking they might transfer from one subject to another or from school to work or higher education.
>
> (Herring, 2009, 3)

As it is the diaries that form the majority of the dataset, no student concept maps are actually shown or considered by Herring in his analysis unfortunately. Nevertheless, there is a section in which the students' specific insights into mapping are recorded; it is brief but revealing (note that Herring uses the terms 'concept' and 'mind' maps interchangeably):

> In relation to concept mapping, students cited a range of connections or links which they made with subsequent parts of their assignment completion. These included viewing the concept map as an aide memoire, and about half the students made reference to looking back at the map. Comments included 'A mind map helps by the fact that if I get an idea, I put it on that and I can just go back to that page. It really helped me because I never forgot what I was doing.'
>
> Students also linked the concept map with note taking ('The information can be written down in sections of the map. The information is easy to find as it is in

sections'), with the order in which to write the essay ('A mind map helps me because I can write down ideas I have and I can put them in the order of when I want them in my essay') and with what to include in the essay ('Your map helps you to know what you want to put into your essay and what you don't).

(ibid., 2009, 8)

Structuring of an information landscape is in evidence, with the map being a representation of this process. The map serves as a *record* of the self-structuration, but the significant implication is that the map comes first and plays a constitutive role in the structuring process. It makes tacit understandings of relationships more explicit, as they need to be uttered and given form by being placed on the map. And this record can subsequently be consulted and scrutinised, by its creator, the learner, or by others, whether peers or teachers. The concept map is seen by the learners as having not only present value, but *future* value (ibid., 10), as the basis for later judgements ('your map helps you to know what you want to put into your essay and what you don't').

It is not only concept mapping that the learners believed had a significant impact on how well they could navigate and organise their landscape for the purposes of this task. For example, with the question formulation task:

… students identified different ways in which questions could aid the retrieval of relevant information for their assignment. Students cited having a focus for information retrieval ('I think that writing questions helped with looking for information because you knew what you were looking for – not just looking randomly for information'), using keywords ('I knew exactly what I was hoping to find out and could take keywords from the questions to use when using a search engine') and confidence in searching ('Once I had written the questions I felt a lot more confident for searching for information').

(ibid., 8)

Herring's learners are engaged in a discursive and dialogic process: the act of creating the map and formulating questions has helped make tacit understandings explicit and helped the students define a structure for subsequent practice, that is, the information search. The final quote, about confidence, suggests a connection with affect, and that this graphic and discursive mapping process has helped relieve the students' information anxiety (Kuhlthau, 1993). Herring observes (2009, 1) that these students are relatively high achievers. One can surmise they have an emotional investment in being seen to succeed at the essay-writing and diary-writing tasks. The stages of mind mapping and then question formulation are working well together here as part of a repertoire of IL techniques and there is some recognition by students of the different roles they play in the overall process. The teacher confirms this in a quote from the interview:

I think the questions enabled them to actually have a different kind of experience when it came to research initially and also writing their essays. I think with the search, it gave them a far greater sense of direction and clarified aims – their own personal aims. When it came to writing the essay, it made it more likely that they were going to be more able to convey a distinct line of argument and that the essay itself would read as a whole.

(ibid., 8)

Note, though, how the teacher has a perspective on what constitutes 'good' practice in this area, that is, 'convey a distinct line of argument' and a product that 'would read as a whole'. Students also take this discourse on board:

Students related confidence to: structuring their essay, e.g., 'I felt much more confident about writing my project when I had done my questions because it gave me a strong structure to have for my project'.

(ibid., 9)

The idea of a 'strong structure' is not clearly defined (at least, not in this quote). They have adopted the discourse of the teacher in this case (cf. Walton and Cleland, 2017, discussed in Chapter 6). This student, however, perceives an alignment between his/her practice and the practice that is sanctioned by the architecture in this setting. Confidence flows not only from students having a sharper focus for the search (Kuhlthau, 1993) but achieving greater clarity on which information practices they are expected to show in the assessment: 'What the teacher wants'. Recall that it was this informational discrepancy, this lack of confidence about how they were 'supposed to' do the task, that caused the students in Badke's study such anxiety (2012).

The mapping and question formulation practices are therefore directed towards the teacher's schema and aim at optimising the students' landscapes by narrowing them, honing them more closely in line with practices that are valued in this setting. The assessment process – the student diaries, in this case – has allowed these practices to become visible, to be scrutinised by the students: the kind of self-reflective IL awareness that Herring's paper suggests is valuable. Nevertheless, Herring eventually remains ambiguous regarding whether these skills are transferable, or would be transferred, outside this context. The teacher doubts it, saying: 'I'm not so certain that they would transfer these skills without me reminding them of what they did' (Herring, 2009, 11). This is a meaningful concern, but it is also a subjective opinion: nevertheless, it does suggest the importance of *facilitation* to the mapping process and this issue is returned to below.

In the end, Herring's study contains several points of interest. The dearth of reporting on the data is regrettable and a limitation of the academic journal paper as a way of really exploring the context and the practices that come into play in this setting.

Mark Hepworth and Geoff Walton, in their book *Teaching IL through Enquiry-Based Learning* (2009), describe the use of concept mapping as a learning intervention that can help develop information literate practice. They apply it as part of an IL-focused unit on a postgraduate course in Development Studies (which is itself of interest as it is an example of IL-focused teaching taking place in the disciplinary setting and outside the library 'silo').

Mapping metaphors and tropes are liberally used by Hepworth and Walton to both justify and describe their method. The opening section of this chapter has already cited a passage from this book that showed their awareness of how spatial metaphors are pervasive when we discuss information landscapes, and they build on this further:

> Cognitive constructivist learning, from an individual perspective, relates to building a mental map of the information landscape. Presenting, explaining and justifying this 'map' helps the learner concretise and internalise this view. From a social constructivist perspective the learner is learning about the information artefacts and tools that a specific 'community' uses and values. Learning involves learners presenting and discussing their conception of the information landscape, exchanging and defining categories of sources and information either face to face or via social media such as e-mail, discussion lists or blogs. They learn to use the general language of sources, such as 'portal', 'full text', 'open access' or 'creative commons', or those specific to the domain. Discussion and possibly consensus could be reached with others in this community of practice about what is valued and how to evaluate such sources.
>
> (Hepworth and Walton, 2009, 156)

This passage shows Hepworth and Walton's concern with dialogue and how through this, members of the group can reach a collective agreement on the shape of the information landscape, stewarding it (Wenger et al., 2009) by 'learning the general language' and fixing on the definition of terms. The approach acknowledges that in complex and unfamiliar informational landscapes, new entrants may well get lost, or at least feel lost, and will need guidance, or scaffolding (Hammond and Gibbons, 2005), accordingly; but this scaffolding draws not only on the authority of the teacher (e.g. 'read this paper') but of peers sharing their own ideas. As learners 'present and discuss their conception of the information landscape', they are learning not only from the academic, the disciplinary expert in this setting, but from each other as they become more effective practitioners within this landscape, developing autonomy when it comes to navigating it.

Mapping and landscape metaphors are also to the fore in the passages where Hepworth and Walton offer details of the mapping activity:

Prior to starting the task a metaphor was used to introduce the activity. This was to show that this was part of a wider process of discovery. Hence the 'journey' metaphor was used and a further geographic metaphor 'mapping the subject'. Students were asked to imagine the subject as a 'landscape' which was inhabited by clusters of knowledge, in a sense 'villages' that represented the interests of the community of practice. The flip chart was used to draw the landscape … The journey metaphor set expectations showing that there was no direct route, and that students were likely to experience dead ends, retrace their steps – it was an iterative process – and that the task would be associated with feelings of uncertainty and frustration.

(ibid., 142)

And:

… the 'journey' and 'travelling through a landscape' metaphor was used and drawn on the flip chart to indicate how the students would be 'travelling' through and trying to identify sources of information in the information landscape. The concept of 'tools' that would help them explore this landscape was introduced, including people and organisations.

(ibid., 144)

Thus, the task overtly raises students' awareness of the equipment that exists in this landscape to help with its exploration.

Once again, though, it is unfortunate (at least for my concerns in this book) that more is not said about the mapping sessions themselves and how the maps were talked into being. Hepworth and Walton include two photographs (ibid., 146–7) that show students presenting their hand-drawn maps to the group, with one having a much more 'web like' structure and the other being hierarchical and with fewer concepts. They note that the two show 'very different styles for visualising and presenting information' (ibid., 148). There is also some evaluation reported; the activity was popular with students and active, in-class reflection helped students 'concretise the process they had gone through' (ibid.). Presenting the maps to the rest of the class also helped with other transferable skills like presentation and communication. Hepworth and Walton also note that with most of the students not speaking English as a first language, this helped the whole group firm up some of the terminology used to define an information domain: 'Presentation and discussion meant that students had to use the language of the domain and consciously verbalise connections and define in their own minds what it was they were interested in' (ibid., 144).

Ketso maps

The remaining studies discussed in this chapter are based around a graphic concept mapping tool, Ketso, developed at the University of Manchester. (See www.ketso.com and other publications mentioned in the text to follow.) I am not personally involved with the commercial side of Ketso and no attempt is being made to endorse it as a product. Many other concept mapping tools are available. But the development and subsequent application of the tool has been well documented and so is a rich case study of the information practices that have developed around it and which it supports as a piece of equipment (Schatzki, 1996, 113–15).

Hughes and Hay (2001) raise the possibility that concept mapping can be used to bring together views and perspectives from different stakeholder groups in a setting. Ketso is a tangible, material concept mapping tool that manifests this possibility, being specifically designed to be the focus for the conversation of a small group. It consists of a felt mat, around 1 x 1.5 m in size, on which 'leaves' can be placed, moved and repositioned. Each can be written on with a fibre-tip pen, the ink of which is easily wiped off. The leaves come in four different colours (brown, yellow, green and grey) and there are additional map elements provided in the kit, including smaller pieces for comments and symbol markers (exclamation points, warning triangles, tick marks) that can be used in various ways to highlight areas or leaves on the map. Relationships between concepts – the leaves – can be indicated by simple proximity, but there are also other markers within the kit, such as lines or small 'connectors', that can be used for this purpose. In terms used by Wenger et al. (2009, 60) to classify tools that could help communities of practice with stewarding, Ketso is *group-oriented, participatory* and *synchronous*. Figure 5.2 shows Ketso in use.

Figure 5.2 A Ketso session (photo by the author)

The likeness of the elements to trees, leaves and (though not apparent on this monochrome image) natural colours is deliberate, and the tactile nature and visual appeal of the tool are considered important (Furlong and Tippett, 2013, 631, 636). The size and form of the kit is also seen as optimal for group work. With digital concept mapping tools, it is often difficult to have more than one person working on the map simultaneously: even if a shared virtual space exists, the ability of users to interact physically as they co-create the map is limited. Ketso's physical presence and size – aspects of its materiality – defines an optimum group size of 6–8, as is apparent from the photograph.

Within such a group, the tool can be used to initiate and structure the *exploration* of the information landscape, using this experience to help participants 'develop a discourse amongst themselves' (Furlong and Tippett, 2013, 632). Tippett stresses the kit's worth at eliciting contributions from those who are less confident (Tippett et al., 2009, 111). The focus is not on getting 'right answers', but on building the discussion in stages, using answers to one question to help with the next after confidence develops, using what is on the workspace to build further insight. 'The fact that the leaves could be moved and clustered allowed participants to place their leaves in relation to each other. Participants could see further important themes emerging from the grouping of their individual ideas' (Furlong and Tippett, 2013, 635). The symbolic markers, such as the 'warning triangles', can also be used in various ways to provoke dialogue and the scrutiny of what has been placed on the map. Furlong and Tippett note that:

> The section on highlighting key issues using icons was generally the most animated part of the workshops. Further debate was engendered as people assessed their initial ideas. Participants spoke of implementing new practices within their households at this stage. The fact that these useful practices emerged from within the groups, as opposed to being interjected by the researcher, demonstrated that peer learning had occurred.
>
> (2013, 635)

Furlong and Tippett conclude that 'participants' thinking was becoming deeper as the workshop progressed' (2013, 633). Thus, the tool is a way of structuring a group conversation and gathering data and ideas from groups in a relatively short space of time (Tippett et al., 2009, 23). 'The ability to see and develop patterns promoted a richer dialogue than if there was no physical record of the ideas' (Furlong and Tippett, 2013, 635). Quoting one of the study participants, Tippett, Handley and Ravetz state that:

> … [s]eeing the issue displayed visually has a much greater impact than merely using words. Also, the physical action of changing the direction of the arrows is very

empowering as it demonstrates that solutions exist and that it takes a refocusing of
activities and effort to achieve sustainable outcomes.

(2007, 65)

Positioning and repositioning of map elements is therefore not just an abstract act,
but represents a specific move in the dialogue, a point of agreement among members
of the group that this concept or relation is relevant; or is not relevant and should be
removed. Thus, each map element, and its placing, is an utterance, made in response
to what has gone before and inviting further utterances in response, whether made
on the Ketso field or in the dialogues taking place around it, and whether at the time
or in the future. Thereby, this process of agreement and review can be iterative: the
record of the conversation immediately opened up to scrutiny through its
representation on the Ketso field.

A final practical feature of Ketso maps is their durability. To store a map requires
only that it be folded up and replaced in its storage pack. Better still, it can be hung on
a wall for easy future reference. It is not a file format that will become obsolete.
Photographs can be taken of the maps nevertheless. The information on the map can
also be transformed into a matrix using a spreadsheet (see Tippett et al., 2009, for
examples).

At a material level then, Ketso – the physical kit, the events which take place
around it, the texts and other practices (e.g. research) that sustain it – can be
characterised as 'equipment', as outlined in Chapter 1. Its various tangible and
intangible elements are 'objects used in the performance of [mapping's] constituent
actions' (Schatzki, 1996, 113). From the practice theory perspective, Ketso is also
something *discursively* understood as useful for mapping: that whatever 'mapping' is
understood to be at the level of dispersed practice, to *integrate* it into the other
practices of the setting in which it is used, participants collectively find intelligible the
way that 'the settings are set up to facilitate the efficient and coordinated performance
of its constituent actions' (Schatzki, 1996, 114). Thus, to understand how a graphic
mapping tool like this can be used requires defining it as more than just 'equipment',
but as a *practice architecture*.

In the remainder of this chapter I therefore investigate how Ketso, as a practice
architecture, can facilitate participants' learning to navigate an information
landscape, and whether they do so in ways that may help distribute authority over the
practices that constitute that landscape or, at least, help raise awareness of what
constitutes expertise in this landscape.

Ketso in use

Ketso, first called DesignWays, was originally developed through work on
participatory ecological planning, particularly around water and river basins,

undertaken in both southern Africa and the Irk valley in Manchester (Tippett, 2005; Tippett, Handley and Ravetz, 2007). Tippett and colleagues then applied the technique in a workplace learning project with Britain's biggest retailer, Tesco, focused on sustainability planning (Tippett et al., 2009). The theme common to each project is ecological sustainability. Ecological issues, by their nature, are complex and usually there is no single solution acceptable to all stakeholders, whether they make a rhetorical commitment to 'sustainability' or not. Stakeholders often also act as advocates for interests (of ecosystems, marginalised groups and/or future generations) that cannot contribute directly to the debate (Whitworth, 2001). In such circumstances, if a dialogue is to take place, and a consensus – a collective, informed judgement – is to be reached (at least in principle), then stakeholders' participation in a joint planning process has to be meaningful, not tokenistic. Meaningful contribution requires the use of each participant's knowledge and skills, not in an exploitative way, but with an aim to enhance the knowledge and skills through a participatory, inclusive process (Tippett, Handley and Ravetz, 2007, 67). In short, it requires that the planning process be inclusive.

In decision-making fora like these, authority plays an important role in determining what gets brought 'to the table'. What knowledge about the landscape, its flows, fixities and resources is considered of value? In her work on water management in Africa, Tippett established that those with key roles in the associated practices are often women (Tippett, 2005; Furlong and Tippett, 2013), who lack status, particularly in rural areas. They would often not be invited to participate in planning sessions at all; even when they were, if male and/or more elderly members of the community were present, the younger women, despite being most directly involved with water collection and management, would often not contribute their knowledge to the dialogue taking place in focus groups and thus their perspectives were absent from any collectively-generated map of the landscape. This, plus the low literacy levels of many participants, led to Tippett developing a number of graphical tools to help with these, and subsequent, projects, for example a 'jigsaw' tool and graphics which illustrated certain ecological relationships. Ketso – the word means 'action' in the Sesotho language – was one of these.

The original work of Tippett and her collaborators displays several themes related to mapping, practice and information landscapes. Unlike the mapping of information horizons as outlined by Sonnenwald et al. (2001), Tippett's approach 'made useful advances in terms of enabling knowledge to be *generated and shared simultaneously*, such that the process of generating data was in and of itself a useful learning experience for those taking part in the research' (Furlong and Tippett, 2013, 636, emphasis added). Furlong and Tippett used Ketso in a water management project in Peru as a specific way of bringing 'scientific' knowledge back into the community of practitioners most directly concerned with applications of that knowledge (ibid., 630), thereby situating that knowledge in a specific chronotope and, therein, establishing a dialogue between the scientific and lay communities, to the benefit of both:

> The ability to engage participants in peer-led learning and interactions with scientific knowledge in a non-threatening and open dialogue represents an important advance, as it is well known that lack of knowledge of the local context and lack of consideration of local perceptions often leads to failure of drinking water improvement schemes.
>
> (ibid., 636)

Wengel, McIntosh and Cockburn-Wootten similarly note the value of 'creative and reciprocal knowledge transfer between researchers and the stakeholders aiming to make a difference to our communities' (2019, 1, see also below).

Ketso is therefore a tool not just for concept mapping, but for *collaborative knowledge production*, a way of translating and transforming information and cognitive schema between contexts. In Tippett's projects, the focus was also on making connections between the physical and information landscapes. What information did the community possess about the location and quality of resources, particularly water, in the landscape? Involving local communities in the preservation and sustainability of resources is not the only approach needed to combat environmental deterioration – we must also be concerned with macro-level processes such as economics and national policy – but it nevertheless illustrates that '[p]lanning at the landscape level of scale informs, and is informed by, work at the site level' (Tippett, 2005, 95). In general then, the work from which Ketso originated was based on an epistemology and methodology that are compatible with the site ontology that underpins practice theory and practice-based views of IL.

This conceptual connection between social sites and the wider landscape was even more apparent in Tippett et al.'s later work (2009) with Tesco UK. Like all very large retail organisations, Tesco is distributed across a range of sites that are nationwide (global, if supply chains are considered) and include different types of setting, principally offices and stores. Tippett's team were commissioned to help this company conceive of more sustainable business practices, with Ketso used as a way of brainstorming ideas and creating a space for dialogue between different stakeholders who, in the normal course of things, would not normally encounter or pass through such spaces.

Prior to their intervention, Tippett et al. (2009, §4) reviewed the landscape of Tesco, assessing what support it offered learning. While staff, from both offices and stores, were generally positive about how encouraged they felt to pursue professional development initiatives, it was communication *between* these two key locations that was problematic, and/or between senior and other levels of the organisation. For example:

Whilst there is a mechanism through which staff ideas can be shared with managers, called 'Ideas Capture', none of the participants in the pilot carried out in Stores were able to explain how this worked. Several of the participants in focus groups in Head Office had not heard of this system, or said that they had not heard of it for some time.

(ibid., 48)

Whatever it is or was, 'Ideas Capture' is not functioning as a boundary zone, a conduit of communication and (shared) learning. Lack of time was also a pressure, particularly when it came to finding and/or being allocated time to discuss longer-term corporate values (like sustainability), as opposed to solving the more immediate problems encountered in day-to-day practice (ibid., 56). The Ketso mapping sessions were thus intended to provide both the time and place to engage in dialogue that was intended to help move Tesco towards more sustainable practices (Tippett et al., 2009, 75; also Forster, 2017, 14).

In the Head Office sessions, participants numbered 35, drawn from two different sites. They represented a wide range of business functions, spanned work levels from administration to senior management, and length of time working at Tesco ranged from four months to twenty-four years. Two-thirds were female. The Stores sessions took place in Manchester, with 17 participants (11 male) from three stores across the region. The participants represented a range of functions within the organisation, including food and non-food, managerial and shop floor, some dealing with customers and some not (Tippett et al., 2009, 26). These groups are diverse, but not particularly large considering the size of the organisation. The questions that structured the dialogue, answers to which were plotted on each colour of leaf, were: How do you understand sustainability? What is Tesco doing well [with regard to sustainability]? What are the key challenges? Why is sustainability important?

The project team continued to work with Tesco and produced a later report (Tippett et al., 2010) that discussed how more sustainable business practices could spread through the organisation, including the design of training programmes, incentivising change via bonus payments and promotions and 'develop[ing] a system for capturing ideas and encouraging them to flow within the organisation, so that they are more likely to reach the people with the capacity to evaluate them, and the agency to implement them' (ibid., 8). But this later report does not return to any discussion of how Ketso was used in the pilot phase. It does, however, illustrate how those concept mapping sessions became a firm foundation for the later work, a way in which information was gathered and shared by both the academic researchers (Tippett and company) and the 'clients' in the field (Tesco).

Other academic researchers have made use of Ketso, such as Alabbasi and Stelma (2018) in work with female teachers in Saudi Arabia, another group that is often marginalised and lacks an active voice in its work and societal setting. Like Tippett, these authors report favourably on the physical, tactile nature of the tool and its inclusivity, both of which are considered to 'activate a wider range of cognitive processes than what may be the case with 'standard' focus group methodology' (Alabbasi and Stelma, 2018, §15). The ideas – and thus the maps – become those of the groups, not the individuals (and dominant personalities) within the group. Alabbasi and Stelma use transcripts of Ketso sessions to suggest how the impact of dominant personalities is reduced and authority distributed (e.g. ibid., §31). They also stress the role of facilitation in helping 'talk the map into being' (e.g. ibid., §33).

As with the Tesco project, but unlike BIE (see below), Alabbasi and Stelma determined in advance how the concept maps would be structured. Their interest is in teachers' use of technology and they present the following diagram (Figure 5.3) as a representation of how the teachers are asked to organise their landscape.

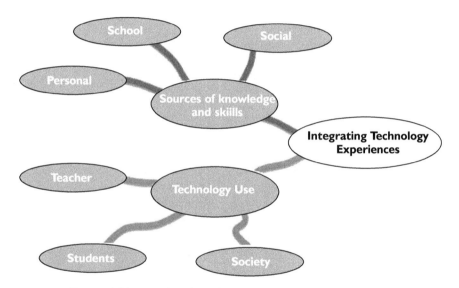

Figure 5.3 From Alabbasi and Stelma, 2018

Leaves were then used as follows (ibid., §24): brown leaves for experiences of learning and using technology, yellow leaves for positive impacts of using technology, grey leaves for challenges associated with using technology, and green leaves for suggested solutions, i.e. ways to overcome challenges. This shows that the meaning of Ketso map elements and the use of the equipment to structure the representation, and thus the dialogue, can vary from application to application.

Wengel et al. (2019) use Ketso in co-creating knowledge in tourism research. The intention is to co-ordinate discussions between multiple stakeholders regarding the rebuilding of Christchurch, New Zealand, after the earthquakes of 2010–12. Again, the intention is to open a place in which stakeholders can co-produce a map of the landscape (both physical and informational). Wengel reports on how Ketso can then be helpful in supplementary data analysis; its 'interface' making it possible to rearrange and restructure the leaves around themes, consolidating from 12 themes down to four and also noting priorities (Wengel et al., 2019, 7).

McIntosh and Cockburn-Wootten (2018) use Ketso with refugee-focused service providers in New Zealand. This latter paper is clearer about how the data on the Ketso map can be transformed and visual maps reduced to matrices in order that they can be more easily analysed and amalgamated. But in this paper Ketso is discussed only in passing and is reduced to a method for recording the outcome of the focus group.

These projects also note limits on the use of a tangible, synchronous tool. Getting busy people in the same room at the same time is not easy and Wengel et al. (2019, 8) note that while their eight participants is a good number for a focus group, it was from a list of over 200 invitations sent out. Tippett et al. (2009) also note that some of their sessions had few attendees: for example, one clashed with a management meeting that was seen as a higher priority.

To use a 'Ketso-style' method does not necessarily require the purchase of the special kit (to some extent it can be mimicked with Post-It notes, for instance), but it is helped by having this equipment. Either way, skilled facilitation is required as well as space and time to run the session (Wengel et al., 2019, 9). These all impact upon the cost and convenience of establishing boundary zones like this, for all that they might be useful at enhancing the 'operational proximity' of different work groups in a setting (Tagliaventi and Mattarelli, 2006).

Bibliotek i endring

The remainder of this chapter reports on a project called *Bibliotek i endring* (BIE) – Norwegian for 'Changing Libraries'. Elements of this discussion have already appeared in a different form in Whitworth et al. (2014; 2016a; 2016b; 2016c) and Whitworth (2015) and the next few pages are essentially a resumé or summary of these, focusing on aspects that are of most concern to the present book.

BIE was a collaboration with two Norwegian university libraries, which I will call A and B, from 2013 to 2015, with the active phase of data collection lasting between October 2013 and September 2014. Twenty-eight participants, 13 at library A and 15 at B, were involved in this phase, around 50% of the full-time staff at each location. These participants engaged in a series of six Ketso sessions held over the year. Each also took part in a short interview before the first session and another at the end. (The initial interview covered matters that are less relevant to my concerns in this book and so I have omitted discussion of insights gained therefrom regarding the social networks which existed at both libraries and how they changed over the course of the project. However, conclusions can be found in Whitworth et al. (2014; 2016c).)

The concluding interview drew out participants' reflections on the Ketso sessions and the changes that had occurred in each library over the last year. Retention of participants was good: only one voluntarily withdrew from the project, stating after the third session that she did not see the relevance of her continuing participation; another left because he got a different job. Not all participants were able to come to every Ketso session, however (their absence at times giving rise to interesting points about responsibility and territorialism, to be discussed further).

Both libraries underwent significant changes to their information practices over the period of the project. Library A is located at an institution that in 2014 merged four of its five campuses (and hence libraries) at a new location. Staff that had worked in separate locations were thereby being brought together in one physical setting. The level of operational proximity (Tagliaventi and Mattarelli, 2006) and the connections that existed between staff and workplace within this organisational structure were shifting. Practices that had developed in the different campus libraries were no longer insulated from each other through geographical separation. The librarians also faced a complex logistical task, needing to physically pack and move stock and the contents of offices, either into the new library, storage or recycling, while still offering services to users (except for a short period in summer 2014 when the main move took place).

Library B operates across three campuses, one principal and two satellite. The majority of staff work at the main campus but there is still a need to reconcile practices across the space that separates it from the satellites. In the period of the project, this library's significant organisational change was the appointment of a new Director in January 2014. While not in quite the same way as the merger for library A, as it involved changes to management style and priorities but not roles or practices, this remains a change that the staff needed to learn about and which would impact on the judgements about the relevance of resources. We sought originally to use library B as something akin to a 'control group', one where we were expecting a year of more stable operation. Its original Director announced his departure, due to ill health, as our work had just started. However, the two transitions are still different in form and there are ways in which they impacted on the groups' learning about Ketso in different ways, a point I return to in the chapter conclusion.

The BIE project was a collaboration between myself, as an academic researcher, and the practitioners in both libraries. Of the other authors named on prior publications (e.g. Whitworth et al., 2016a), Bodil Moss was employed from 'outside' as the research assistant on the project: she facilitated the sessions with me and (as did the others) worked on data analysis. Our three other colleagues, Maria-Carme Torras i Calvo, Nazareth Amlesom Kifle and Terje Blåsternes, were librarians. Therefore, as with the other Ketso-based projects discussed above, this was an attempt to do more than just position the librarians as the 'subjects' of research but as co-producers of it, developing knowledge about the information landscapes and practices of these workplace settings in ways that could be *immediately* relevant and applicable in that setting. To develop such knowledge was also the presumed intention of the funders of the project, as this is how we described the work in the funding bid we submitted to the Norwegian National Library (Norsk Nasjonalbiblioteket).

At each library, six Ketso sessions were spaced 6–10 weeks apart through the twelve-month period (October 2013–September 2014). In each, attendees were further split into two groups, each of whom worked on their own map. These groups remained constant through the series except after the departure of the staff member from library A, when a participant was moved from one group to another to balance numbers. When these sessions are referred to below, the following labelling convention is employed: §[n][A | B][x] where n represents the number of the session in the series (1–6), A/B is the library, and, where necessary, x the group within the library (1 or 2). Thus §5A1 indicates that the data referred to were generated in the fifth session, library A, group 1. Where participant names are mentioned, these are pseudonyms. The gender of a participant is not necessarily reflected in their pseudonym.

Each group was engaged in a series of structured conversations, as a result of which a map of their shared information landscape emerged on the Ketso. This dialogue was audio-recorded, capturing the conversations of both participants and facilitators as the map was talked into being. These, and the interviews, were coded and reviewed by all members of the project team. See Whitworth et al. (2016a and 2016c) for more details on the process of data analysis.

The questions used by the facilitators to structure the dialogue were as follows:

- *Tasks*: What tasks require attention at work? (The brown leaves were used to record answers. The answers were grouped into topics, clustering around larger ovals; see the example below.)
- *Needs*: What information do you need to attend to these tasks? (Yellow leaves.)
- *Sources*: From where, or whom, could this information be found? (Green.)
- *Blocks*: What obstacles might be in the way of acquiring this information? (Grey.)
- *Actions*: What actions can be taken to fulfil needs or remove obstacles before the next session? (Also grey, but with an added star to distinguish from 'blocking' leaves. Our desire to have five focusing questions was not quite supported by the design of Ketso, with its four colours of leaf. But we adapted the equipment to meet our informational needs.)

In line with guidance given in the Ketso documentation (see www.ketso.com), each group member was encouraged to write answers to these questions individually, in a minute or two of silence, before engaging in dialogue with their colleagues and the facilitator to agree whether all answers should be placed on the map. Thus, what is plotted on the map field was a provisional agreement, reached through the structured dialogue – but not a final one, as any leaf could subsequently be removed, rewritten or repositioned. Leaves were written in a mixture of English and Norwegian throughout all sessions and discussions were held in English when I was facilitating them, in deference to my mediocre Norwegian. In the final interviews, many participants noted they felt comfortable in either language but those with less proficient English felt that using a second language had been a barrier to the task.

After these structuring questions were addressed by the group and the map plotted as a whole, each group marked three *priority areas of concern* on each map (using the 'tick mark' symbol), and then, after a final examination of the map, concluded each session by specifying *actions* that should be taken after the session. Thus, the maps depict group perceptions of each community's tasks; information needs; sources; obstacles; priorities; and actions at each of a series of six time-points throughout the study period.

The map was preserved from session to session. Except, for obvious reasons, in the first session, all sessions began with a review of the actions that had been listed at the end of the previous session, with the facilitators using this discussion to prompt the initial review of the map. An excerpt of this dialogue follows, as it shows how facilitators and participants worked together to 'talk the map into being':

> FACILITATOR: What about the opening event for the new library, how are things going with that?
>
> MARY: The programme is done. We have a plan. We have a programme already. So everything is prepared. It's just we need to send out the invitations. The people have to say yes …
>
> FACILITATOR: So you need to do that, send out the invitations?
>
> MARY: Yes, we have to send out the invitations.
>
> FACILITATOR: Can we put that down as a task [brown leaf]?
>
> MARY: Yes, it's a task, 'send out invitations'.

What is evident in this dialogue is an *explicit* representation of tacit knowledge by an utterance on the map. As suggested by Harvey, this shows 'shifts in language from free flowing processes to a crystallised causal schema' (1996, 82) – a schema that here, and in all the similar utterances made during the concept mapping process, becomes fixed as part of the map.

Figure 5.4 opposite displays one quadrant of a map. It shows two topic clusters, one entitled 'Teaching' and the other 'Kompetanse utvikling', which translates from the Norwegian as 'professional development'. Four tasks, five needs, four sources, two blocks and one action are clustered around the first topic, and this action – 'Adapt course to need of group' – has been marked as a priority. (Note, the smaller white number markers placed around 'Teaching' are later annotations.)

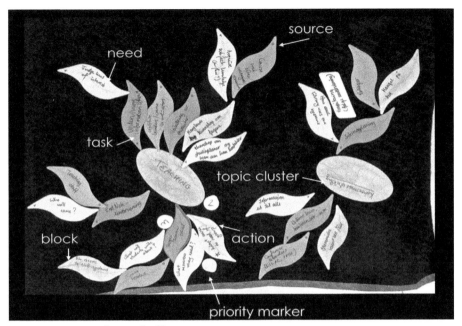

Figure 5.4 A quadrant of a Ketso map

In visual terms, this image depicts only 6.25% (that is, one-sixteenth) of the data generated in just one session across both libraries, and 1.04% of the overall Ketso data across all six sessions. To discuss the contents of all maps in more detail than this would lead to little insight. The maps are unique to the contexts from which they emerge. What can be highlighted, though, are the general patterns and trends on the maps, and how these patterns and trends may change over time. Alabbasi and Stelma (2018, §35–7) suggest it is less the individual leaves that matter and more the clusters into which they form, though unlike in their project, core themes (the ovals) on the BIE maps were not determined in advance. In BIE, topic ovals were placed after the first question in session 1, and the laying of task leaves in answer to that question ('What tasks require attention at work?'). While participants had the opportunity to review whether these elements, the topic ovals, continued to be relevant to their depiction of the landscape, in practice they changed little.

There was only one occasion (§3A) where a completely new topic was introduced by the participants, this being the 'professional development' topic depicted in Figure 5.4. Significantly, it appeared at this session on the maps of both groups in the room, having been 'talked into being' in the first stages of the session where both groups, together, discussed actions set in §2. And only one topic was ever removed from the maps, that of 'reorganisation' in §5A, this coming after all the sub-tasks relevant to the move to the new campus were completed in summer 2014.

Nevertheless, if we see the topic ovals as defining the 'top level' of the data structure on the map – key landmarks or orientation points in this landscape, like Seaford Head or Crowborough town centre – then this structure emerges from the first session and the intersubjective agreement, between participants and facilitators, that creates these clusters.

There are notable variations in volatility between regions of the map. Some areas stayed fairly static over time whereas other regions had leaves (tasks, needs, etc.) added and removed in all sessions. But there was no obvious relationship between the level of volatility and whether participants perceived these as priority areas by the placing of markers. Some topics were designated as priority areas throughout but still saw negligible changes. See the two images in Figure 5.5, for instance, which both show a region of one map, group B2's 'Teaching' quadrant, first at §3B2 (February 2014) and then at §6B2 (September 2014). The region just below the topic oval contains a task leaf and associated information needs (the four leaves lined up more-or-less vertically) marked as a priority for attention. Yet six months later, that representation of part of the landscape remains unchanged, despite it continuing to be designated a priority at each session. This does not necessarily mean no work activity is taking place, but it does indicate that there is a *perception* of stagnation, with the map being a representation of group perceptions and judgements.

The maps were group creations, but that does not mean all group members played an equal role in their construction. Some participants made significantly more alterations to the map than others: in other words, their voices were more dominant in the produced map compared to those of colleagues. This was seen in the data across all the sessions (for detail see Whitworth et al., 2016c) and with reference to specific areas or 'territories' that developed on the maps. In certain areas, a particular individual took on the majority of the responsibility for managing regions of the map where these were considered the province of staff members with particular expertise: that is, with *authority* in that area of work. This was also evident when certain people were absent from sessions, when there was a reluctance among other group members to make adjustments to map regions that they perceived as the territory of these absent colleagues. This is from §B2, though is not the only example:

Figure 5.5 The development of a map over time

FACILITATOR: These [leaves] seem to have become detached … to do with the Archaeological Museum?

ANGELA: Yes, but we have to leave these, because Matthew is not here.

This map contained a territory that in earlier sessions had been laid and managed largely by Matthew, but in his absence, the other members of the group agreed, informally, that they would leave this area of the map untouched.

It may seem self-evident that those with expertise in, and formal responsibilities for, a given area of work would be most active in mapping that area. But this misses the way in which the mapping process became an explicit *articulation* of this expertise, allowing the judgements made by the staff member possessing authority to be scrutinised by other members of the group *if they desired it*. In §4A2 there is a nine-minute passage of the recording where the dialogue is almost wholly between facilitator A and Dawn. At one point the facilitator says to Dawn, 'your handwriting is all over this …', thus acknowledging that this area of the map is mostly plotted and managed by her. However, the discussion still contains interjections and observations from other group members and her having a conversation with the facilitator (as opposed to completing the review alone, in silence) ensures Dawn's judgements about the ongoing relevance of information sources and needs are not made *in camera*.

Thus, the mapping process has become a way by which staff members not involved in a day-to-day way with certain areas of library work can nevertheless *acquire knowledge* and *engage in dialogue* about these tasks, help set priorities, suggest sources and so on. Frank said:

> … if there were areas which were my [formal] responsibility, then colleagues would ask me for my input, sure. But it's not like I only contributed to those areas that I personally work on.

Thus, the map becomes a way for the expertise of individuals to be displayed: a representation of their tacit knowledge and their understanding of the elements and relationships that make up this region of the information landscape. By exposing these representations, it also allows these understandings to be scrutinised by others who occupy different communities across the landscape of practice. Even the revealing of the map to the territorial 'manager' (Dawn's role, in the case of research support and digital resources in library A) is valuable, particularly bearing in mind the presence of a facilitator who could here take on a 'counsellor' role with respect to the information needs arising in this area of the library's work (cf. Kuhlthau, 1993). This scrutiny was also taking place as a result of the practice architecture in place here, namely the structure of the sessions themselves, with each involving explicit procedures of scrutiny and review.

Facilitation

In these procedures, *facilitation* was very important, and as this was also evident in some of the earlier discussions about Ketso and other concept mapping interventions, the nature and impact of facilitation deserves closer attention.

Facilitators are active agents of various processes that coalesce around the mapping tool and the places in which it is employed. In BIE, the facilitators helped create a conducive environment for dialogue: they are part of how the practice architecture in this social site was 'set up to facilitate the efficient and coordinated performance of its constituent actions' (Schatzki, 1996, 114). This extended across both the material and discursive aspects of the environment. Materially, meeting rooms needed to be prepared beforehand and the Ketso kit laid out. Facilitators also made sure coffee and refreshments were available. In the interviews it was noted that having a 15-minute 'prelude' in which these refreshments were served was a valuable transitional period, helping attendees gather their thoughts, particularly as most admitted they did not otherwise prepare for the sessions in advance. During the meeting, the facilitators compensated for and/or anticipated limitations of the mapping process; for example, keeping the group to time (mapping discussions could not last indefinitely: they were 90-minute slots in the work diaries of busy people).

Once the basic environment was established, facilitators were an integral part of how the map was talked into being. At the most basic level, facilitation helps 'crystallise' what is in the group mind, reflected in their dialogue, and thus helps a concept be plotted on the map, or removed if it is no longer relevant. Participants frequently checked procedure with the facilitator: take these passages from §5B1 (the bold text highlighting repeated requests for confirmation from 'Jacob'):

> LUKE: Do the tasks need to be completely fulfilled to be removed?
>
> FACILITATOR: No, not necessarily, but you might want to write new leaves as well, if the goal or the task has changed in some ways.
>
> JACOB: We can leave it on, because there will be some restructuring etc **can I just leave it?**
>
> FACILITATOR: Yes, but you could also add a comment.
>
> JACOB: Yes, but … we have a perspective of one year from now, **should I write that** on some kind of a note?
>
> FACILITATOR: Yes, take a square comment-note.
>
> JACOB: I write time horizon of one year, or I say Sept. 2015, **is that ok?**

Similar insights can be gained from other reported studies of the Ketso process, such as that of Alabbasi and Stelma (2018, §33).

As well as being agents of *structure*, facilitators acted as agents of *scrutiny*, prompting group members to review every leaf on a map and making sure no regions were neglected. And facilitators did not just 'shepherd' the participants: at times they would also write and plot leaves for participants, serving as agents of *consensus*. This from §4A2:

> FACILITATOR A: 'So is that an obstacle, or an action?' [asking for clarification on an existing grey leaf – 'Hang lende kunnskap om fagene' – though it's obvious once translated that this is an obstacle ('Lack of knowledge about subjects')]
> CAROL: Well, it's that I'm not an engineer but I still have to teach engineering students about IL – it's up to me to extend my knowledge of the subject …
> FACILITATOR: I see, so getting this knowledge is an information need for you?
> CAROL: That's right.
> [Facilitator writes out the 'Acquire subject knowledge' yellow (need) leaf]

Group A1 did not require a great deal of input from the facilitators, but A2 and B2, particularly, saw a significant increase in the amount of plotting (the laying of leaves) by the facilitator: in fact, in sessions 5 and 6 for group B2, all new leaves were laid by the facilitator. There are various ways to interpret this phenomenon. The most negative (at least from the perspective of critical and radical approaches to IL) is that it shows a concentration of authority. Group B2 may have 'gone into reverse'; members seeming unwilling to shape the landscape and leaving it up to the facilitator. A more positive view is that the facilitator was not imposing his perception of practice onto the group, but helping the group find an agreed, effective way to record their collective perception on the map, which they were otherwise finding difficult. The facilitator may well be the best agent of consensus there is, a summariser, a judge in his/her own right, acting effectively with the best interests of the group in mind. The problem would come if all, or even the majority, of decisions were ultimately those of the facilitator: just as it would be if a teacher in a more formal setting was always the one solving the problem or answering the question.

Significantly though, in other groups, facilitation diffused, with participants spontaneously adopting the role in later sessions. This excerpt from §6A shows Fay being persuaded by Mary and Dawn to lay on the map a leaf that represents an information need. She needs to know from the operations team (a source) whether there have been changes to certain routines since the opening of the new merged campus library:

> MARY: You depend on Drift [Norwegian for 'operations']?
> FAY: Yes I depend on them, but I don't need to know anything.
> DAWN: Well, you need to know whether there are changes …
> FAY: Ok, I'll write 'change of routines'.

In §5B1, the group members reach out to a non-member (Frank, part of group B2), who is temporarily admitted to the conversation to confirm that websites will need updating due to new technology. This is done without facilitators' prompting; group members themselves determine that fresh input is required and the boundaries of the community of practice are made permeable to new information. That is, Frank's input is considered relevant at that point.

These observations show how facilitators act as agents of structure; of scrutiny; of consensus; and ultimately, of learning. They do not impose their agency on other participants in a rigorous and inflexible way, but they do police the parameters which shape the dialogue, help give it direction and form, and thus help see it recorded on the maps in ways that best reflect the dialogue. But the handing over of control of the practice, which should be the case with scaffolding, is more evident in some groups than others.

Managing conflict

There was one particular moment, in §6A, which is worth highlighting. This reveals how much potential existed for conflict in the different histories and practices of the previously separate libraries. (Session 6 took place in September 2014, after the move to the new campus had been completed.) It also shows how affect and emotion arose as a result of the mapping practice and, as noted by Reckwitz, affects 'are a constitutive part of the social life which incessantly produces them' (2017, 118). This was the only overt manifestation of conflict in the project, but though it was singular, this does not mean it was an insignificant occurrence. Tagliaventi and Mattarelli (e.g. 2006, 304–5) noted that in their study of an oncology unit in a hospital, '[r]eaching consensus about the unit's values has sometimes been a stormy process', even if open conflict was very rare (they cite a figure of less than 1% of all informational exchanges). What this event reveals is how the group had, by this point, learned how the map might be used to attend to the issues revealed by the altercation, if not actually resolve it.

In the session, conflict arose between Bill and Fay regarding a practice – librarians delivering books to academics' offices – that had developed over time in one of the campus libraries. This practice was objected to by Bill, who had worked at a different campus. The disagreement became about more than whether the book delivery service should continue in the new (shared) setting. It represented a dispute over the underlying value of 'user service' that both librarians agreed was fundamental to their roles, but they disagreed over the manifestation of this in practice. The disagreement was severe enough to provoke a strong emotional reaction in one of the disputants.

Joanna, library A's Director tries to cool the dispute via her role as Director but also with reference to the mapping practice, as the bold text here indicates:

BILL: …we are delivering very bad service to the researchers, this is not possible!
FAY: What do you mean?
JOANNA: Ok? Is this something that needs to be addressed? … If it is an obstacle
or a challenge, **it is very important that it is written here** [on the map].

Bill suggests how the mapping process has raised awareness of practices elsewhere in
the library but in a manner that he perceives as problematic. He uses the term
'uneven' (in Norwegian: *ujevn*) to refer to how attitudes and values have developed
in different ways across the broader landscape of library A. As the disagreement
becomes apparent, another staff member, Kirsty, says three times 'this is not the place'
for it, but Bill replies that the issue is on the map so they should discuss it. Eventually,
despite the tension an 'obstacle' (grey) leaf gets talked into being and placed on the
map and the discussion moves on.

The conflict has not been resolved, however, and recurs when the group discuss
the setting of priorities. Bill is insistent that the user service issue be prioritised,
justifying his stance by drawing on specific items plotted on the map, saying: 'What
I have written here shows a problem we have, user understanding …' Eventually,
Joanna states (drawing on her authority in this setting, as Director): 'I agree that we
put this as a priority in the short term and take a look at the quality of our services.'

The conflict developed not just through divergent practices, but through
conflicting ideas about roles and how members related to other people outside the
community (in this case academics). The group's collective identity, as librarians in
this particular setting, was unsettled by conflicting interpretations of practice. These
had been concealed when the sub-groups had worked on different campuses and
operational proximity was lacking. But the differences became relevant with the
merger and were given a medium of expression in the Ketso session.

When asked about this altercation in her interview, Joanna said:

Middle management did sense that there was some divergence which could lead to
trouble and said they were going to address it, but the Ketso session then brought it
out, provoked it to come out? It did at least give me the chance to see this conflict
from the grass-roots, whereas if we'd waited for the meeting this would have been
mediated by middle-management – not that this would have distorted things, but it
at least gave a different perspective.

This event shows how the mapping sessions acted as more than just a way of
recording the outcomes of information handling practices that had already occurred
in the past. Instead, the mapping sessions were, in their own right, an information
practice. These groups of workplace learners were incorporating the mapping
technique into their repertoire and using the map to make informed judgements
about information practice. These decisions included ongoing evaluations of the

relevance of information sources to needs; the setting of actions and priorities; and reviewing the impact, on the information landscape, of those actions that had been listed at the previous meeting. As noted earlier, this learning community included the facilitators.

Recognising the constraints

Further evidence of how the group learned to incorporate this practice into their repertoire comes with the moments where members recognised its limitations. One example occurred in the recording of §6A, in which Bill reflects on the fact that all the Ketso leaves are the same size. He notes that one thing the map cannot therefore depict is scale; there is no way to measure the relative significance of tasks:

> We should have something very big, to show how much time some things take, because some of these are tinier things we do, others take up 50% of our time, it doesn't show on one little leaf.

He believes that Ketso would be a more effective aid to making judgements about the comparative relevance and priority of information if it was more able to depict this relative significance.

Group members also began, in later sessions, to note how the structure of the earlier maps was serving as a constraint. They perceived that the maps laid down before – the lower layers of the palimpsest – no longer reflected their perspective on the information landscape. For instance, group A2 complained, in both §4 and §5, that the topics of 'reorganisation' and 'moving' had, in their first session, been combined on one topic oval. Both were consequences of the campus merger in library A's institution, but while 'moving' referred to the physical relocation of books, equipment, etc., into the new library, 'reorganisation' related to changes in jobs, management structures and so on. In §1A2 these had become combined, but by §4A2, six months later, the group stated that this was confusing their judgements about relevance:

> MARY: Reorganisation and moving are on the same leaf, but are not the same thing ...
> FACILITATOR: I think we're OK to pick out the differences?
> DAWN: But 'flytteprosjekt' [the project to physically relocate the libraries] isn't directly connected to the reorganisation.

No changes were made, but in their next session participants reiterated the point. Carol defends combining the topics on the grounds that it separates them from others. The bold passages in the quote below highlight how she perceives their depiction and proximity on the map as a way of helping to make judgements in this area of work:

> CAROL: … **they are put together here**, in my view it is because **they are things that are connected with what is happening now in the organisation**. They are **not things that we normally work with** in a normal situation. It is a way to prepare the establishment of the new college.

These passages suggest that Carol and her colleagues are not just learning to map, they are also developing shared understandings about how their maps depict the configuration of the information landscape, as they learn about how to manage the informational, logistical and social demands of this challenging period at work.

Conclusion

What has BIE shown, in terms of the elements of mapping practice explored in Chapter 2?

The bounding of the map has been intersubjectively defined by the group, not imposed upon it by an external authority. In §1, in principle, anything could have gone down on the maps; the Ketso was an almost-literal *tabula rasa*. But as with my Seaford psychogeography, the implicit 'blankness' of the slate was illusory. The map was pre-framed by assumptions about what the task would involve and what information was therefore *relevant* in this chronotope. Assumptions about what behaviour was expected of participants in that first session were shaped partly by the fact that the research team and the project itself were not complete unknowns. They had already had their initial interview and prior to that we had talked to them about the project as a group, they had read participant information sheets and indicated their informed consent to the project – informational practices that were essential to establishing the validity of the project as research as far as all three involved institutions were concerned (the two Norwegian institutions and the University of Manchester).

Thus, when asked that first question, 'what tasks need attending to at work', no one wrote 'renewing my car parking permit', for example, even though this might have been a pressing work-related task. The focus of attention – what the soon-to-be-populated Ketso mat represented as a *field* – was 'the library'. But what 'the library' actually meant to each of these different participants was unknown in advance, not only to us as researchers, but to each of them – until the landscape coalesced on that first map. In that session, the boundaries were set and, as noted above, overtly and covertly structured how the landscape was perceived in subsequent sessions.

Ketso has given this mapping process a specific *materiality*. In practice theory terms, Ketso is 'equipment', integrating the dispersed practice of 'mapping' into this social site; as it did with Tesco staff, the Sesotho villagers, the Saudi teachers and so on, each in different ways. Each Ketso map acts as a *physical*, *tangible* focus for the dialogue of the group, a way of recording data about collective judgements for analysis but also becoming an outcome of the discussion; a 'generative means' (Corner, 1999, 228) that represents collective insights and subsequently becomes a prompt for reflection and further discussion. Adding concepts, revising them, removing them when a task is complete or a source is considered no longer relevant: these are practical manifestations of judgements about relevance and temporality (map creators must ask: is this process still ongoing, has it changed somehow?). Thus, the map is a material, as well as a social, site of knowledge. The act of writing out a concept and placing it on the map is an explicit articulation of a reached agreement, however provisional. Positioning the concept relative to others gives the connections made between concepts (e.g. needs and sources) a sense of permanence; but because it has been visualised, this also means that these and other judgements could be scrutinised and, if judged necessary, easily removed or changed. The process of placing or removing something on the map represents more than just an abstraction. Three separate BIE interviewees pointed out the sense of satisfaction that was achieved in library A when all remaining map items concerning the move to the new campus could finally be removed in June 2014. This removal was more than just a technical device of representation but became symbolic, at least within this setting, of the end of this complex and time-consuming project.

Also, note the *spatiality* of the activity. Everyone (including the facilitators) has to make *time* and *place* for it; in other words, to share a chronotope. Being in the same room at the same time is important: it is not that a map could not emerge without this (see Chapter 6) but it would happen in different ways that, in this case, would have been less likely to meet the specific learning needs of these groups. One of the changes that the library A Director was concerned about when it came to the physical move to the new library was that colleagues would lose certain shared places, not just formally but including lunchrooms, which provided a regular place for informal dialogues about work matters. Culturally, there were motivations in this setting to provoke the development of new connections in the social network and to define these in spatial terms, anticipating how the new library at A would be physically configured in different ways.

The question of how power and authority within this social site shaped the project is more ambiguously answered. It is difficult to directly assess the impact of the fact that the Director of library A was present in each of the Ketso sessions there, whereas her equivalent at library B was not. There is little evidence from the transcripts of sessions, or the maps themselves, that her voice was more dominant than others. She did not show evidence of managing areas of the map territorially in the way that Dawn did (see above).

However, power issues, defined around the *place* of the BIE project as a whole, did have a subtle impact on how the mapping practice was positioned at each of the two libraries. The agreement to use library B as a case study was made with the Director in place at the time of the funding bid (late 2012), but very shortly after we began the project, he announced his retirement due to ill health. Yet the change of Director, while obviously significant, did not impact on the *practices*, and thus the *information landscape*, at library B at anywhere near the same level as the relocation and reorganisation did at A. The BIE project as a whole, and the Ketso sessions specifically, had not become integrated into the short- and medium-term planning work of staff at B in ways that it was at A, who were perceived as the 'owners' of the project. Although we have no direct data, as we did not interview the new Director, the library B staff member who was on the project team had their time allowance for it stopped at the conclusion of the original project: when we secured a small second tranche of funding to continue with the analysis and find ways to take the project forward, we had to do this only with team members from A. The implication is that at library B generally, and particularly in the eyes of the new Director, BIE was perceived as a *research* project only and not a *learning* and/or *staff development* project.

Nevertheless, at both libraries it was noted that there were few opportunities, in normal work patterns, to get together for discussions of this depth. Strategic 'away days' had a similar function, but were hard to arrange, so were less frequent and more formal. On the other hand, team meetings, while more regular, did not typically involve 'frontline' staff and, again, were more formal, mediated by the structuring (but not shared) object that was the agenda – a discursive map. In Joanna's words:

> I got more out of it [the mapping] than from the normal monitoring and meeting process. The amount of information I would normally get would be a lot less, particularly the perceptions of the staff. Previously contact would be mediated through middle management, but even though they were there in the [mapping] sessions, the mediating aspect was removed .... Socially it's nice too, constructing together. There is a team-building aspect to it.

It was the mapping *sessions* that became part of the information landscape of these communities, more than the maps themselves. From the perspective of the participants the map was a *focus* for dialogue and a way of *structuring* it, but it was not the primary *product* of the dialogue. The maps 'anchored' the sessions and provided continuity between them, and the process of producing/modifying them generated discussion and reflection. But participants did not take away copies of the map and refer explicitly to them between sessions (though interviews indicated there was some implicit use of them in subsequent practice). The map per se was therefore mainly an artefact generated for the benefit of the researchers.

Yet the map and the process of its production can be seen as complementary. Without the map itself, the mapping sessions would have been less likely to become part of the participants' landscape of practice, a liminal space in which diverse viewpoints could come together and negotiate the 'intersubjective agreement' (Lloyd, 2012, 773) that constitutes the connection between resources across this landscape. The maps are representations of the intersection between *the practice of the mapping community* and *the resources in the wider landscape of practice that it both shapes and is shaped by*. These representations are collectively created and constitute a record of the shared intersubjective agreement that has been facilitated within the community around the map. Thus, the map is a way of recording and facilitating group judgements of relevance (cf. Saracevic, 2007, 2134).

As equipment, the maps built in BIE and the other concept mapping projects described in this chapter can help integrate the (dispersed) practice of mapping into specific practice settings and have further practices develop around the map. Produced maps are unique to the chronotopes from which they emerge: they are shaped by the particular concept mapping method in each setting and, corporeally, by the dialogues, decisions and (on occasion) conflicts that emerge at the place and time in which the map is being drawn. The different studies all show how in each chronotope, the map becomes an informational resource that allows learners to understand the configuration of resources available and make connections that were previously concealed. The maps are a substantive part of the dialogue between the learner and a facilitator, whether that be a peer, a 'teacher' of some kind or a researcher. Whether created individually or through the work of a small group, these maps can be the basis for further judgements about the relevance of information; they help with the organisation of that information; and they are ways of communicating understanding to others, indicating pathways through a landscape, and also representing changes in that landscape over time.

Chapter 6

Discursive mapping of an information landscape

Introduction

The previous chapter focused on learners creating graphical maps of information landscapes, whether individually or collectively. But the value of this to the learners was seen as much in the *mapping* as the maps; the process, as much as the product. The discussions so far have suggested that mapping has value in learning to use, nurture and steward information landscapes because it is a means by which representations of relationships between relevant landscape elements can be developed, communicated and scrutinised within communities. It has already been suggested that these processes do not have to result in the production of some kind of cartograph or other graphical map (like a concept map) for mapping to nevertheless be occurring – and, therefore, for these kinds of representational and communicative processes to still be taking place.

The aim of this chapter is therefore to look more specifically at the practices involved in *discursive* mapping and how these are manifested in dialogue between learners; an outcome of which is a more effectively, or at least differently, organised information landscape. Two key themes underpin this discussion. The first is how a learning environment, designed around the principles of informed learning (Bruce, 2008) and incorporating techniques and supporting technologies that promote the discursive mapping of an information landscape and the modelling of good practices, can build and validate the information literacy of small groups of learners in an HE setting. According to Bruce et al. (2017), effective design for informed learning has three key principles:

- It takes into account learners' existing experiences of informed learning, using reflection to enhance awareness;
- It promotes simultaneous learning about disciplinary content and the information using process;

- It brings about changes in learners' experience of information use and of the subject being learned.

Chapter 4 was based around a real but wholly informal 'educational' situation. In Chapter 5 the focus was on either workplace learning and/or the use of mapping to generate data for academic researchers. In this chapter, the IL intervention being discussed is a formal one, part of an organised programme of study. This formalisation adds elements of power and authority that must also be discussed: this being the second key theme of the chapter.

The research reported on in this chapter is drawn from a project known as SPIDER (Stewarding and Power In Digital Educational Resources). SPIDER has worked since 2015 with a large corpus of text and other data that records how small groups of learners stewarded their information landscapes during a course of study. This dataset has so far been analysed in different ways, and with differing intentions, by myself and other colleagues, including Lee Webster and Helen Gunter at the University of Manchester, Linda Corrin of Swinburne University, Australia, and Camille Dickson-Deane of the University of Sydney, Australia. Publications in which these other insights are discussed include, at the time of writing, Webster and Whitworth (2017; 2019), Webster and Gunter (2018) and Whitworth and Webster (2019). These publications will be directly cited where necessary. However, what I offer in this chapter is a supplementary – and, due to space constraints, selective – analysis of the data that is specific to my concerns in this book, namely, what these dialogues and utterances illustrate about the use of discursive mapping to develop IL.

Studying online discussions

Before embarking on the discussion proper, let me place this study in context, as an example of a research genre. SPIDER is a study of information seeking within an academic setting, but the approach – in line with the views of practice theory – is not focused on assessing cognitive change in learners. Rather, the attempt is to capture the richness of practice and dialogue that emerge from the interaction of the individual and the context. In this regard, its approach is akin to other studies of online communication and decision making. This line of research flourished with the opening up of Usenet and its online discussion boards in the 1980s; new communicative spaces that sparked the interest of enthusiastic participant/analysts such as Rheingold, with his studies of the WELL group in San Francisco (1993); Baym, with *rec.arts.tv.soaps* (2000); and Schneider's study of *talk.abortion* (1997). Each author is enthusiastic about how these boards, and the communities which they see developing around them, might revitalise the ideal of the public sphere (Habermas, 1989), offering an asynchronous space for dialogue in which valuable informational resources could be shared and co-developed, free of the constraints and structural limitations of the traditional public sphere and its domination by powerful media companies and other institutions. For example, Rheingold recounts the following anecdote:

> In the summer of 1986, my then-two-year-old daughter picked up a tick … and we weren't quite sure how to go about getting it off. My wife, Judy, called the pediatrician. It was eleven o'clock in the evening. I logged onto the WELL. I got my answer online within minutes from a fellow with the improbable but genuine name of Flash Gordon, MD. I had removed the tick by the time Judy got the callback from the pediatrician's office.
>
>   What amazed me wasn't just the speed with which we obtained precisely the information we needed to know, right when we needed to know it. It was also the immense inner sense of security that comes with discovering that real people – most of them parents, some of them nurses, doctors and midwives – are available around the clock, if you need them.
>
> (1993, 1)

Rheingold concludes that 'virtual' community can exist and be just as effective at giving access to information – and the affective structures that help link these 'sayings' with 'doings' or actual practice – as the geographic community, and in some cases, as the professional community.

On the other hand, his citing the help of 'Flash Gordon MD' would doubtless raise alarms in writers such as Keen, whose position on the great expansion of online information can be summed up in the title of his book *The Cult of the Amateur* (2007), and Thompson, with *Counterknowledge* (2008). Keen, Thompson and other commentators of their ilk do not agree with Rheingold that a reduction in 'gatekeeping' is a positive step. What checks now exist over the quality of this information? And it is not just concerns about the content of Usenet and, subsequently, other popular online resources like Wikipedia, which bother these critics, but also how the structure of the information landscapes might obscure learning. As early as 1999 – and in fact, these concerns are little different than those of Bush (1945) – Shenk was warning how online 'data smog' obscured people's attempts to navigate between different communities. Usenet was seen as a technology of fragmentation, isolating micro-communities from each other: once people find their informational niche (like the WELL, say) they make fewer excursions outside it; the weak ties prized by Granovetter may be deteriorating, not being strengthened, through online dialogue. More recently, Pariser (2011) warned how the operations of Google and Facebook create 'Filter bubbles' in which we tend more and more to only encounter information that supports our perspectives (and personal constructs), rather than challenge them (see also Gilroy-Ware, 2017).

These concerns are obviously valid; no educational approach that claims the mantle of IL can ignore them. But this is exactly why it is important to look at the epistemological, knowledge-formation practices that are actually occurring in online groups like this. Baym and Schneider's detailed and (for Schneider at least) quantitative approach to content analysis is therefore significant. Both show how important it is that certain members of the community take on stewarding roles. Schneider draws attention to the existence of 'opinion leaders' on *talk.abortion*, with an evident concentration of posting duties: among 3,000 individual posters over the year of study, just 15 of them contributed around 45% of the messages: 80% of posters posted fewer than five times. What is interesting is that he notes (1997, 98) how it is the more frequent posters who (in relative terms) post less content that is *directly* related to the subject matter of the group (abortion) and more what he calls 'metacommunicative' content: that is, discussions that are about the board itself, community policy, the behaviour of other posters, etc. Evidently these individuals are acting as stewards of the information landscape of the community as a whole.

Baym (2000) studied *rec.arts.tv.soaps* in similar depth. She noted that 'flaming', quite prevalent on *talk.abortion* (see Schneider's Appendix), was not tolerated on this group. Members acknowledged that some discussions became heated but in general this was a friendlier group than others. Baym notes that 'the creation of friendliness in r.a.t.s. is not given but rather a communicative accomplishment … friendliness is something a group *does* rather than something it *is*' (2000, 121). Relevant discursive techniques that she observes include phrasing that manages disagreement and reduces tension (e.g. opening a possibly contentious statement with 'I may be wrong, but …') (ibid., 124); pulling threads back onto topic; ways people introduce themselves at the point of 'unlurking'; and use of real names rather than pseudonyms or nicknames. All provide evidence that the group had developed a structure of social norms, displayed in the text (what people said, to whom and when) – and thus in the dialogic practices of the group (ibid., 158).

Posters on the group have varying levels of 'cultural capital'. In this setting, such capital arises in two main ways. Firstly, by being a *provider of information*. Some posters develop a reputation for knowledge of the histories of particular shows or their detailed archives (ibid., 160–2). On the group there was one person responsible for writing an update about a particular soap opera each week. This is a time-consuming task: the only pay-off is status and authority within the group, but this is considered enough motivation for people to regularly undertake the work. The other source of cultural capital is 'performance' (ibid., 162); those who were witty, humorous, could write well and succinctly, were given credit for this and seen as valuable resources within a value system, one that prizes 'honesty, information, insight and wit' (ibid., 174); these are informational values that are relevant to the context and not just generic 'soft skills'. Baym's study shows, therefore, how the members of this community, through dialogue and without any formal instantiation of this agreement, either in writing or through the application of technology beyond the existence of the board itself, created a practice architecture that kept the board a congenial and *relevant* space for its users.

Can, or should, communities like these be created in formal educational settings? Hodgson and Reynolds (2005) adopt a nuanced view of the benefits of 'community' and of asynchronous communication, noting the importance of creating authentic, commonly-held goals for the group. Compare this with points made earlier, via the discussion of Saracevic, who noted that the problem with studies of group judgements of relevance was that the groups were artefacts of the research study, but members otherwise had no connection with each other. In educational settings, we should not expect such shared goals to emerge because a discussion board is presented to a group of students with an expectation that simply from this, dialogue will flow. Rather, thinking about how the learning activities can be structured and facilitated in ways that might, at least for the duration of the task, give rise to this sense of community is a key pedagogical design task. Pai et al. note that '[s]tructures, such as scripts, roles, and group rewards, have been identified as critical for fostering greater learning in groups than in individual contexts …' (2015, 80); such 'scripts' can be: 'designed to increase specific cognitive behaviors associated with learning, such as summarizing, providing explanations, or asking questions …' (ibid., 81). They also cite Aronson's 'Jigsaw' approach, in which:

> Each group member studies a subtopic of the material, meeting in 'expert groups' to share information with peers from the other jigsaw groups specializing in the same subtopic, and then returning to their groups to teach their peers about their subtopic. Each student is like a piece in a jigsaw puzzle. Each part is essential for full understanding of the final product (Aronson 2002).
>
> (ibid., 2015, 81)

Most importantly:

> … when working in groups, *multiple perspectives on the problem need to be negotiated to a common representation.* Therefore, the representation tends to be abstract to be able to bridge various views. Collaboration provides an environment to generate more abstract representations which is not normally available when working alone …. While working collaboratively, individuals *have to generate and explain their thoughts to each other.* Vocalizing one's thoughts can help to produce an *organized cognitive structure* of the material…
>
> (ibid., 82–3, emphases added)

These points strongly allude to the notion of discursive mapping and the value that this process can have. This was evident from the studies reported on in Chapter 5, but Pai et al. do not mention the need for a graphical map (see, however, Hughes and Hay, 2001, 558): the suggestion is that by *articulating* their positions, a common representation, an 'organised cognitive structure', can emerge among the student group. This structure is not something imposed on them by the teacher. Schunk describes the importance of *peer modelling* here. The peer is someone 'roughly equivalent in development to the observer … [and] whose actions, verbalisations, and expressions are attended to by one or more observers and serve as cues for modeling' (Schunk, 1998, 185). But following the model of a peer is not done automatically, there needs to be a *perception of relevance*: 'students are likely to attend to, retain and produce modelled actions that they feel are important' (ibid., 186). Nor are all peers treated equally when it comes to judging their cognitive authority: 'Especially when there are multiple models, students are more likely to attend to those with prestige and competence' (ibid., 187).

Neither Pai et al. nor Schunk are specifically discussing the use of online discussion boards to facilitate such work, but introducing such technology does give rise to significant points both for researchers and educators in IL. Unless specifically recorded by video and/or audio, face-to-face discussions between group members may well have outcomes in terms of a product, but the content of those dialogues, and hence the process, may well be lost. For either a teacher or researcher to stimulate reflection on the process, the only option is to elicit post hoc reflections from participants on how judgements were made in these conversations or what 'organised cognitive structures' emerged from them. Online boards, on the other hand, allow for observation of these dialogues both at the time and, potentially, some time afterwards.

That being observed impacts on one's behaviour is an effect that has long been known. The question of how learners adapt their dialogue when they are aware it is somehow being recorded cannot be avoided and so will be returned to below. But putting this aside for now, the value of the corpora of text that are recorded in spaces like these has been exploited in SPIDER and other studies, for example, those of Geoff Walton and colleagues. Walton et al. (2007) studied postings on a VLE and, more recently, Walton and Cleland undertook a study which has a:

> … focus on the notion of discursive competence (Foucault 1972) within a practice architecture as a means of revealing to what extent individuals gain the ability to produce contextually appropriate texts within the online peer assessment construct.
>
> (2017, 588)

Walton and Cleland are specifically noting that 'discursive competence' is manifested not in generic ways, but *within a practice architecture;* indeed, that competence is integrated with the development of the practice-arrangement bundles in a given social setting. Their study is of a three-week IL activity performed by undergraduates studying sports science at a UK university. These learners were asked to use a discussion board to comment on essays written by peers. The authors cite a few examples of these feedback comments; the following is typical:

It [the essay] is effective how you focus on one particular idea and you use good examples to back your arguments up. The way in which you structured your paragraphs allowed a clear transition from each one and your grammar made it clear and easy to read. One area of improvement could be to use 'do not' and 'could not' as opposed to 'don't' and 'couldn't'. Overall referencing was done well, however, make sure every key point made is backed up with a reference. Also try to use academic references instead of autobiographies [i.e. texts by famous sports people].

(ibid., 588–9)

What Walton and Cleland are primarily concerned with – hence their citing Foucault – is how the practice architecture in this setting shapes views of what practice is considered 'desirable' and how this is reinforced by the online peer assessment. Are these learners being empowered to develop their own information practices or are they reproducing dominant practices? Take the comment above and its phrase, 'use academic references instead of autobiographies'. Walton and Cleland suggest this shows how references are seen as 'better' if they are what is defined as 'academic' in the prevalent discourse and that these are superior 'in some agreed fashion (the notion of validation)' (ibid., 590) to autobiographies written by sportspeople. Postings that were recognised as more authoritative or 'strong' from students were those that achieved status by imitating the approach, the discourse, used by the tutor on the group: the architecture thus 'has the function of reproducing the discourse of the subject context or the academic tutor – especially the notion of what constitutes valid scholarly work' (ibid.).

As well as this observation, Walton and Cleland offer methodological support to the SPIDER study. They link their use of the board's postings directly to practice theory:

In practice architectures (Lloyd, 2012) 'sayings' are the words and phrases members of a practice group use in their day-to-day situated interactions … It is argued here that this definition could be extended to include online textual postings generated by learners because: these communications are a demonstration of their comprehension as defined in Bloom's taxonomy (Walton & Hepworth, 2011); they are carried out in an environment (Virtual Learning Environment) which provides a cognitive space (Garrison et al, 2003); they embody more considered utterances about a topic than face-to-face conversation … and finally, they can form the basis for shared meaning within a community of practice …

(ibid., 585)

These points are significant. The environment – that is, the VLE – is not just an inert space, nor even just a recording device; it is a constitutive part of the information landscape and has a variety of features and affordances which students can bring to bear when it comes to selecting, organising and communicating information. The board itself, 'the basis for shared meaning', needs therefore to be considered as *material* equipment which allows these educational practices to coalesce around it. How certain features of this equipment were used by students to organise – and thus, discursively map – their information landscape is a key theme in the discussion to come. Such attention to organisation is necessary because:

> Collaborative information behaviour in COGs [completely online groups] is challenging because members share some information resources in common, such as those contained within the collaborative tools they use, but also rely on information resources unique to each individual's physical location and internet use habits…. Patterns of collaborative information behaviour emerge as COGs perform tasks, maintain social relations and coordinate member responsibilities.
>
> (Goggins and Erdelez, 2010, 110)

In this process, Goggins and Erdelez stress the importance of what they call 'social navigation', meaning 'the capacity for members to see and follow the work trails of their group mates in an online forum' (ibid., 112). As with the landscapes of Crowborough, Seaford and any similar town, signposting is a helpful navigational aid; but in a COG this can only be done verbally via each individual's posting, each one being a manifestation of their inner cognitive state at the time. The dialogue builds up, utterance upon utterance, to create these 'patterns'. Goggins and Erdelez also suggest that groups like this should have broader *information horizons* than physically co-located groups (cf. Webster and Whitworth, 2017), but this in turn means that it is a harder task for these learners to find common ground within these different horizons.

A final point from this study that is worth making here is where Goggins and Erdelez note that while groups, as stewards should, bring in other tools to help them communicate and meet their shared learning goals: 'the selection and adoption of online tools by each of the groups in this study shows collaborative information behaviour in COGs is easily influenced by the technology choices of assertive members' (ibid., 120). This can be benign, but in two of the eight groups they studied they concluded this choice 'emerges out of an assertive member's explicit attempts to control group discourse' (ibid.). Skype is cited (ibid., 121) as a tool brought into the habitat even though it was inconvenient, and thus less relevant, for some group members (they lacked broadband or found it difficult to create time for synchronous discussions).

Summary of the context

The SPIDER data are drawn from two academic years (2015–16 and 2016–17) of student work on a UK-based postgraduate course in educational technology, which hereafter I will refer to as DET ('Developing Educational Technology'). This is IL education taking place firmly in the disciplinary setting, rather than the library, as advocated by many authors already cited (e.g. Badke, 2012). As described in Webster and Whitworth (2017; 2019) DET's course design is based around the principles of informed learning (Bruce, 2008). Christine Bruce's distinctive approach to IL education was first promoted in her study (1997) of workplace learning and developed into the 'six frames of IL education' (Bruce, Edwards and Lupton, 2006) and the book *Informed Learning* (2008). In the latter, Bruce summarises the approach as based around:

> … the view that learning involves coming to appreciate the different ways in which it is possible to see or experience the object of learning (Marton & Booth 1997). These differences are usually referred to as the variation in ways of seeing or experiencing particular concepts, professional problems or forms of professional practice.
>
> In this view, the primary task of the teacher is to understand students' ways of seeing, whatever it is they are learning. As educators, we then need to help students encounter different ways of seeing the phenomenon we are teaching so they will understand those differences and have a sense of which lenses are more appropriate for them to use.
>
> (2008, 23)

The notion of learners enhancing their IL by experiencing variation is integral to the design of DET. A key feature of this setting is that the course is part of a degree programme that recruits both on-campus and distance learners (DLs). As part of the assessment, students are placed into groups of 5–7. In the two academic years covered by SPIDER, each group contained 2–3 distance learners. Groups are colour coded: the Blue Group, Gold Group, etc. When group discussions are referred to below, references take the form 15/Blue or 16/Gold, where the number indicates the academic year in which the group started work, 2015 or 2016 respectively. Posts have been reproduced verbatim, with spelling and/or grammatical errors uncorrected. Student names have been reduced to a first initial.

The presence of DLs in the groups, as Goggins and Erdelez noted, broadens the horizons of the groups as they bring to the dialogue the quality of *alterity*, or 'outsideness' (Linell, 2009; Webster and Whitworth, 2017). DLs are not only physically located away from the university, but on this course they also tend to be older, have more years of professional experience (almost all the DLs are studying part-time, while working in a professional setting) and are more likely to have English as their first language. Most of the on-campus students come from outside the UK, tend to be younger and are less likely to have professional experience: some do, but many have come onto this MA course direct from their undergraduate studies. As Webster and Whitworth (2017) discussed, supporting the aforementioned observations of Goggins and Erdelez, the alterity which this diversity brings to the groups is valuable when it comes to learners experiencing variation about the objects of study (to be outlined shortly); but the variety of contexts also provides a pedagogical challenge.

Informed learning is evident in the DET course design in the ways that, within their groups, students collaborate on a series of tasks of increasing complexity. Following an initial 'icebreaker' designed to introduce group members to one another and familiarise them with the discussion boards, there are three assessed activities:

- *Activity 1:* students are asked to read a provided academic text (Mishra and Koehler, 2006), and discuss the relevance of its core idea (the notion of 'technological-pedagogical-content knowledge', or TPCK) to their shared learning needs.
- *Activity 2:* the groups are provided with a scenario involving a fictional HE institution, 'Mackenzie College', seeking to enhance its use of educational technology. Each group plays the role of a stakeholder (e.g. management, academics, IT services, students). The task parameters require each group, through consulting academic literature and subsequent dialogue, to establish a collective position on 'Mackenzie's' situation, then contribute information to the management group who draft a decision that is publicised to the other groups. Each group should then respond to this document. Thus, in terms used by Steinerová (2010) and cited in Chapter 5, the task has two stages: an *orientation* stage (what is our interpretation of the scenario, what are our priorities?), then an *analytic* stage (what do we think of the management group's draft decision?).
- In *Activity 3*, which is discussed in detail in Webster and Whitworth (2017), groups must propose designs for technological enhancements to two educational settings: specifically, two museums. They can propose solutions such as new exhibits within the museum space, mobile apps, videos, a change to the museum's website, etc. Unlike in the first two activities, the information students need is not provided to them, but gathered on a field trip. DLs are expected to arrange their own field trip at a museum local to them; on-campus students all visit the National Football Museum in Manchester (hereafter, NFM). As members do not all visit the same museum, to make a choice about which to work with, they need to share information about these contexts within the group and discursively map them: which in this case means reaching agreement on what aspects of the museums are relevant and how these relate to the proposal they must collectively publish. (Museums were chosen as the setting for two main reasons. First, their stability. One can determine in advance

what will be present in the museum environment and, largely, predict what will occur within it on a given day; this is harder with a more dynamic educational environment, such as a classroom. There are also simple logistical, material factors; with 30-plus students on any given field trip, taking them into a museum is far less disruptive than to a classroom.)

All in all, the students are being asked to act as practitioners, to use and handle information in ways common in the field (Bruce 2008) – in this case, the field of the educational technologist, making *informed* judgements about which technologies might be most applicable in a given setting. DET's pedagogical design obliges students to *articulate* that understanding. Reifications of agreements constantly crystallise out, as students apply their developing disciplinary knowledge in contexts, whether simulated (Mackenzie) or real-world (the museums).

The tasks, especially activities 2 and 3 (on which the bulk of the following discussion is based), are too complex for one person to complete in the two weeks allocated for each and thus require collective action, the 'jigsaw approach'. There needs to be organisation of the task, temporally (time management) and informationally: groups must establish who is going to do what and when. Tasks build from simpler into more complex tasks in terms of what information is provided to them in advance. There is a dialogue with the tutor, who gives feedback between the tasks and helps scaffold things in tasks 1 and 2, but this is withdrawn; though in activity 3 there remains some monitoring from a teaching assistant (TA).

The most significant feature of these activities, for my concerns here at least, is that it is the *process* which is subject to assessment, not the product. The marking rubric for the task (which is available to students from the start of their studies) is provided in Appendix 3. It is evident that what is being graded is not the 'correctness' of the outcomes of the discussion: that is, the content of the decision made by each stakeholder group in Mackenzie College, nor the design for either museum. Instead, groups and their individual members are given credit for effective information practices, such as the adoption of different roles, the rooting of their claims in authoritative sources (including the academic literature, but also, where appropriate, first-hand knowledge and experience), the inclusivity of the group, keeping to deadlines and so on. The tutor provides formative feedback after each activity, by e-mail, and this also shows how it is the process that is more of concern here than the product. Take this feedback given to the 16/Red group as a whole for their work on activity 2:

> You were certainly a well-organised group. This included both how you went about taking the decisions you needed to take (and communicating them), on schedule, and also how you used the discussion board format to help with these tasks. Threads were clearly distinguished from each other, phase by phase, and clearly labelled, rather than having everything lumped in one discussion. Generally you

were inclusive of the whole group, though not everyone at every phase, and your reflection was more a set of individual posts than a final discussion. I liked the summary you provided and the ideas were good, but although the chart looked interesting at first, it is really just a representation of the different groups in the game and I'm not sure that it communicates much new information. You seemed a little put out that the management team were not consulting you but I think largely they got what they wanted from the summary post.

The tutor is also a participant in the dialogue on the boards for activity 1 and 2, though not in 3 (see also below). The TA remains on the boards throughout and will occasionally remind groups about task parameters. For example, the assessment specification notes the importance of students backing up any claims made with reference to the literature. In a post made in activity 3 in the 15/Gold group (see also below), the TA here validates [S]'s last utterance then notes how [A]'s good practice – relating her idea to theory – should be followed by the rest of the group:

> I'm really enjoying your discussion and think it got off to a great start with [S]'s thorough description of the museum as related to her experience watching a [football] match. I think it is more difficult to consider the 'non fans' in terms of what you would be aiming for pedagogically with this group and how to achieve it, and you have made a really good start in addressing this.
> Nice connection between the referee activity and learning theory [A] it will be great if you can all continue to draw on this and other theories you have studied to justify the ideas you have, theoretically as well as practically.

In Appendix 4 there appears a list of the resources introduced by these groups and it can be noted that all citations that group members bring in arrive after this prompt.

In all, the assessment specification, the marking rubric and structures of facilitation and support within DET are designed in ways that promote certain informational practices, conducive to informed learning, over others. The design of these activities offers a framework or *practice architecture* in which students get practical experience in building around them an information landscape that helps them meet *collective* learning goals. They must set up a sociotechnical information system, one that helps them make selections, organise information and disseminate findings. And as it is what is posted on the discussion boards that is graded, the dialogues taking place as the group work together are not happening *in camera*, but are visible, open to scrutiny by the course tutor, the students themselves: and finally, the SPIDER research team.

Stewarding the landscape

In order to illustrate how discursive mapping takes place in this setting and helps the learners navigate and steward the information landscape they use to work on these tasks, let me first show how each group's landscape dynamically evolves over the period of the course, as learners adopt certain technological tools and discursive practices into their landscape. Like all information landscapes, the landscape of DET is not a flat structure without temporal depth, but a palimpsest with many layers: layers that continue to sediment out of the discussions and interactions that students have with each other and with the tutor and TA.

The course landscape is one that students know they must learn to navigate effectively, but it has not been created through their own efforts and contains many unfamiliar resources, discourses and connections. The tutor has used a range of structuring devices including the curriculum, intended learning outcomes, the assessment specification and marking rubric, and the features of the VLE to represent to the students potential pathways to this landscape and delineate a number of sub-regions to explore, whether in terms of disciplinary ideas (e.g. accessibility, the social shaping of technology, to name but two sub-topics from the curriculum) or different types of resource (e.g. web pages, a reading list, tools like the discussion boards). At the start of the course, this is a landscape without inhabitants and, in this respect, is the same for each group. Yet this landscape, explicitly or otherwise, has gaps within it: areas of the landscape which students are directed to – and hopefully, feel motivated to – explore for themselves. The design of the assessment provides a structure for this enquiry that is tighter than the general, vague notion of 'doing research' or 'writing an essay' of the kind that Badke laments (via his frustrated student). The activities are also located in specific places and in two main ways: first, the sense of their information landscape being a place that is conducive to learning; and second, the specific contexts to which they are being expected to apply their disciplinary knowledge.

I will look initially at how students co-create their information landscapes as conducive places for learning. (The discussion on the next two pages also appears in Whitworth and Webster, 2019.) This co-creation takes place through the introduction of resources and how these become organised into a discursive map. Based on their prior experience and judgements of relevance, oriented by influences such as their own subjective understanding of tool affordances and their interpretation of how best to set up the landscape so the group can meet its shared learning needs most effectively (Wenger et al., 2009), groups introduce new resources into this 'starter' habitat. These resources may be informational, and come from online sources and/or the literature, as these quotes illustrate:

Here is the link for the text 'Knowledge for Literacy' as a reference:
www.shankerinstitute.org/blog/knowledgeliteracy [15/Purple]

In my university ... to be innovative in technology or deliver teaching in a
different way is questioned, not by the faculty, but by higher management who see it
as not conforming to the standard norms students are used to. [15/Black]

Since technologies are changing very fast, we must also relearn and readapt our
own teaching practice. Mishra and Koehler say that technological knowledge is 'the
ability to learn and adapt to new technologies' (page 1028). [15/Purple]

We see here, respectively, the provision of information via URL; via narrative and
personal experience; and via academic citation.

As well as these informational resources, students introduce technological tools
into the landscape. This is rare in activity 1, but after that experience, groups
frequently note that the discussion boards have limited functionality and so, through
a series of informed judgements, introduce other resources. For example:

Me, [D] and [S] just had a Skype planning meeting to think things over; here's a
summary of the discussion and what we will be doing [16/Blue]

Other groups use different tools. For example, Padlet becomes part of the habitat
configured by 15/Blue, 16/Diamond, 15/Black and 15/Gold, but not the other groups.
Student [B] here introduces Padlet to 15/Blue. He draws on his professional
experience and suggests associated information practices to align the group's work
with expectations defined in the starter landscape, referring to instructions given by
the tutor:

In class I like to use padlet.com to create discussion boards and students have even
used it to do group work. I've created a padlet with the information. It's a huge
poster board where we can all add information. I've added all the information
[tutor] has provided and a quick comment. Let me know what you think? Should
we give it a try? http://padlet.com/[URL truncated]

If you want add information, please add you name to posts or register (it's free) so
[tutor] can view it for assessment. [15/Blue]

On occasion, individuals suggest reasons to avoid particular technologies (remember,
these utterances are made to other group members as they work, not post hoc to an
interviewer):

The main problem I find with LinkedIn is that it's overrun with recruitment
agents, so I rarely use it. Twitter is OK for some stuff, but because it's so transient I
find I miss things a lot and it feels like a lot of effort to keep up with it. [16/Blue]

By the end of the series of activities, each group's learning environment looks different from those of other groups and different from the starter landscape (see the Appendix for three examples). The group's landscape has become a record of the judgements of relevance that have been made by members. These judgements are based on the prior experience of individuals and their application of IL in work and everyday life, but are then validated by colleagues according to their relevance for the specific, shared task that the group has to fulfil. The group learn to develop practices that help them work together as a group and that are in a dynamic, mutually-reinforcing relationship with the technologies and sources that they introduce into the landscape. As Wenger et al. write: 'Shared assumptions about how to use [the technologies] constitute practice' (2009, 137). These practices are taken forward from activity to activity without needing to be renegotiated. Groups also reflect on their prior performance and consider how the practices, technologies and resources in the habitat might be better used this time:

> Me, [Y] and [S]... have already discuss on how we should form our thread in this forum so that it'll better organized than our previous discussion (Hehehee ... we think it was pretty cluttered). [16/Black]

In each group, what is emerging is a set of shared assumptions about the landscape and ways of navigating it most effectively.

The 16/Diamond group

Let me now present extended dialogues from two groups that stewarded their landscapes well, then some content from a less effective group. The first is the 16/Diamond group, comprised of two DLs, [A] (a UK national) and [G] (Polish, resident in China) and five on-campus learners, [J], [Y], [H] and [X] who are all Chinese, and [S] who is Arab. With respect to the characteristics of the cohort, 16/Diamond is a representative group.

16/Diamond effectively establish divisions of labour, taking on responsibility for different areas of the landscape and/or the task of stewarding it. These divisions of labour are evident in activity 1, but at this early point in the course have not been explicitly negotiated. Instead they are based on prior experience and the perceived credibility this gives certain learners, particularly (but not only) distance learners. In their first posts to the board, the two DLs [A] and [G] display their professional experience openly:

> I teach online, using Blackboard Collaborate, so when I talk about technologies and technological knowledge, I'm generally referring to digital technologies, over more 'standard' technologies ... I use a number of the Adobe products for creating

teaching materials Photoshop, Illustrator, InDesign and Captivate. I've been using Photoshop since the beginning of my undergraduate degree … [A]
In my current job, I mostly design online courses and various online components for my University, support teachers with designing their VLE (Moodle) modules and part of my job also requires me to train teachers in the use of technology in the classroom, delivering best practice workshops etc. [G]

[H] immediately contrasts this with her own lack of experience and [J]'s first post says 'I have no experience in teaching before and I am looking forward to your answers … can you [give] examples about the aspects you use the applications (you have already mentioned like Moodle and Blackboard) to give support….?' [G] answers, 'Sure, I'm happy to help but perhaps drop me an email so we can communicate outside this discussion forum.' Already then, [G] is suggesting expanding the landscape and making judgements that any subsequent discussions about [J]'s query, as not directly relevant to their assessment task, would be less appropriate for this forum.

In activity 2, the role-playing game, which is appreciably more complex than activity 1's reading task, groups benefit more from divisions of labour. The groups have plenty to do and tight, fixed deadlines for when they need to communicate their conclusions to each other and to the tutor. They need to make group judgements about relevance, but the landscape is more complex, with new sources of information coming into play. In activity 1, the only sources of information they needed to draw from the wider landscape, and manage, were their prior experiences and the Mishra and Koehler text, but here they are being expected to find for themselves some texts to justify their stated position. They can also communicate with other groups to discover, at second hand, information that was part of the starter landscape for this activity but which, due to their positioning in the game, was not initially available to them.

Returning to the 16/Diamond group, in the very first post of activity 2, [A] suggests good stewarding practice and invokes the authority of the tutor to back this up by indirectly citing his published activity guidance:

As suggested by [tutor] it is better if we have different roles to make the whole process easier …

(Note, the use of the tutor's name as part of statements such as 'As [tutor] said' or 'According to [tutor]' becomes more significant, as a locus of the student's authority, in activity 3; see the discussion below.)

Student [J], who calls her 'Captain A' while doing so, responds by volunteering to take on the role of the public board checker and group 'spokesperson'. [G] announces that he will: 'be the IT expert since I currently work in a very similar role …' and [H] feels confident enough to claim similar expertise (and thus authority, within this task) as an 'IT expert' 'since I majored in related course when I was in previous university'. Both students are *positioning* themselves within the structure that is being negotiated as a prologue to the substantive, decision-making dialogue. But [A] then uses her authority to suggest that there may be too many IT experts; she asks [H] if she can reallocate the role of source checker to her as she 'was the last one to comment'.

[X] volunteers to take on the role of summariser. Note how he asserts the value of particular practices as he does so, those (such as staying on topic and frequent checks of the boards) that he perceives as linked to the group's collective success in this task:

> I would like take the role of group relationship and summariser too, based on your help. This activity request us to participate actively so all of us can get a good mark. Come on guys, let us do it in collaboration and help each other together! Please check the discussion board frequently, and help people who is off topic …

[A] now not only organises the work into different 'feeds' (threads), she explicitly signposts this for the others, telling them what she is doing and why. She divides up the information seeking according to the divisions of labour that have been mapped out ([X] as summariser, [H] as source checker) and also prompts [Y], who has contributed little thus far, for her opinion:

> [X] our summariser, any suggestion?
> [H] can you suggest any other sources that support what have [G] and I said?
> [Y] can we get your opinion as well since we have only three days before reaching to final decision?
> we need your support guys…

The division of labour has thus become a structural element of the information landscape, something which the group can use to streamline its information searches and better organise and communicate found information. This is not mapped out on any kind of 'organisation chart', but nevertheless there is a record of the division, which can be scrutinised, and used as the basis for subsequent judgements: the postings themselves. These are not abstract representations. The manipulation of the equipment in the landscape is creating a structure within 16/Diamond's landscape in an embryonic way. There are no formally expressed rules as to what relates to what or how information should be classified, rules which could be manifested as code in a database, expressed as an SQL query, etc. Nevertheless, a schema has clearly emerged by which the group is organising its information and making the landscape easier to navigate.

The group's developing facility with these practices is even more evident in activity

3. The dialogues around this activity show a passing of the 'chief steward' baton away from [A] to [S], although not until after [A] makes several excellent stewarding moves in the first post. Her very first sentence is encouraging. She provides information that she has worked out, in advance, will be relevant: as much because of what is *not* in her visited museum as what is, and related to the goals that give direction for the task to come. She tells the group that she has posted her field notes (information about the Maritime Museum) to a separate 'feed' (thread) and makes suggestions as to how they should use the affordances of the board to structure their dialogue:

> Looking forward to working with you all again! Our first job is to decide on the two museums we will be focussing on. I'm looking forward to hearing about your experiences at the National Football Museum.
>
> I visited the Maritime Museum in Hull ... [this] is a fairly 'traditional' museum in terms of its presentation with minimal opportunities for interaction with the exhibits and very minimal use of technology therefore, there's great scope for creating a technology based exhibit here.
>
> I've typed up some of my field notes and added them to a separate feed in an attempt to keep everything organised – there's a link to some photographs in there too. I think it would make sense to have a separate feed for each museum as there's likely to be a bit of back and forth in order for people to understand the context and content of the museums they haven't visited.

The 'summary' info in the second paragraph is then expanded upon in her second post, to the other thread, where she provides a URL, photos and a narrative account of the Maritime Museum, with headings to structure the information.

However, in response to a post from [G] about whether [A] is willing to 'lead us to victory again', [A] notes she is 'willing to let someone else have a go this time' and, as noted in Webster and Whitworth:

> [A] credits the group as a whole with good performance in tasks (e.g., 'backing up our points with literature') that represent good information practice and are specifically cited in the marking rubric for the activity. But she and [G] both also recognize the instrumental and the communicative benefits of establishing divisions of labor within the group.
>
> (2019, 124)

The group have honed their stewarding practice over the three activities. [A] has been the exemplary model for her peers most of all, but the group's effectiveness cannot be attributed only to her presence. The practices have spread and their diffusion is evident in how the group now populate and structure the landscape. The list of resources provided in Appendix 4 shows how they have used the discussion board technology to create two different types of thread: one related to deciding on the products (the designs), into which more informational resources are introduced, and the other type being 'metacommunicative' (cf. Schneider, 1997): threads entitled 'Selecting the two museums', 'Roles?' and 'The final discussion: suggested structure'. No resources come into these threads except one, a Google Form which the group use to take a vote on which alternative museum to select. [A] does introduce the most resources, a third of the total of 57, but other students take up the load, most noticeably when it comes to their chosen alternative, the Maritime Museum. Only [A] had first-hand experience of this place, but all the students introduce something to the dialogue at some point, judging it to be relevant. Thus, they have discursively mapped and organised their landscape both thematically, allocating resources to different areas of the landscape, and geographically, meaning, with clear reference to the real-world context and the material, embodied experiences of visiting the museum.

In this first phase, while they set up this configuration, there are few discussions about what their actual proposal is. But then, having volunteered after [A]'s 'abdication' to take on the moderator role, [S] enhances the discursive map as she signals the transition into the next phase:

> Now we're moving to the design stage … this thread is to discuss the design of new technology for the NFM. To have an easy flow discussion, I suggest that we start focusing on
>
> 1   what are the areas that need to be improved/ developed in the museum
> 2   suggest how it can be targeted/ improved
> 3   Then, collection these aspects will help us rich to a design of a needed technology?
>
> Anything to be added?

A similar post is made by [S] to a second thread, concerned with the Maritime Muscum.

[A] is aware of the iterative nature of the task, announcing on day 10 that she went 'back to the [Maritime] museum and took some more photographs'. She uses these to focus on the specific exhibit that the group has decided they will look at (a whaling ship), as until they made this focusing judgement they did not have this specific information need. Thus, the group have an iterative and dynamic view of their landscape and are not assuming everything is in place and all information needs have been met after the initial field trip.

16/Diamond are thus an exemplary case of effective stewarding and the use of discursive mapping to gradually focus on the problem and come up with solutions, marshalling a large number of informational resources.

The two Gold groups

To investigate the dialogues of all twenty groups in similar detail is obviously impractical. But I will, more briefly, look at how two other groups engaged, or did not engage, in similar discursive mapping processes and what evidence there is of this having an impact on their work. Both groups were designated as 'Gold' in the respective academic years, hence, 15/Gold and 16/Gold. As with 16/Diamond, the structure of threads and the resources introduced into their third activity discussion have been provided in Appendix 4.

15/Gold are effective, from the beginning of activity 2, at structuring their landscape and verbally 'signposting' colleagues to the right area of work. For example, they set up a Facebook group at this point and [R] asks straight away: 'Is our first task to decide the division of labour? is the best way for us to communicate through this discussion board?' [Y] answers 'I think we can use discussion board to post our thoughts, and use facebook to inform group members that we made a thread ...' and [S], 'We built a facebook group in order to talk more convenient. Can you just add me on fb, and I can drag you into our group!'. [Y] also restates the deadlines for the activity.

They separate out the discussions into threads early on. They leave the initial thread as the place to set up the task and agree a work schedule and move the discussion of the problem into a new thread. The structure for the group and its work on this activity is thus set up before [L] makes her first post, three days in:

> Hi guys, Sorry for my later than usual response to the discussion board. I have just arrived back in the UK from Australia for the xmas holidays.
> My email is b_____@hotmail.co.uk. Are we just using FB or email or both? Getting confused as to how we will be communicating. I don't want to have to keep checking various different means of communication, can we just stick to one?

Within four minutes [R] tells her, 'Welcome back to the UK! So far we have just been using the discussion boards to communicate ...' And within an hour [L] has provided her own summary of what she perceives as the key issues from the discussion so far, presenting this map for scrutiny and validation by the others: 'From reading through the main problem and your discussion I can see the main facts/issues that we face are; [...12 bullet points follow].'

[R] validates this exemplary catch-up with the following post that provides further information about the group's landscape, checks that [L] is now properly oriented and offers affective support:

great summary [L], thanks. Totally agree with all the above.
can you find the threads now? they are just seperate threads within this forum. Any problems or you want to clarify anything you can email me
r_____@hotmail.co.uk or call me 07_____. I got confused at first so please call if you want to talk it over.

The group take this effective stewarding forward into activity 3. Their number of introduced resources is lower than in the 16/Diamond group and they do not use 'meta' threads, but the organisation of the landscape is established clearly in the very first post from [A]:

Hi everyone,
I am pleased to work again with you in this discussion =)
For this task we are asked to design two plans for technological improvement as applications of digital technologies, one for National football museum and another one that [R] or [L] visited.
So, to start I would suggest at this stage to introduce our museums to each other supporting this with photos and discussing the general messages of the museums and trying to deconstruct the context of the museums. We also need choose one either [R]'s museum or [L]'s museum. In order to make our work organised from the beginning, I suggest to launch 3 threads one for each museum.
We can call this 'Analysis stage' until we come up with a clear and specific issue then we can move to 'design stage' in responding to the previous stage. We may also use this thread for organisation or general discussion and reflection. What do you think? Do you agree?

Again, discursive mapping is clearly evident, here encompassing thread, time and task management. Note also how the posting is verbally inclusive, bookended by social hooks, like the salutation and 'Do you agree?'.
In response, 15/Gold group members all immediately provide resources such as narratives, videos, photos of the NFM and the two DL museums (Alcatraz and an Artillery Museum in Australia), slotted into four threads (see Appendix 4). [R] provides validation to two fellow students and plenty of her own information in this post. She suggests how she has used these resources to develop an understanding of a context, the NFM, that she has not visited:

Hi [H], thanks for your post, it was really interesting and informative and really helped me understand the football museum. Also I watched a good video of it here is the link https://www.youtube.com/watch?v=1DA3iiiJfbM, this also helped me to understand the museum and how it was different from my expectations of a football museum. The venue for one thing ... I would have assumed it was in a football stadium.

[Y] I like your idea about The Holographic Laser Projection and I think we should consider it but also I want to suggest an idea. One of the things that you mention was the atmosphere of the fans when you went to the match, for me as well at Alcatraz it was the sounds of the prison on the audio headset that invokes the most emotion and atmosphere. How about some audio as well as the projection. What I realised at Alcatraz was the power of audio especially when it is through a headset somehow more powerful and personal.

In the end, [R] herself comes up with reasons to not choose this seemingly rich setting for the task, judgements made based on her own, material experience of the setting:

For Alcatraz I find it hard to improve on the museum and its content and use of technologies. Mainly this is because the place is relatively unchanged and so it has the sense and feel of a real place and therefore it is possible to experience it in reality as opposed to virtually. In the same way would you want to put any e-technology in say for example the Colloseum? … I felt that I learnt about Alcatraz through sound, touch, sight, smell, and empathy and feeling. When I asked my son (aged 13) did he think any technology would improve it he said no.

So straight after that decision is made, [L] now presents further information in a new thread:

Seeing as we are in agreement about creating a digital technology for the Artillery Museum I thought I would start this thread as suggested so we can discuss our ideas on here ….

And on they go. The 15/Gold group do not discuss roles, but this makes little difference to their performance on the task: again, as Appendix 4 suggests, each member contributes to each phase of the discussion and the stewarding of the group's landscape is equally distributed among the members (with the possible exception of [S], though she is not significantly behind her peers).

The 16/Gold group, on the other hand, was less effective at creating this kind of meta-structure for their activities. Whereas members of the two exemplary groups discussed above got started on activity 3 straight away by making initial discursive mapping moves, and quickly reached agreement on how they would structure the space, 16/Gold are noticeably more sluggish than other groups. They make fewer posts and more sporadically; on days 4 and 5 there are no posts at all. After eight full days of the activity (there are 14 in total), student [C] is moved to say that 'since our second museum has not yet [been] decided…' and after another day of inactivity the TA is moved to post 'Guys … you are falling behind the others :-('

As confirmed by the data in Appendix 4, the group introduce significantly fewer resources than the two groups discussed above: a total of 24 (fewer than half 16/Diamond's total). Five of the six group members post first-person narratives (one does so twice, in two threads); 12 posts contain citations to the literature (one of which is simply a large block of copy-and-pasted text); three posts contain images; and only five contain URLs of some kind. No mention is made of other technologies, for example, spaces like Facebook and Google Docs which might have been used for dialogue, nor are there posts which discuss threading or divisions of labour.

There are fewer connections made between posts and ideas than in other groups. Posts are made in declarative ways that lack hooks for responses. [M] particularly tends to post long summaries of readings or publications without signposting how these are relevant and generally pushes the discussion into areas that other group members do not see as relevant. For example, early in activity 2 and without any prior mention of there being a need for this, [M] publishes an agenda for a team meeting. [B] shows his confusion; an on-campus student, he just about keeps up with the discussion but his on-campus colleagues [D] and [C] are largely absent from this activity.

It is not just [M], however, who is guilty of this style of posting. Also in activity 2, this initial post from [A] is immediately 'in character' but it is a declarative utterance that uses 'I' instead of we and promotes a sense of authority:

Dear Members,
You will all probably be aware of the difficulties at our University, mainly with the distance students and the VLE in use. I feel that it is inadequate and outdated, especially since it does not allow the efficient embedding of Web 2.0. As a result, our teaching is suffering. I have some ideas on how to rectify this situation... [3 bullet points follow]:

[K] posts next, but not as a response to [A]'s initial utterance; rather, her post is a separate statement in which she restates key principles from the assessment specification ('we are being asked to ...') and then mentions a role but only in the sense of it being a self-appointment:

... can we please hear from other group members. Thanks, [K]. (I will be taking on the moderator's role in this discussion)

[K] also undertakes the work of the public board checker, notifying the rest of the group that there are two messages for them requesting information from other groups. She posts these messages one evening, but when no one in the 16/Gold group has replied by the following day, she then says (in two separate messages referring to both requests), 'I have replied to this group on the public discussion board'. Nothing is posted regarding what answers she gave, nor whether her posts reflected a group consensus. She feels moved to say, 'I'm not sure if I actually spoke your minds as there were no more response from you guys.'

All in all, the 16/Gold group, while by no means dysfunctional, is less inclusive. The group do not form *agreed-upon* bases for dialogue. It is less clear that judgements of relevance are being made by the group as a whole and the landscape is less clearly organised than in the other two groups.

Group judgements of relevance

So far, stewarding and discursive mapping have been discussed in terms how group members used equipment (the discussion boards) to establish a structure for their information landscapes and the informed judgements based on them. What can now be shown is how mapping also applied to the contexts – the material places – which acted as foci for activities 2 and 3, giving these internally diverse groups a *single, shared* focus for their judgements of relevance. The groups jointly create an agreed-upon representation of a landscape and use this as the basis for further judgements. This is most evident in activity 2 in which the groups are being asked to make judgements about a context that is imaginary: or put another way, it exists (at first) only as the scenario presented by the tutor, outlining a situation faced by 'Mackenzie College'. They also manage to collaborate on judgements about museum contexts of which some members had no prior first-hand knowledge. As noted in Whitworth and Webster (the discussion on the next two pages is also drawn from this paper):

> Members of the groups can be observed introducing and validating informational and technological resources to other group members, and working to configure their information landscape in ways that then allow them to make judgments about found or encountered information in ways that *could not have been possible for them prior to the dialogue.*
>
> (2019, 1, emphasis added)

The 'Mackenzie College' scenario, which outlines the problem and offers brief notes about issues that each group might like to consider in their discussions, is the tutor's initial discursive map of this context. But the landscape it provides is a limited one and students are told this. The assessment specification and marking rubric encourage practices whereby, in the orientation stage, group members must broaden their information landscape, incorporating other resources that they judge to be relevant: these include citations from the literature and information that can be gleaned from other groups who are playing different roles in the simulation. The stakeholder groups in each game are: senior management; IT services; the student body; an innovative group of 'tech-savvy' teaching staff; and other teaching staff.

As a result of these searches and dialogues, each group develops their own perspective on the scenario and the question of how 'Mackenzie' should develop its e-learning strategy. There is no 'right answer' to find, so these perspectives differ from group to group. Contrast these posts, from groups playing the same role, that of the IT services department. These groups begin with the same initial information, but eventually agree on different priorities: Wi-Fi for the Diamond group, the virtual learning environment (VLE) for Green; for the Diamond group, training and teaching are also considered important, but the Green group's focus is more on speed and students accessing the environment after graduation:

> So far our ideas seem to be around:
> Changes in infrastructure: potential investment in wifi; Changes in teaching: potential changes in the adoption of apps as an IT team we need to look at how we could support this both through infrastructure and possible training. This might be a potential digital change agent project (students and staff working together) [15/Diamond]
>
> Questions we (the IT team) have to deal with by the end of this week: What should/can we do to make the VLE a faster platform? Can we get in touch with the provider and see if they have any updates coming up next year? For sure, we don't want to move into a different VLE. Is there a possibility for us to help the students maintain their access after they graduate? This might be a real satisfier for the students. [16/Green]

What is significant is how this interpretation of this context – a discursive map of Mackenzie College and what is important within it – is carried through into the analytic stage and used as the basis for judgements made there. The transition from one stage to the other takes place after the group playing the managers in this simulation use the public discussion board to post the outcome of their own group deliberations: a draft e-learning strategy for 'Mackenzie'. The other groups are then asked to present their (group) reaction to this judgement. This quote, made in response to that post by [R] from the 15/Gold group, highlights a significant issue:

> ... this is good information for us to use and saves us time ... this strengthens our argument for 'going it alone' and they recognise us as being well trained [15/Gold]

The basis for the judgement made in it – that the conclusions of the 15/Silver (management) group strengthen the argument of the 15/Gold ('innovative teachers') for 'going it alone' with educational technology – is *authentically* made, even though it refers to a *simulated* context. There is no external 'reality' to Mackenzie and therefore no criteria against which the group can base its judgements *except those which they negotiate and agree upon* whether through intra- or inter-group dialogue. Through these dialogues, each group agrees certain basic informational constructs such as priorities and problems for 'Mackenzie'. These constructs subsequently become the basis for the judgements of relevance that each group makes regarding the decision posted by the 'senior management'. For example, the 15/Gold group – largely because of the presence of [R], who was a DL student working as an academic librarian – were the only one of the 20 groups in the game to question why the library was not mentioned in the Mackenzie scenario. The rest of the group agree and from this point, the role of the library becomes an evident part of 15/Gold's discursive map of Mackenzie in a way it does not for other groups. Thus, when responding to the management group's decision, [R] writes:

> Have the management integrated the librarians, the students want this and we do too. How is the new situation an improvement for us? Will it make any difference to our teaching and delivery of our courses and our research? I think we need more support from the management and more recognition. [15/Gold]

[A] brings in information from the starter landscape (the provided scenario) to integrate it into the mapping (the indented text in the quote below), then builds on it to make judgements about what is best for, and what 'happens' within, this simulated context:

> we already have long experience with this issue because we manage to teach distance learners. In other words, our expertises have formed as a respond to learning process which is distance learning.
>> 'Mackenzie's distance learning programmes are highly rated and are led by a team of academics/researchers who are internationally regarded as innovators in the teaching of History at a distance.'
> So, I suggest to contact with managers team to discuss the idea of introduce our experience to other colleagues either IT team or other academic team? [15/Gold]

[R] agrees with [A] that this will have benefits for their group:

> … this could be a good opportunity for us to improve our profile at the university and therefore to get some recognition for the quality of teaching we deliver in the department. [15/Gold]

These things can be stated confidently about an unreal context because the agreed discursive map that they have negotiated has been integrated into their information landscape and for each group is now no less 'real' than their collectively negotiated perception of the assessment task. There is a 'register of correspondence' (Cosgrove, 1999, 1) between the place about which decisions are being made (Mackenzie and, later, the museum) and the discursive map that the group have performatively created via their discussion on the boards, which can guide their own self-assessment and help them scrutinise judgements made. The map has helped the group make connections between informational resources and it has become an agreed-upon basis for action that does not need to be renegotiated and can serve as the basis for group judgements of relevance regarding found and offered information. A map makes propositions; and that these propositions can then be explored in the world, that is, the place represented upon the map – it does not matter that Mackenzie has no physical cognate: it nevertheless acts as an *information ground*, a 'sociophysical location' (Hultgren, 2009, 140) *which both facilitates access to information and makes it relevant*. Mackenzie only exists as a PDF (in effect), but it has enough depth for the task at hand. The museums, even more explicitly.

The value of alterity

The importance of peer modelling in these activities has already been mentioned. The existence of two distinct groups of students on DET, brought together in shared places, is not a trivial aspect of the pedagogical design. Webster and Whitworth (2017) have already analysed the impact of *alterity* in this setting: that is, the value of the 'outside' perspective, the learners in the groups with a different *positionality*. The distance learners in this setting may be liminal, that is, in a 'border' area, but this does not mean they are marginalised or peripheral. Liminality can alternatively be seen as a privileged position (cf. Harvey, 1996, 101). Writing about the notion of alterity, Linell states:

> The other's 'outsideness' brings in a 'surplus' of vision, knowledge and understanding other than you had before or you had expected to encounter. The other may see things from points-of-view that have so far been strange or unfamiliar to yourself, and this forces you to reflect and try to understand, thereby possibly enriching your, and our collective, knowledge ... The other's discourse may function as a counterpoint, and it gives the individual opportunities for integration of others' knowledge. Since this is a mutual process among interlocutors, it provides for the development of socially partially shared knowledge.
>
> (2009, 85)

Recall (from Chapter 3) the reference to Haraway (1991, 195), and her assertion of the value of *partiality* as the basis for valid knowledge claims. Each and every claim made by the learners in this dialogue is specific to a time and place. Their worth as utterances cannot be judged against generic criteria, but only with reference to the task being undertaken, its overarching practice architecture (the assessment process) and the discursive maps that have developed differently in each group. The assessment obliges learners to develop knowledge about contexts they have not visited. They lack first-hand knowledge, so must therefore use second-hand knowledge, and cognitive authority (Wilson, 1983) thereby comes into play. As Schunk (1998, 186ff) said about peer modelling, cited above, the actions of peers are not automatically accepted by learners and when multiple models are present, some judgement of prestige or authority is made to distinguish between them.

For a student to make any proposition to their peers – asserting the value of an online resource, say, or offering an idea for a new technology for the museum – they must articulate that proposition on the board, make an utterance of some kind. Responses to these utterances – whether they come from the tutor/TA or, in more in-depth ways in this setting, from peers – thereby validate and position each claim to knowledge. As exhorted by Bruce (2008), they are learning to see the world from multiple positions, 'experiencing variation'. Through this dialogue, the students *triangulate* on the landscape (Harvey, 1996, 283–4); bringing multiple perspectives together in a single interpretive framework or discursive map. At least transiently, that is, for the duration of the activity, this becomes a locus of collective memory.

Webster and Whitworth (2017) show how this is not just a formless abstraction, but that these different experiences can be shown coming together in each group's landscape, through the choices they make, via dialogue. They provide the example of one group's discussion in activity 3. Student [U], an African DL student, had visited a local war museum, and when other group members began suggesting it for their second location, used her local knowledge to point out how the surface layer of information on display in the museum was that presented by the government and obscured the viewpoints of minority and subordinate groups in the country. [U] stated:

> I think [the museum] have got a good marketing ability or strategy that is why people keep coming there as a tourist centre. Basically I think that foreigners are the ones who will believe their message because some of them are naive of the political situation in [country] right now. [15/Diamond]

Her locally-based 'surplus of knowledge' (Linell, 2009, 85) is then shared amongst the others; in response, [F] acknowledges her previous ignorance of the context (and, along the way, validates [U]'s provision of an information source):

> Hello [U], I've just watched the video from the official website you gave to us ... Thanks for your explanations of this [war museum]. You point surprised me that the facts in this museum are not very real ... I don't really understand the background of your society. [15/Diamond]

However, as well as just allowing access to other funds of knowledge, alterity was a locus of various forms of perceived authority, or prestige, in this setting. Webster and

Whitworth (2017, 76) observe that the on-campus students tend to be younger; are less likely to have English as a first language and/or be confident about using English; and are less likely to have experience of professional practice in this area. As a result, more experienced students in the setting – ones with more sophisticated initial maps of the landscape – bring their tacit understandings of practice to bear in organising the work of the group as a whole. This has already been seen with [A], the primary steward of 16/Diamond, who had worked as an online teacher (of children excluded from school) for several years and employed 'next-to-hand' behaviour to organise the landscape for the benefit of her group. Others did the same. Webster and Gunter quote one interviewee:

> There were some occasions, however, when I felt that we were not going anywhere by saying we agreed on doing whatever the others thought was going to be fine or keeping on asking if the others agreed to doing one thing or the other and waiting for everyone to respond before making a decision. I have been a manager before, and making these sorts of difficult decisions is part of being a manager. That's why I felt the need to take the lead sometimes and make certain decisions for the team.
>
> (2018, 77)

Lloyd notes how in practice settings, the experience of information is, typically, 'managed and directed by experienced members of the group' (2010a, 20). In groups that worked well, such as 16/Diamond and 15/Gold, these differences were exploited for the benefit of the group as a whole. This is evident from the discourse and the maps they have created. Although particular group members, usually those with professional experience, are seen as authoritative at first, this expertise diffuses through the group and in terms of what is posted – whether resources, suggestions, or metacommunicative posts like new threads – few differences between group members are evident from activity 2 on. But in less inclusive groups like 16/Gold, the more declarative style of posting evident there does not help develop these links across the 'border'. This is one area where interventions can be made and feedback given by the facilitator/tutor.

Power and empowerment

As well as 'intra-student' authority, institutional power also has a significant role to play in influencing how the students discursively map their landscapes. Webster and Gunter (2018) discuss how the power of the university is manifested in various symbolic and practical ways. Symbolically, the use of honorifics and titles, the formalism of the graduation ceremony and other representative devices offer legitimacy to the academic body when it comes to defining their role as authorities. They are 'authorities' in a given disciplinary field, but also have authority over the 'incentive structure' (Dowling, 1996, 5) within which students form practices. Most of all, this structure – a practice architecture – forms around the assessment process, the awarding of grades and academic credit. Being a 'learner', and in this case a 'university student', is a position one adopts with respect to a practice architecture and the power invested in it. IL remains an 'interplay of the agency of the student and the structuring impact of university systems' (Webster and Gunter, 2018, 66). The university is a 'representational machine' (Salvatore, 2006, 665), a complex nexus of real and symbolic places and practices that shape information flows (and accumulate capital as a result). To succeed there, that is, to have one's practices align with those that are rewarded by the system, means 'learning to read the semiotics of [these] institutionalised landscapes' (Harvey, 1996, 112).

That this process, and the form it takes in particular chronotopes, affects students' information practices has already been recognised. For example:

> … Biggs (1979) discovered that students who were told that credit would be given for factual recall adjusted their study methods for recall, which was detrimental to overall understanding and critique of written material. Students who were told that credit would be given for understanding and higher order thinking adjusted their study methods to achieve that task ….
>
> (Badke, 2012, 120)

Thus, students try to anticipate *the tutor's* tacit understandings of the assessment process, aligning their activity with what (they think) they are being asked to do. Yet recognising this also permits the design of the assessment in ways that *model* good information practice: as suggested by Bruce et al. (2017, see the beginning of this chapter). Badke again:

> Thus, while professors may not be able totally to overcome student tendencies to work primarily to meet the requirements of an assignment or an exam, it is possible to alter learning approaches by making deep learning the intended goal of instruction and informing students of the requirements to achieve success in such an environment.
>
> (Badke, 2012, 120)

Students on DET obviously are aware that what they post on the boards forms a visible 'performance' that is subject to assessment. If they perform in ways that the tutor judges as poor, then they will be awarded lower marks and this may ultimately endanger their chances of passing the degree. The work of Walton and Cleland, discussed above, and ideas developed in Chapter 3 of this book, suggest that what might be happening in DET is the imposition of 'approved' practice. Students may be self-disciplining, giving the tutor 'what he wants', or at least, what they perceive he wants. And interview data makes clear how some students discipline themselves and others when it came to making contributions to the dialogue. One interviewee states:

> There were many times I didn't want to contribute to the discussion but I knew I had to do it. In fact I had an interview with another person yesterday who asked if the discussions had not been marked would you have contributed? I don't feel I would have contributed as much, if I didn't feel it would have impacted my grades I would speak but not as much.
>
> (Webster and Gunter, 2018, 79)

There is also evidence that the presence of the tutor on the boards, and the perception of surveillance, leads to students self-censoring, particularly when disputes arose. They were keen to promote the appearance of consensus and politeness on the board, but this did not preclude them using other spaces (e.g. WhatsApp) to engage in discussion that they felt was more contentious and/or developing ways of posting that disguised true feelings. This from another of Webster and Gunter's interviewees:

> If you see my discussion board posts the posts that I refer to [Student N]. The ones where I put a ':-)', it means I don't really agree with you but I'm not going to say anything. The ones with him where I put a ':-)' they hide you know, well, [laughs].
>
> (ibid., 80)

'Compulsory visibility' (Webster and Gunter, 2018, 71) is 'a relation of surveillance … inscribed at the heart of teaching … as a mechanism that is inherent to it and which increases its efficiency' (Brookfield, 2005, 136). Nevertheless, Webster and Gunter also note (2018, 78) that most of the groups set up some kind of space outside the boards, away from the tutor's gaze. This was done partly for stewardship reasons, with other tools perceived as having better functionality and more applicability to the learning task than the discussion boards, as stated by this interviewee:

> Our own VLE proved to be tricky sometimes … I valued that, as a team, we made use of different ways to communicate, group our ideas and give shape to our preliminary decision and strategy. Gmail, Facebook, Google Drive, and the chat room in Blackboard helped us explore the use of social media and Web 2.0 tools to better communicate and write collaboratively.
>
> (ibid., 79)

But these tools were also incorporated into the group landscape to create a space away from the panoptic gaze of the tutor and engage in freer dialogue. Webster and Gunter consider this a positive step vis-à-vis information literacy and the informed learning basis of DET:

> By choosing to move outside of the discussion board space the students were shaping their information landscapes, demonstrating digital stewardship and distributing authority in line with the aims of [the tutor].
>
> (ibid., 79)

Even on the visible boards, the influence of the tutor is not wholly directive. He possesses a cognitive authority in this setting that students recognise as legitimate – and, significantly, draw on to justify their own claims. In activity 3, across all 20 groups, the tutor withdraws from the discussion, although the TA continues to monitor the groups in case some (like 16/Gold) need any assistance. Yet in every group discussion of the museum task, students make at least one direct reference to the tutor as a proxy authority, to back up their own claims. For example:

> The main point of our last activity, as I have understood it, is first, sharing experiences and photographs related to the museums we visited (something that we have already done and it was really interesting) and secondly discuss and share ideas and knowledge about the design of one application. Also as [the tutor] has said **everyone in this group should apply frameworks and theories which were introduced in the course and use our field notes from the museums.** [16/Purple]
>
> This reminds me of what [the tutor] was talking about last week when he explained the social model of disability, when a bad design makes some people less able to access a space or perform a task. What I want to say from this point is that **we as instructional designers should understand that it is important to design with the accessibility needs of learners in mind.** [16/Orange]

The bold passages are claims made *by the students*; utterances to the rest of the group regarding what that student perceives as being good practice. But they draw on the tutor's authority *as a proxy*, justifying their own claims with reference to their interpretation of the tutor's perspective. This is certainly not blind conformity to an institutional discourse, nor imposed practice. The authority within this setting is diffusing out from the tutor, as he withdraws from direct participation in the dialogue but remains a symbolic participant.

Adopting Foucault's view of power as generative (see Chapter 3), for all that it indicates how power seeps into the micro-level of discourse and each utterance made on these boards, also suggests that the visibility and assessment of these dialogues is itself empowering for the students. Learning to read these landscapes is a desirable outcome of this or any other course of university study. The tutor does, indeed, want students to 'know their place' in this landscape: hence the design of the starter landscape and the task itself and the dialogue that he engages in, including the provision of formative feedback. Effective pedagogical design for informed learning involves this *placing* of the learner, giving them a *position* from which they can develop a *perspective* on the landscape, a starting point from which they can learn to navigate. That does not mean it is desirable for students to *stay* in this place, but that is how the design of activities, the signposting by tutors and peers of additional resources that may be useful in the landscape, turns the assessment specification from a *plan* (which 'extinguishes contextual potential') into a map, a tool for exploration, 'a generative means, a suggestive vehicle that "points" but does not overly determine' (Corner, 1999, 228). This is illustrated by the variety of 'Mackenzies' which come into being and the different practical settings (museums) in which students actively apply their knowledge.

If Foucault's view of power is accepted, then the power flowing through the discourses, available to be wielded to affect behaviour in this setting, cannot be fundamentally different for the tutor than for the students. Thus, what empowers the students in this setting is the same feature of the discourse as gives rise to the power inherent in grading and assessment – the *visibility* of the dialogue. Articulations of positions, and the ways these coalesce into the groups' different discursive maps, have been made explicit through the assessment process, but the marking rubric and feedback dialogue also give students the chance to hone their own and each other's practices and diffuse expertise throughout the group, learning how to optimise their information landscape on their own account, as the 16/Diamond and 15/Gold case studies indicated. Bringing in new sources is behaviour they are encouraged to adopt (that the TAs prompt them, and they respond, in the groups discussed is a clear sign of this). The discussion helps them configure these additions and place them with regard to a particular aspect of their joint enquiry.

In any case, learning to become a practitioner and developing effective informational skills (particularly around communication) will at times require students to understand how discourse is controlled and surveilled in such settings, not only by shadowy institutional authorities but by peers, as part of the self-regulation of language and expression that is characteristic of many social settings. An interviewee cited in Webster and Gunter is revealing with his/her last statement (in bold):

> I certainly didn't feel free to write anything … I definitely felt that I modified my behaviour **but only as far as what I would do in a professional environment** …
>
> (2018, 78)

Conclusion

In summary, the pedagogical design of this assessment clearly incorporates more than just the epistemic modality: in this case, information drawn from the discipline of educational technology. The groups are indeed drawing from this fund of knowledge, but the design of the activities also means that, to succeed, they must effectively articulate that disciplinary knowledge within task settings that also demand the use of social and corporeal modalities of information: and of not only the settings (Mackenzie and the museums) as they are interpreted and mapped in the present time, but of understandings of practice that are being drawn from past experiences and comparable landscapes. Mackenzie College and the museums are places, loci of collective memory, even if only for a brief time, and rooting their dialogue in shared places helps the groups establish the relevance and value of information, requires them to organise their landscape and effectively communicate their understandings. It is the interplay between these modalities of their information landscape that opens up their claims to authority to scrutiny, as they must not just make propositions rooted in the literature (the epistemic modality), but make them *about shared places* and *to each other* (the social and corporeal modalities).

The SPIDER data also illustrate how the learners were making use of all three 'avenues' of linkage between the doings and sayings of IL as a practice (Schatzki, 1996, 89); first, *understandings*, manifest in students expressing to each other what they believe should be done; second, *explicit rules*, manifest in what they are told to do in the assessment specification (though even here there is scope for groups to establish differing interpretations of these rules); and third, *teleoaffective structures*, manifest in students expressing desires regarding what they wanted to happen: not just that they wanted a good mark but noting the desirability of keeping on topic, posting regularly and so on.

In Chapter 5 it was demonstrated how the Ketso maps, as a material artefact, became a representation of the information landscape of the groups of workplace learners. Here, it can be shown how it is not the physical device that is Ketso but the existence of a communicative space, structured in certain ways, that allows this representation to come into being, and that this is a discursive, not graphical process. Following this, that these representations, these discursive maps, become the basis for group judgements. Compared to graphical maps, these maps are somewhat elusive; they are not 'immutable mobiles': at least, not without a considerable amount of further cognitive work (akin to, but in the end, greatly extending beyond what I have undertaken in this chapter). Propositions about the landscape of the groups are made within them and conclusions can be drawn about this landscape through 'reading' the maps via the research methodology used in SPIDER, but this was not a process done as easily as with a cartograph, nor even with a Ketso map. Yet, evidently, the map/dialogue is a *locus of collective memory*; it was acting as one while it was being created, and, as the record of the dialogue still exists, it remains one. The assessment and subsequent research processes have given the dialogue a permanence and helped reveal the dialogic moves that are made by the learners as they construct, map and navigate their information landscapes.

Chapter 7

Conclusion

Mapping the field of mapping

Growing up in Crowborough (see Chapter 4), the English Lake District felt far away. And in English terms, it is, lying in the opposite corner of the country from Sussex. Yet despite this geographical separation, and before I had ever visited there, the Lake District felt like a familiar place, it having been brought into my life by my parents' copy of the seven-volume *Pictorial Guide to the Lakeland Fells*. Even when young I appreciated that these books, written between 1952 and 1965 by Alfred Wainwright, are different from the norm. Rather than being conventionally typeset, the pages are photo-reproductions of a manuscript that, in its entirety – the text, illustrations, maps and the whole layout – Wainwright had hand drawn. This is impressive enough, even before one takes account of the scale and detail of this undertaking. For example, across more than 1,000 pages, all the text is fully justified to both margins without any use of hyphenation. To make the diagrams of mountain ascents most useful, Wainwright altered the perspective as the reader's eye moved up the representation, a technique that is innovative even today (Hutchby, 2012, 26–9). And in addition to his skills as a draughtsman, Wainwright's *Guide* is exhaustive in terms of its coverage of this area of natural beauty, erudite and possessing a dry wit. Little surprise that the books have become classics of their genre. Those who seek to climb all the fells, or mountains, described in the books are now said to be 'doing the Wainwrights'.

In both cartographic and discursive terms, Wainwright's *Guide* is a map of great depth and, thanks to revisions undertaken in the 2000s (by Chris Jesty) for a second edition, still with much relevance to the contemporary walker as a guide for practice. Its classification schema influences this practice, with the chapter titles defining some fells as 'Wainwrights' and others as mere supporting players, perhaps less worthy of time and effort as a result. A wide range of emotional reactions are evident in the book (Wainwright does not even try to be an objective chronicler of his pathways and perspectives) and can be provoked simply by reading its pages, let alone following its guidance and immersing oneself in the landscapes it articulates.

Remarkably, Wainwright created the *Guide* while in full-time employment as treasurer for Kendal council. In the evenings he would write up data gathered from fieldwork trips made each weekend. And yet for all the exemplary communicative techniques, the skill and artistry, that are brought to bear in this map, consider this: in terms of time spent on writing and fieldwork, the work was completed over 13 years of more-or-less the same amount of time that one would spend on a full-time job. I have so far been in my current job a year longer and even in the age of increasing workplace mobility, this is not exceptional. What if I, or any other professional, aspired to document, organise and communicate those experiences, just for one's own satisfaction, as was originally the case for Wainwright (and for A. A. Milne, with the stories he first told his son about his toy bear, Pooh)? In his own words (see the 'Personal Notes in Conclusion' of volume 1 of the *Guide*), Wainwright did not initially create the *Guide* with an eye on publication. (All profits that he eventually made from the book were donated to an animal rescue centre in Kendal.) Could others not aspire, at least in principle, to create maps of different form, but still with value in helping others navigate the landscapes with which one is intimately familiar, through these years of experience?

Of course, it is unrealistic to imagine that maps as detailed and inspirational as Wainwright's could be created within most professional settings, particularly by anyone already feeling themselves stretched by more immediate workplace tasks. But this is not the point being made here. What I am drawing attention to is that the *fund of knowledge* on which Wainwright drew was extensive and largely self-generated (though he pays frequent homage to the prior efforts of the Ordnance Survey), but no more so than that which the average professional accumulates over an equivalent period of time. It was his skill at *organising, representing and communicating* the information he gathered that sets Wainwright's map apart, and his possession of the will to document his practice (the walks) in the first place.

In the digital era, information accumulates in ever-greater quantities. Documenting our experiences within the world is becoming easier. On top of what we consciously create and post on blogs, social media or YouTube, in an era of 'big data', records about our lives accumulate without our conscious intervention. In professional settings, or in civic life, or with regard to keeping oneself healthy, there is, at least in principle, more information available to each of us than there has ever been. Our landscapes, their geographical and informational elements, are now complex and multimodal. As has been noted at several points in this book, information literacy cannot only be defined as skills at finding and discerning good quality information; it must also incorporate attention to how that information is subsequently organised and used, and further insights communicated in ways that keep the landscapes healthy and sustainable.

Thompson (2008) highlights the dangers of an excess of information and a concomitant loss of what he perceives as quality control. But quality is not just a matter of content. Even 'fake news', or misinformation, can be of value if it is recognised as such and if this leads to a challenge to the validity of the claims based on it. 'Quality' is therefore also a factor of how the information is *positioned*, what *dialogue* takes place around it. IL involves judging the relevance of found information, certainly; but information literate practice also involves organising this information and scrutinising it, accepting expertise where that is valid and relevant, but also being prepared to review claims made, and the maps and practice architectures, which are governing our practice. If we are to make *informed* judgements (Bruce, 2008), what informs them? Are the bases of these judgements still appropriate and relevant? To answer such questions, we must not only raise cognitive schema up for scrutiny but *learn how* to do so. Mapping provides one such means.

This book is called *Mapping Information Landscapes*, not 'Maps of information landscapes'. I have displayed and discussed only a few graphical maps, although Chapters 4 and 6 offered more detailed mental and discursive maps. But I do not believe much would have been added to the argument had I done so. Maps are always unique to a context. They have much use as tools that can discern things about that context for the benefit of researchers: as several of the case studies have shown. There is, in consequence, an archaeological value to the maps produced: they can give one a sense of what an information landscape consisted of at a particular chronotope and how actors in that social setting perceived it in that place and time. But one will never be able to discern everything of value in a landscape simply by looking at a map of it. One must visit the landscape, immerse oneself in it. As my discussion in these pages was not about the *contexts* – about issues arising when running and relocating Norwegian academic libraries, say – I chose not to focus overly on the content of the maps.

My principal concern has instead been with mapping as an *educational practice*, something that helps us learn how to navigate our information landscapes and establish the basis for judgements about the relevance of found information, and thus of IL. Mapping is a way of teaching IL that is based on the theory of the information landscape and what is understood about information practices in the landscapes of HE, work, community and civic life. Mapping has been hinted at by authors such as Lloyd, Hepworth and Walton, and Badke; researchers such as Sonnenwald et al., Hultgren, Tippett et al. have explored its richness as a method offering insight into information horizons. Wenger et al. (2009) also offer detail to the practitioner. But these prior studies are underdeveloped when it comes to *education*. And where work like that of Herring, or Hepworth and Walton, does use mapping with an explicit focus on learning, detail is unfortunately lacking on how the maps were talked into being, how the mapping practices took shape in the setting. These various studies thereby stand as signposts, but there is no further, detailed guide to points beyond them. What is going on dialogically as one learns to be an effective steward of an information landscape and how can an educator, of whatever type, understand these dialogues and intervene in them to help learners develop relevant and transferable navigational, organisational and communicative skills?

I have attempted to provide this detail, relating these prior studies and some of my own research and experience to relevant theories of information, communication and practice, and through doing so, map the field of mapping. I have tried to offer an experience of variation, viewing the practice of mapping from a variety of perspectives, and triangulating them, with a goal of establishing what mapping practice might offer educators who, within a formal, workplace or informal learning setting, strive to help develop learners' IL – and their own. In this pedagogical landscape there have been many regions, including the application of different techniques (for example, Ketso, psychogeographical wandering, online discussions); the theory of mapping; the historical background; and the unavoidable and complex issue of power.

Some of these regions, particularly the last, I have only begun to explore. Certainly, there remain gaps. For example, I have said very little about how the students of DET or the librarians of BIE might go on to use their discursive or graphical mapping skills in later life and/or transfer them to other settings. This is valuable follow-up research, but as yet remains just a plan. But with these lacunae admitted, I nevertheless hope that this book does serve as, at least, a starting point for further exploration and that it inspires educational interventions, while not dictating them.

What has been learned

Throughout the book, the case studies have illustrated different aspects of maps and mapping. The historical review in Chapters 2 and 3 established that the making of a map requires the mapmaker to be positioned at focal points of information flows, within nexuses of practice. Maps emerge from social, intersubjective learning processes, and are ways of organising and communicating understandings of landscapes that can, as with the Hereford Mappa Mundi, be of immense depth and durability: they can also be transient, sketched on a scrap of paper, used once only. But all maps make propositions that can be explored in the world. They are utterances, reifications of singular or multiple perspectives that can be the basis for future judgements. Their representational form serves to carry the information on the map into different contexts: not all maps are 'immutable' mobiles by any means, but even when their representations are open to multiple interpretations, the map remains a medium with significant discursive force. Mapping is explicitly oriented to ensuring people 'know their place', with all the implications of that term, for good and bad.

The psychogeographical investigations in Chapter 4 illustrated the durability of mental maps, but also their adaptability *when new information was perceived as relevant*. Mental maps are not necessarily precise in every detail but are built around a combination of knowledge and/or availability of key locations or points in the landscape, and an understanding of the broader configurations of districts and regions, and the pathways that connect key points. Points of orientation exist at all scales, down to the micro-level, such as the ongoing confirmations provided by street signage. In a familiar landscape, next-to-hand behaviour also comes into play as we navigate by habit and routine as much as by on-the-spot observations and deductions. Judgements are made about contexts as they existed in the past, not only the present; landscapes are not temporally 'flat', with no history, but are palimpsests, layers upon layers, earlier judgements remaining visible and still influencing the present chronotope. Affective reactions also filter information into and out of perception and thus are integral to our making judgements about relevance.

Chapter 4 also, in passing, suggested the value of an autodidactic approach; self-reflection can be a way of learning about the maps one uses habitually. 'Having a good sense of direction' may well have come into play in my navigation of Manchester, Crowborough and Seaford, but that was also an outcome of the fact that, for the purposes of writing this book, I was working at raising it into awareness. Navigational competency, if it can be called that, is not a spiritual capacity, but a factor of how well certain equipment is used in the landscape and how the incoming information is organised and integrated with the existing mental map. Techniques like finding a vantage point and there taking a survey, bringing in knowledge of comparable landscapes, observing the pathways of others and updating maps as new information was encountered, were all aspects of good information practice when it came to these psychogeographical assignments.

Chapter 5 showed how concept mapping practices open up a discursive space in which equipment (Ketso in the case of BIE and Tippett's various projects, but other tools, including pencil and paper, and Le Louvier and Innocenti's game board approach (cf. Corner, 1999, 243) are used across the case studies) and, more significantly, *facilitation* provide ways of articulating knowledge and understandings that otherwise might remain tacit. At group and individual levels, the produced maps can be the basis of ongoing judgements about information. Some of the case studies take only snapshots of a particular place and time, but in others, including BIE, there is a specific focus on how the maps represent change over time and reveal other temporal phenomena, like obduracy. The case studies show how groups with different views on practice can use the mapping process to develop a shared perspective. Maps can reflect improvements in information literacy and be a means to achieve these improvements: organisational tactics like focusing, prioritising, scrutinising and fixing on terminology are evident in some or all of the cases discussed in this chapter.

Chapter 6 revealed the discursive mapping processes that come into play as learners steward the information landscapes they need to meet their shared goals. Through dialogue, they develop representations and cognitive schema that allow them to make group judgements of relevance and reach agreement on what resources are relevant and how they should be organised and used. Stewarding is evident in how technical, social and discursive features of the discussion board environment – for example, the use of threading, allocating roles, posting summaries – are used to orient participants and are examples of peer modelling. Stewarding capacity spreads through the groups as the facilitator's role reduces.

Chapter 6 also revealed the power relations implicit in all mappings: most obviously these are instantiated in the assessed nature of the process, though note also the stratification within the groups on the basis of prior experience and facility with the communicative medium. Yet there is evidence that this power, at least at times, is drawn on and used to generate knowledge in (and by) learners and empower them, rather than to impose practice. The modelling of good practice and the development of the learners' ability to scrutinise and review the maps and practices in this setting are integrated into the assessment. The shared, teleoaffective aspects of practice (goals, in this case) of the participants in the dialogue gives the group cohesion. The format of the assessment and its explicit, process-oriented schema for grading obliges the learners (and tutor) to *articulate* the navigational practices in use here and thus gives them permanence and value as learning objects.

On the whole, these various cases support notions that IL is inherently dialogic (Whitworth, 2014, 1). Maps and mapping are social and intersubjective and thus a means for exploring information landscapes inherently suited to work with small groups and communities (cf. Harris, 2008). Objective maps – 'immutable mobiles' – can be one outcome of mapping, but there are many examples of where dialogic representations of information landscapes are created without this necessarily being manifested in a graphical map, or even a permanent text. Yet these discursive maps have a more elusive character. As an outcome of dialogue, they may quickly sink back below the conscious level of group awareness. There are no data nets, no conventions of representation to preserve them. Discursive maps remain as guides for practice, but tacitly; to articulate them to those unfamiliar with the landscape becomes a challenging task. But this is exactly what Lloyd means by noting how immersion in an information landscape means learning to navigate it *from within*, engaging in dialogue with 'insiders'; just as Wenger's insurance claims processors learned most of their skills on the office floor rather than in the training room. Embedding the principles of informed learning into the design of learning environments, as with the DET course, explicitly recognises this.

As understanding these processes, and generally how we learn to navigate a landscape individually and collectively, is one key to understanding how IL becomes manifested in real-world settings, then we cannot continue to design for and theorise about IL as if it did not exist prior to Zurkowski (1974). The ways we are taught to navigate information have been, like other core skills such as language use, instilled in us through a variety of means and media, in formal education but also informally, as we mimic and try to learn from our parents, colleagues, teachers, role models and peers. These practices, and the equipment developed to help us along the way, have been developing for millennia. And while the current era of digitisation is bringing about obvious changes in terms of mobility and ubiquity of access points to information, geographical and information landscapes remain indivisibly intertwined. We use interchangeable metaphors, similar navigational techniques. The skills, equipment and information (in its social, epistemic and corporeal modalities) that are useful in one, have cognates in the other (landmarks, signposts, maps, memories, routines). Our location in space and time and our material engagement with the equipment available in that chronotope and its practice architectures, remains an integral part of how we make judgements about information in practice. Mapping shows how central *place* remains to our ability to learn and how these places become loci of collective memory, the basis against which judgements are made. Within these places, IL then becomes *performed* and has material, tangible effects on the world.

The layouts and configurations of settings matter greatly, even when a site has the appearance of 'virtuality'. Even if the landscape being mapped is principally informational, this does not make it *immaterial*. The practice of configuring and organising space cannot be understood – cannot be *made intelligible* to others – without some shared representation of how the landscape is being structured. Propositions made on the map can be explored because there is a sense of permanence to the map, and reliability in that people may share interpretations when they interpret the same map against the same *elements* of a collective matrix of interpretation. There needs to be at least this level of recognisable shared interpretations otherwise the whole notion of a 'map' as a communicative (instead of just cognitive) device evaporates into air. The empirical chapters have demonstrated, however, that even discursive maps, and inner mental maps, have durability, and a variety of dialogic and material devices can be used to articulate these maps, give them permanence, raise them into visibility and thus make them useful in all the stages of an information system (selection, organisation, communication). For these purposes, mapping can be *designed into* a social site, in a variety of ways.

A good map also functions at an affective level. The eruptions of emotion that occurred at points in the empirical studies were not just methodological noise, but evidence that the maps were working, having an impact. Positive affect is an essential aspect of developing a sense of place and of care for that place. Chapter 4 showed this, not just through my own wanderings but the reference to work like Willard's and Milne's. The studies in Chapters 5 and 6 also suggested how the distribution of authority is important for this sense of place. Institutions, as Harvey understood, sustain themselves through an extensive architecture incorporating many actual and symbolic places. Maps of such landscapes reflect stratification, power relations and the imposition of cognitive schema on subordinates. But in more inclusive social settings the distribution of authority and power is part of what gives rise to a sense of place and community: something surely evident from environmentalist literature from *Walden* (Thoreau, 2006) on, as well as studies like *theirwork* and Tippett's original Ketso work. Care for an environment, the idea that landscapes should be managed in sustainable ways: these values can apply, indeed must apply, to information landscapes too.

Journey's end

In the theoretical sections of this book, the suggestion was made that IL is an *epistemology*; a way of knowing and, specifically, a way of making effective judgements about, and with, information and the technologies we use to find, select, organise and communicate information. Maps help with each of these phases. This process – find, select, organise, communicate – is not linear, but holistic, with each part supported by the others, and for each, mapping can help form utterances that are part of this broad dialogue. But each map (the product of the process) is then a *reification* of that utterance. This gives it value because its relative permanence makes it something that can be used to make an *informed* judgement. Yet as soon as anything is reified in this way, the continuing applicability of that artefact – the map – to the present situation requires scrutiny (Habermas, 1993).

Developing information literacy thereby also requires developing the ability to recognise and agree on when such scrutiny should take place: on when the trade-offs of depending on prior cognitive schema have become too large, when they make judgements in the present chronotope less reliable and/or sustainable. IL means being then able to wield the necessary armamentarium of technologies and practices, align it with goals (teleoaffectivity) and thereby apply appropriate cognitive schema to practice. This is what makes IL innately political. Authorities, and the cognitive schema on which they base their authority, are not easy to challenge. Of course, the notion of 'authority' is diverse (see Wrong, 1995; Whitworth, 2019) and many claims to authority quite legitimate and justified. But as demonstrated by Wilson (1983), authority is nevertheless an inescapable aspect of how we make judgements about information. Thus, in the landscape, how we are positioned with respect to the *places* in which this authority is invested, the practice architectures which shape activity (albeit not deterministically), will shape the definition of information literacy in that context, perception of available pathways, criteria for information selection and so on. The emphasis on the epistemic modality in how work in HE is typically assessed is a clear example. But Lloyd's assertion that through learning to explore a landscape, one can empower oneself within it, becoming a practitioner who can articulate their understandings of practice in effective ways, suggests strongly that those who learn to navigate the landscape most effectively will acquire authority within it in legitimate and justified ways.

Writing shortly after Zurkowski first introduced the term 'information literacy', Hamelink (1976) offered a more radical perspective on IL, defining it as the *collective* capacities needed for subordinate populations to create and maintain their own 'information banks', located both in particular geographical locations in the community (like the 'information centres' mapped by participants in the studies of Sonnenwald et al., Hultgren and others), but also located in those communities' shared sense of identity and place. Whatever the sociophysical basis for a community – whether it is shared geography, practice, learning needs, suffering from the same disease – if that community is, as Hamelink exhorted, to undertake this task as a form of political resistance to the hegemonic pushing of information into their landscape by the mass media, then groups are going to have to learn the necessary skills and do so in ways that keep the skills relevant to the community. This book has shown how keeping information landscapes sustainable and navigable requires at least some attention to how equipment is used to map and organise the landscape. How we collectively think about and solve problems in the present time inscribes maps and positions them as resources in whatever landscapes we will draw on in the future.

I will leave the final words in this book to David Harvey, whose work has been so influential on this one:

> Our future places are for us to make. But we cannot make them without inscribing our struggles in space, place and environment in multiple ways. The process is ongoing and every single one of us has agency with respect to it.
>
> (Harvey, 1996, 326)

Appendices

Appendix 1: 'Rutters' for the walks in Chapter 4

Walk 1, Manchester

I walk this regularly in both directions. I describe it here as done from my office to the station; from station to office I simply reverse the route.

Ellen Wilkinson Building — Oxford Road — University Place — National Graphene Institute — Booth Street East — Upper Brook Street — Princess Street — Canal Street — Abingdon Street [see note] — Portland Street — Nicholas Street — Booth Street — Pall Mall — King Street — Cheapside — Chapel Walks — Cross Street — Exchange Square — National Football Museum — Victoria Station.

Abingdon Street has been closed since summer 2018 due to building works and remains so at the time of writing. During this time I have omitted Canal and Abingdon Streets from my route and turned straight from Princess Street into Portland Street, but the day Abingdon Street is eventually reopened I will go straight back to using the route as defined.

Walk 2, Crowborough

Day one: Railway station — Crowborough Hill — path behind the social club — Forest Rise — Palesgate Lane [**Limekiln Football Ground**] — through the woods, down to the Ghyll — Forest Rise — Burdett Road — Crowborough Hill — Church Road — Beacon Road — Melfort Road — Warren Road — Fielden Road [**B&B**].

Day two: Fielden Road — Beacon Road — Sheep Plain — footpath — Manor Way — Southridge Road — Whitehill Road — Gladstone Road — Queens Road — Blackness Road — Luxford Road — Old Lane [**my house**]— Poundfield Road — footpath [**Beacon school: Fermor school**] — Crowborough Hill — New Road — Beacon Road — Mill Lane — Croft Road — High Street [**lunch at Crowborough**

Cross pub] — St Johns Road — Goldsmiths Avenue — Glenmore Road East — Rannoch Road — Warren Road — Fielden Road.

Walk Three, Seaford

Seaford station — Station Approach — Dane Road — Esplanade — past the Martello Tower and beach huts — up onto the cliffs — along cliff edge — past end of golf course [**Viewpoint**] — retrace steps a couple of hundred yards — path to South Hill Barn — (unnamed?) road down to houses — Chyngton Way — Arundel Road — Sutton Avenue — Bramber Road — Bramber Lane — East Street — High Street [**The Old Boot**] — Church Street — Dane Road and back to station.

Appendix 2: Concept map of this book's key ideas

I sketched this concept map as a way of breaking out of a bout of 'writer's block' which held up progress on the book during May 2019. I present it here as it was drawn, including notes, though some illegible scribbles around the edges have been cropped. The point is both to offer another example of a concept map and to suggest to readers some connections between key ideas in the book. However, note that this map shows my cognitive structure as it stood when the map was drawn: three more months passed before the book was finished and so the final manuscript may not be entirely represented on this map, though I think the correspondence is still mostly sound. For this reason, I present it in an appendix rather than the main text.

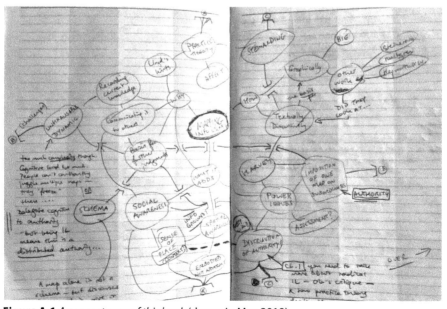

Figure A.1 *A concept map of this book* (drawn in May 2019)

Appendix 3: Marking rubric for the discussion board tasks

This rubric, reproduced here in full, is available to the students from the start of the course. It is calibrated using the convention in UK universities for converting performance into (essentially arbitrary) percentage grades: at postgraduate level, 50% is a pass mark, and anything above 80% is of exceptional distinction. This differs from conventions adopted in some other HE contexts.

Individual marks (out of 10):

0 marks: No contribution.

1–2 marks: Irrelevant or cursory contribution.

3 marks: You have made a contribution that tries to address the issues under discussion, but it is very limited, probably because you have only posted once and/or you have not tried to back up your ideas with reference to any of the literature or teaching on the course.

4 marks: There is some attempt to engage in a discussion but without any real justification for your point of view.

5 marks: Passable contribution, but still rather limited – largely, you will be following the ideas of others, rather than showing signs that you have come up with new ideas of your own throughout the discussion.

6 marks: Fair contribution. You will have engaged with discussion, shown signs of developing new perspectives, and are prepared to criticise the work of others if necessary. There may still be some weaknesses in how you present arguments however: e.g. posting too much, wandering off the topic, not always rooting your ideas in the literature, etc.

7 marks: Good contribution. Your posts are efficient, effective and justified. You have clearly shown signs of a developing perspective as the discussion has gone on.

8 marks: Substantial contribution. As for #7, but you have also shown signs of taking on a leading role in the discussion and acting in at least one of the roles of moderator, summariser, or source searcher, on behalf of your group.

9–10 marks: Excellent contribution. You have led a discussion from start to finish and introduced new ideas to the group that are fully justified and relevant. Marks of 10/10 are awarded very rarely, so please do not be disappointed if you do not get 10 – though they have been known.

Group marks (out of 5, shared between all group members who participated):
[NB. Group marks may be withheld from members who did not make adequate individual contributions. This has helped reduce complaints about 'free riders'.]

5 marks means you introduced creative solutions or perspectives that I had not seen before in the playing of the game. Also, that all group members were included; you developed decision-making processes, channels of communication and divisions of labour that brought in every group member, despite any limitations on participation they may have had.

4 means full participation as a group, still very good work but more in line with what is typically seen in terms of technique and approach.

3 might mean that there was some exclusion of group members, or that your decision, while collaboratively reached, was not particularly explored or justified.

2 would mean you really struggled to work together as a group, and to be honest I would not expect to give a mark of 1 here unless a group was really dysfunctional.

Appendix 4: Lists of resources created by three groups (16/Diamond, 15/Gold, 16/Gold) in activity 3

These lists show the threads that each group created and any informational resources that were introduced into each, with the initials indicating the identity of the student who first introduced them. At the end, total numbers of resources per student are calculated.

15/Gold

[First thread – 'To start']

1st person narrative (Alcatraz)	R
Facebook videos	R
1st person narrative (artillery museum)	L
URL, museum website	L
Word document (musings on Alcatraz)	R
3 x URLs, museum website	L
Text from the assessment specification	S
YouTube video	L
URL (resource on VR)	L
URL, museum website	R
Info from artillery museum website	A

[Thread: NFM]

1st person narrative (NFM) [with 2 images]	S
1st person narrative (additional museum)	Y
YouTube video	R
1st person narrative (additional museum)	L
1st person narrative (additional museum)	L

Images from NFM	A
1st person narrative (NFM)	Y
3 x YouTube videos	A
2 x video (.mov) files	A
Text from the assessment specification	R
Citation	L
Text from the assessment specification	R

[Artillery Museum]

Additions to 1st person narrative, Ar.Mus.	L
Citation to literature	A
[note that all citations follow a TA prompt]	
Text from the assessment specification	R
Citation to literature	L
1st person narrative (additional museum)	R
Citation	S
Citation	R
URL (other tourist attraction website)	A
Twitter account – recommended to follow	R
Image (additional museum)	R

[New thread – San Diego Art Institute]

1st person narrative (SDAI), 1 image	R
Citation to literature	S
Several citations	A
Citations	S
Citation	Y
Citation	R

R = 14, L = 10, S = 5, Y = 3, A = 7
TOTAL: 39

16/Diamond

[Starting thread – Selecting the two museums]

Google Form (poll)	A

[Hull's Maritime Museum]

1st person narrative (HMM), several images + link to Flickr site, URL	A
Citation from literature	A

Citation   H
PDF of online article   X

[Roles?]
Google Doc (summary)   A

[Natural History Museum Shanghai]
1st person narrative (NHMS), URL, link to
   Flickr site   G
Quote from DL tutorial   G
Screen shots from NHMS website   X
URL (360° photograph technology)   H
Citation, with URL link to Google Book   S
YouTube video   A

[National Football Museum]
1st person narrative (NFM), URL, several images   H
1st person narrative, URL, screenshot
   of comments from TripAdvisor   X
1st person narrative   Y
1st person narrative   S
Citations   H
20+ images of NFM   X
Citation from literature   S
1st person narrative, additional museum   H
1st person narrative, add. museum + URL   X
Image   J
Embedded Video   H

[The last discussion, suggested structure]
None

[The suggested designs for the NFM]
Citation   S
URL (site about QR codes)   X
Citations   A
URL (site about Indoor Positioning System)   A
URL (site about QR codes)   Y
Embedded video   H
Citation (with URL)   A
1st person narrative (additional museum)   A

Citation	G
Citation	X
Citation	J
Citation	Y
URL (info on 3D film technology)	H
Citations	A
Citation from Wikipedia	J
Google Doc (summary)	A

[The suggested designs for Hull's Maritime Museum]

URL (Wikipedia)	A
URLs (newspaper articles + govt report)	G
Citation	A
URL to interactive mapping tool	A
Citations (link to PDFs)	S
URL (re: QR codes) + citation (with PDF)	X
URL (content management platform)	A
Citation	S
Citations to academic papers & Wikipedia	H
URL (3D models)	G
URL (blog post)	J
Citation	A
URL (sound manipulation technology)	H
Images from revisit to museum + URLs	A
URL (example of artwork style)	A
Citations	S
Google Doc (summary)	A
URL (co-operative games)	J
URL (blog post)	A

A = 19, J = 5, S = 7, H = 10, G = 5, X = 8, Y = 3
TOTAL: 57

16/Gold

[Starting thread: The 2nd museum]

URL to museum website + citation	M
Field notes (as attachment) + article as PDF	A
Citation	A
URLs (additional museum websites)	A

[National Football Museum (Museum 1]

1st person narrative + citations	K
1st person narrative + images	C
Field notes (as attachment)	A
1st person narrative	B
Citation	K
1st person narrative	D

[Virtual reality and online applications]

Citation with URL + URLs of add. mus.	A
Citations	K
Citations	D
Power Point slides (prototype design)	D
URL (interactive movie)	B
Citations	D
Citation	C
[actually a long copy-and-pasted block]	

[Appropriate technology]

Citations	K

[Putting our thoughts together, time is running out!]

Citation to Wikipedia	K
Image	D
Images + citations	A
Images	C
Citations	M
URL (virtual museum)	M

M = 3, A = 6, K = 5, C = 3, B = 2, D = 5
TOTAL: 24

Bibliography and references

ACRL (Association of College and Research Libraries) (2000) *Information literacy competency standards for higher education*, ACRL.

ACRL (2015) *Framework for information literacy for higher education*, ACRL.

Alabbasi, D. and Stelma, J. (2018) Using Ketso in qualitative research with female Saudi teachers. In *Forum Qualitative Sozialforschung/Forum: Qualitative Social Research* (Vol. 19, No. 2, p. 24), DEU.

Alkemeyer, T. and Buschmann, N. (2016) Learning in and across practices: enablement as subjectivation. In Hui, A., Schatzki, T. and Shove, E. (eds), *The nexus of practices: connections, constellations, practitioners*, Routledge, 20–35.

Andretta, S. (2005) *Information literacy: a practitioner's guide*, Chandos.

Argyris, C. (1976) Single-loop and double-loop models in research on decision making, *Administrative Science Quarterly*, 363–75.

Arlander, A. (2012) Performing landscape as autotopographical exercise, *Contemporary Theatre Review*, **22** (2), 251–8.

Ausubel, D. P. (1960) The use of advance organizers in the learning and retention of meaningful verbal material, *Journal of Educational Psychology*, **51** (5), 267.

Badke, W. B. (2012) *Teaching research processes: the faculty role in the development of skilled student researchers*, Chandos.

Bakhtin, M. (1981) *The dialogic imagination: four essays by M. M. Bakhtin*. Ed. M. Holquist, University of Texas Press.

Bakhtin, M. (1984) *Problems of Dostoevsky's poetics*. Tr. C. Emerson, University of Minnesota Press.

Bakhtin, M. (1986) *Speech genres and other late essays*. Eds C. Emerson and M. Holquist, University of Texas Press.

Barnes, B. (2001) Practice as collective action. In Schatzki, T., Knorr Cetina, K. and von Savigny, E. (eds), *The practice turn in contemporary theory*, Routledge, 25–36.

Barry, D. (2019) https://www.telegraph.co.uk/science/2019/05/29/google-maps-increases-risk-developingalzheimers-expert-warns/

Bartlett, F. C. (1932) *Remembering: a study in experimental and social psychology*, Cambridge University Press.

Bassett, K. (2004) Walking as an aesthetic practice and a critical tool: some psychogeographic experiments, *Journal of Geography in Higher Education*, **28** (3), 397–410.

Baym, N. K. (2000) *Tune in, log on: soaps, fandom, and online community*, Sage.

Belk, R. W. and Groves, R. (1999) Marketing and the multiple meanings of Australian Aboriginal art, *Journal of Macromarketing*, **19** (1), 20–33.

Benson, A. D. and Whitworth, A. (eds) (2014) *Research on course management systems in higher education*, IAP.

Binder, T. (1996) Participation and reification in design of artifacts: an interview with Etienne Wenger, *AI and Society*, **10** (1), 101–6.

Blaug, R. (1999) *Democracy real and ideal: discourse ethics and radical politics*, SUNY Press.

Blaug, R. (2007) Cognition in a hierarchy, *Contemporary Political Theory*, **6** (1), 24–44.

Bonnett, A. (2015) *Off the map*, Aurum Press.

Bookchin, M. (1986) A note on affinity groups. In *Post-scarcity Anarchism*, 2nd ed., Black Rose, 243–4.

Breivik, P. S. (1986) Library based learning in an information society, *New Directions for Higher Education*, **56**, 47–55.

Breivik, P. S. (1991) Information literacy, *Bulletin of the Medical Library Association*, **79** (2), 226.

Brody, H., Rip, M. R., Vinten-Johansen, P., Paneth, N. and Rachman, S. (2000) Map-making and myth-making in Broad Street: the London cholera epidemic, 1854, *The Lancet*, **356** (9223), 64–8.

Brookfield, S. D. (2005) *The power of critical theory for adult learning and teaching*, Open University Press.

Bruce, C. S. (1997) *The seven faces of information literacy*, Auslib.

Bruce, C. S. (2008) *Informed earning*, ACRL.

Bruce, C. S., Edwards, S. L. and Lupton, M. (2006) Six frames for information literacy education, *Italics*, **5** (1).

Bruce, C. S., Demasson, A., Hughes, H., Lupton, M., Maybee, C., Mirijamdotter, A., Sayyad Abdi, E. and Somerville, M. M. (2017) Information literacy and informed learning: conceptual innovations for IL research and practice futures, *Journal of Information Literacy*, **11** (1), 4–22.

Bush, V. (1945) As we may think, *Atlantic Monthly*, July 1945.

Buzan, T. (2006) *Mind mapping*, Pearson Education.

Carr, W. and Kemmis, S. (1986) *Becoming critical: knowing through action research*, Deakin University Press.

Cherry, M. (2016) A picture is worth a thousand words: teaching media literacy. In McNicol, S. (ed.), *Critical literacy for information professionals*, Facet Publishing, 93–104.

Cheshire, J. and Uberti, O. (2014) *London: the information capital*, Penguin.

Coleman, E. (2005) *Aboriginal Art: identity and appropriation*, Taylor & Francis.

Corner, J. (1999) The agency of mapping: speculation, critique and invention. In Cosgrove, D. (ed.), *Mappings*, Reaktion, 213–52.

Cosgrove, D. (ed.) (1999) *Mappings*, Reaktion.

Cosgrove, D. (2005) Maps, mapping, modernity: art and cartography in the twentieth century, *Imago Mundi*, **57**, 35–54.

Cosgrove, D. (2008) Cultural cartography: maps and mapping in cultural geography, *Annales de Geographie*, **117**, 159–78.

Craine, J. and Aitken, S. C. (2009) The emotional life of maps and other visual geographies. In Dodge, M., Kitchin, R. and Perkins, C. (eds), *Rethinking maps: new frontiers in cartographic theory*, Routledge, 149–66.

Crampton, J. W. (2009) Cartography: performative, participatory, political, *Progress in Human Geography*, **33** (6), 840–8.

Crampton, J. W. and Krygier, J. (2006) An introduction to critical cartography, *ACME: An International e-Journal for Critical Geographies*, **4** (1), 11–33.

Crang, M. and Thrift, N. J. (eds) (2000) *Thinking space*, Psychology Press.

Critten, J. (2016) Death of the author(ity): repositioning students as constructors of meaning in information literacy instruction. In McNicol, S. (ed.), *Critical Literacy for Information Professionals*, Facet Publishing, 19–29.

Crone, G. R. (1965) New light on the Hereford map, *Geographical Journal*, **131**, 447–62.

Crowley, J. (2016) New media and critical literacy in secondary schools. In McNicol, S. (ed.), *Critical literacy for information professionals*, Facet Publishing, 115–22.

Csordas, T. (1994) *Embodiment and experience: the existential ground of culture and self*, Cambridge University Press.

Curry, M. R. (2000) Wittgenstein and the fabric of everyday life. In Crang, M. and Thrift, N. (eds), *Thinking space*, Psychology Press, 89–113.

Dahl, R. A. (1961) *Who governs?: democracy and power in an American city*, Yale University.

Debord, G. (1958) Theory of the Derive, *Internationale Situationniste*, 2. Available at: www.bopsecrets.org/SI/index.htm.

Denholm-Young, N. (1957) The *mappa mundi* of Richard of Haldingham at Hereford, *Speculum*, **32**, 307–14.

De Saulles, M. (2007) Information literacy amongst UK SMEs: an information policy gap, *Aslib Proceedings*, **59**, 68–79.

Dodge, M., Perkins, C. and Kitchin, R. (2009) Mapping modes, methods and moments: a manifesto for map studies. In Dodge, M., Kitchin, R. and Perkins, C. (eds), *Rethinking maps: new frontiers in cartographic theory*, Routledge, 220–43.

Dowling, K. (1996) *Power*, Open University Press.

Downey, A. (2016) *Critical information literacy: foundations, inspiration, and ideas*, Library Juice Press.

Edwards, S. and Poston-Anderson, B. (1996) Information, future time perspectives, and young adolescent girls: concerns about education and jobs, *Library & Information Science Research*, **18** (3), 207–23.

Eisenberg, M. B., Lowe, C. A. and Spitzer, K. L. (2004) *Information literacy: essential skills for the information age*, Greenwood.

Elmborg, J. (2006) Critical information literacy: implications for instructional practice, *Journal of Academic Librarianship,* **32** (2), 192–9.

Fisher, K. E. and Naumer, C. M. (2006) Information grounds: theoretical basis and empirical findings on information flow in social settings. In *New directions in human information behavior*, Springer, 93–111.

Flint, V. (1998) The Hereford map: its author(s), two scenes and a border, *Transactions of the Royal Historical Society*, 6th series (8), 19–44.

Fonteyn, M. E., Kuipers, B. and Grobe, S. J. (1993) A description of think aloud method and protocol analysis, *Qualitative Health Research*, **3** (4), 430–41.

Forster, M. (2017) *Information literacy in the workplace*, Facet Publishing.

Foucault, M. (1966) *Les Mots et les choses*, Editions Gallimard.

Foucault, M. (1972) *Archeology of knowledge*, Tavistock.

Foucault, M. (1973) *The birth of the clinic*. Tr. Sheridan Smith, A. M., Tavistock.

Foucault, M. (1977) *Discipline and punish*. Tr. Sheridan Smith, A. M., Vintage.

Foucault, M. (1980) *Power/knowledge: selected interviews and other writings, 1972–1977*, Vintage.

Fraser, N. (1992) Rethinking the public sphere: a contribution to the critique of actually existing democracy. In Calhoun, C. (ed.), *Habermas and the public sphere*, MIT Press, 109–42.

Freire, P. (1970) *Pedagogy of the oppressed*, Penguin.

Furlong, C. and Tippett, J. (2013) Returning knowledge to the community: an innovative approach to sharing knowledge about drinking water practices in a peri-urban community, *Journal of Water, Sanitation and Hygiene for Development*, **3** (4), 629–37.

Gardner, D. P., Larsen, Y. W., Baker, W., Campbell, A. and Crosby, E. A. (1983) *A nation at risk: the imperative for educational reform*, United States Department of Education.

Garrison, D. R., Anderson, T. and Garrison, R. (2003) *E-learning in the 21st century: a framework for research and practice*, Routledge-Falmer.

Gasteen, G. and O'Sullivan, C. (2000) Working towards an information literate law firm. In Bruce, C. S., Candy, P. C. and Klaus, H. (eds), *Information literacy around the world: advances in programs and research*, 109–20, Centre for Information Studies, Charles Sturt University.

Gastil, J. (1993) *Democracy in small groups: participation, decision making and communication*, New Society.

Gibson, A. N. and Kaplan, S. (2017) Place, community and information behavior: spatially oriented information seeking zones and information source preferences, *Library and Information Science Research, 39* (2), 131–9.

Gilroy-Ware, M. (2017) *Filling the void: emotion, capitalism and social media*, Duncan Baird Publishers.

Goggins, S. and Erdelez, S. (2010) Collaborative information behavior in completely online groups. In *Collaborative information behavior: user engagement and communication sharing*, IGI Global, 109–26.

Goldhaber, M. H. (1997) The attention economy and the net, *First Monday, 2* (4).

Goldstein, S. and Whitworth, A. (2017) Determining the value of information literacy for employers. In Forster, M. (ed.), *Information Literacy in the Workplace*, Facet Publishing, 67–83.

Gonzalez, J. (1995) Autotopographies. In Brahm, G. and Driscoll, M. (eds), *Prosthetic territories: politics and hypertechnologies*, West View Press, 133–50.

Gramsci, A. (1971) *Prison notebooks*, Lawrence & Wishart.

Granovetter, M. S. (1973) The strength of weak ties, *American Journal of Sociology*, 1360–80.

Greenwood, M. (2018) *Reading the signals: the meaning of pedestrian crossings in uncertain times.* MA dissertation, University of Manchester.

Gregoriades, A., Pampaka, M. and Michail, H. (2009) Assessing students' learning in MIS using concept mapping, *Journal of Information Systems Education, 20* (4), 419.

Greyson, D., O'Brien, H. and Shankar, S. (2019) Visual analysis of information world maps: an exploration of four methods, *Journal of Information Science*, March 2019.

Greyson, D., O'Brien, H. and Shoveller, J. (2017) Information world mapping: a participatory arts-based elicitation method for information behavior interviews, *Library and Information Science Research, 39* (2), 149–57.

Gull, C. D. (1956) Seven years of work on the organization of materials in special library, *American Documentation*, **7**, 320–9.

Habermas, J. (1984) *The theory of communicative action, vol 1: reason and the rationalization of society*, Heinemann.

Habermas, J. (1987) *The theory of communicative action, vol 2: lifeworld and system – a critique of functionalist reason*, Polity Press.

Habermas, J. (1989) *The structural transformation of the public sphere: an inquiry into a category of bourgeois society*, MIT Press.

Habermas, J. (1993) *Justification and application: remarks on discourse ethics*, Polity Press.

Hacıgüzeller, P. (2017) Archaeological (Digital) Maps as performances: towards alternative mappings, *Norwegian Archaeological Review*, **50** (2), 149–71.

Hamelink, C. (1976) An alternative to news, *Journal of Communication*, 20, 120–3.

Hammond, J. and Gibbons, P. (2005) What is scaffolding, *Teachers' Voices*, **8**, 8–16.

Haraway D. (1990) A manifesto for cyborgs: science, technology and socialist feminism in the 1980s. In Nicholson, L. (ed.), *Feminism/Postmodernism*, Routledge.

Haraway, D. (1991) *Simians, cyborgs and women: the reinvention of nature*, Taylor & Francis.

Harris, B. R. (2008) Communities as necessity in information literacy development: challenging the standards, *Journal of Academic Librarianship*, **34** (3), 248–55.

Harvey, D. (1996) *Justice, nature and the geography of difference*, Blackwell.

Harvey, P. (2010) *The Hereford world map: an introduction*, Hereford Cathedral.

Hay, D. B. (2007) Using concept maps to measure deep, surface and non-learning outcomes, *Studies in Higher Education*, **32** (1), 39–57.

Helbig, A. K. (1982) The Forest as Setting and Symbol in Barbara Willard's Mantlemass Novels, *Children's Literature Association Quarterly*, **7** (1), 35–9.

Heldmann, J. L., Toon, O. B., Pollard, W. H., Mellon, M. T., Pitlick, J., McKay, C. P. and Andersen, D. T. (2005) Formation of Martian gullies by the action of liquid water flowing under current Martian environmental conditions, *Journal of Geophysical Research: Planets*, 110(E5).

Hepworth, M. and Walton, G. (2009) *Teaching information literacy for inquiry-based learning*, Elsevier.

Herring, J. (2009) A grounded analysis of year 8 students' reflections on information literacy skills and techniques, *School Libraries Worldwide*, **15** (1), 1.

Hewitt, R. (2010) *Map of a nation: a biography of the Ordnance Survey*, Granta.

Hodgson, V. and Reynolds, M. (2005) Consensus, difference and 'multiple communities' in networked learning, *Studies in Higher Education*, **30** (1), 11–24.

Hollway, J. and Knowle, J. (2000) Mikhail Bakhtin: dialogics of space. In Crang, M. and Thrift, N. (eds), *Thinking space*, Psychology Press, 71–88.

Holquist, M. (1990) Introduction. In Bakhtin, M., *Art and answerability: Early philosophical essays (Vol. 9),* University of Texas Press.

Holschuh Simmons, M. (2005) Librarians as disciplinary discourse mediators: using genre theory to move toward critical information literacy, *Portal*, **5** (3), 297–311.

Hommels, A. (2005) Studying obduracy in the city: toward a productive fusion between technology studies and urban studies, *Science, Technology and Human Values*, **30** (3), 323–51.

Hornsey, R. (2012) 'He who Thinks, in Modern Traffic, is Lost': automation and the pedestrian rhythms of interwar London. In Edensor, T. (ed.), *Geographies of rhythm: nature, place, mobilities and bodies*, Ashgate, 99–112.

Hughes, G. and Hay, D. (2001) Use of concept mapping to integrate the different perspectives of designers and other stakeholders in the development of e-learning materials, *British Journal of Educational Technology*, **32** (5), 557–69.

Hui, A. (2017) Variation and the intersection of practices. In Hui, A., Schatzki, T. and Shove, E. (eds), *The nexus of practices: connections, constellations, practitioners*, Routledge, 52–67.

Hultgren, F. (2009) *Approaching the future: a study of Swedish school leavers' information-related activities*, Valfrid.

Hutchby, C. (2012) *The Wainwright companion*, Frances Lincoln.

Ingold, T. (1993) Globes and spheres: the topology of environmentalism. In Milton, K. (ed.), *Environmentalism: the view from anthropology*, Routledge.

Jacob, C. (1999) Mapping in the mind: the Earth from ancient Alexandria. In Cosgrove, D. (ed.), *Mappings*, Reaktion Books, 24–49.

Johnson, P. (2006) Unravelling Foucault's 'different spaces', *History of the Human Sciences*, **19** (4), 75–90.

Karjalainen, P. T. (2006) Topobiografinen paikan tulkinta (Topobiographical interpretation of place). In Knuuttila, S., Laaksonen, P. and Kaukio, V. (eds), *Paikka: eletty, kuviteltu, kerrottu (Place: lived, imagined, told),* Suomalaisen Kirjallisuuden Seura, 83–92.

Keen, A. (2007) *Cult of the amateur*, Hachette.

Kelly, G. (1963) *A theory of personality: the psychology of personality constructs*, Norton.

Kemmis, S. and Grootenboer, P. (2008) Situation praxis in practice. In Kemmis, S. and Smith, T. J. (eds), *Enabling Praxis*, Sense Publishers, 37–62.

Kendall, G. and Wickham, G. (1999) *Using Foucault's methods*, Sage.

Kitchin, R., Perkins, C. and Dodge, M. (2009) Thinking about maps. In Dodge, M., Kitchin, R. and Perkins, C. (eds), *Rethinking maps: new frontiers in cartographic theory*, Routledge, 1–25.

Knorr Cetina, K. (2001) Objectual practice. In Schatzki, T., Knorr Cetina, K. and von Savigny, E. (eds), *The practice turn in contemporary theory*, Routledge, 184–97.

Kuhlthau, C. C. (1993) *Seeking meaning: a process approach to library and information services*, Greenwood.

Lakoff, G. (1999) *Philosophy in the flesh: the embodied mind and its challenge to western thought*, Basic Books.

Lancaster, F. W. (1970) User education: the next major thrust in information science, *Journal of Education for Librarianship*, **11**, 55–63.

Landry, C., Morley, D., Southwood, R. and Wright, P. (1985) *What a way to run a railroad: an analysis of radical failure*, Comedia.

Leeson Prince, C. (1898) *Observations on the topography and climate of Crowborough Hill, Sussex*, Farncombe & Co.

Le Louvier, K. and Innocenti, P. (2019) The information mapping board game: a collaborative investigation of asylum seekers and refugees' information practices in England, UK, *Information Research*, **24** (1).

Lindsay, A. D. (ed.) (1906) *Plato: The Republic*, Everyman.

Linell, P. (2009) *Rethinking language, mind, and world dialogically: interactional and contextual theories of human sense-making*, IAP.

List, C. and Pettit, P. (2011) *Group agency: the possibility, design, and status of corporate agents*, Oxford University Press.

Lister, R. (1965) *Old maps and globes*, Bell and Hyman.

Lloyd, A. (2010a) *Information literacy landscapes: information literacy in education, workplace and everyday contexts*, Chandos.

Lloyd, A. (2010b) Framing information literacy as information practice: site ontology and practice theory, *Journal of Documentation*, **66** (2), 245–58.

Lloyd, A. (2012) Information literacy as a socially enacted practice: sensitising themes for an emerging perspective of people-in-practice, *Journal of Documentation*, **68** (6), 772–83.

Lloyd, A., Kennan, M. A., Thompson, K. M. and Qayyum, A. (2013) Connecting with new information landscapes: information literacy practices of refugees, *Journal of Documentation*, **69** (1), 121–44.

Markless, S. and Streatfield, D. (2007) Three decades of information literacy: redefining the parameters. In Andretta, S. (ed.), *Change and challenge: information literacy for the 21st century*, Auslib, 15–36.

Marton, F. and Booth, S. (1997) *Learning and awareness*, Lawrence Erlbaum.

McIntosh, A. and Cockburn-Wootten, C. (2018) Refugee-focused service providers: improving the welcome in New Zealand, *The Service Industries Journal*, 1–16.

McNicol, S. (ed.) (2016) *Critical literacy for information professionals*, Facet Publishing.

Milton, G. (2002) *Samurai William: The Englishman who opened Japan*, Penguin.

Mishra, P. and Koehler, M. J. (2006) Technological pedagogical content knowledge: a framework for teacher knowledge, *Teachers College Record*, **108** (6), 1017–54.

Moreland, C. and Bannister, D. (1986) *Antique maps*, Phaidon.

Morphy, H. (2001) Seeing aboriginal art in the gallery, *Humanities Research*, **8** (1), 37–50.

Morton, O. (2002) *Mapping Mars: science, imagination, and the birth of a world*, Picador.

Nevison, J. (1976) Computing in the liberal arts college, *Science*, **194**, 396–402.

Novak, J. D. (1990) Concept mapping: a useful tool for science education, *Journal of Research in Science Teaching*, **27** (10), 937–49.

Olson, C. F., Matthies, L., Wright, J., Li, R. and Di, K. (2007) Visual terrain mapping for Mars exploration, *Computer Vision and Image Understanding*, **105** (1), 73–85.

Pai, H. H., Sears, D. A. and Maeda, Y. (2015) Effects of small-group learning on transfer: a meta-analysis, *Educational Psychology Review*, **27** (1), 79–102.

Pariser, E. (2011) *The filter bubble: what the internet is hiding from you*, Penguin.

Perkins, C. (2009) Playing with maps. In Dodge, M., Kitchin, R. and Perkins, C. (eds), *Rethinking maps: new frontiers in cartographic theory*, Routledge, 167–88.

Pilerot, O. (2015) Review of: Whitworth, Andrew. Radical information literacy: reclaiming the political heart of the IL movement, London: Chandos Publishing, 2014, *Information Research*, **20** (1), review no. R526.

Pilerot, O. and Lindberg, J. (2011) The concept of information literacy in policy-making texts: an imperialistic project? *Library Trends*, **60** (2), 338–60.

Purdue, J. (2003) Stories, not information: transforming information literacy, *Portal*, **3** (4), 653–62.

Rader, H. (2002) Information literacy 1973–2002: a selected literature review, *Library Trends*, **51** (2), 242–61.

Reckwitz, A. (2017) Practices and their affects. In Hui, A., Schatzki, T. and Shove, E. (eds), *The nexus of practices: connections, constellations, practitioners*, Routledge, 114–25.

Rheingold, H. (1993) The heart of the WELL. In Donelan, H., Kear, K. L. and Ramage, M. (eds), *Online communication and collaboration: a reader*, Routledge.

Robinson, K. S. (1992) *The Mars trilogy (Red Mars, Green Mars, Blue Mars)*, Harper Collins.

Rockman, I. (ed.) (2004) *Integrating information literacy into the higher education curriculum*, Jossey-Bass.

Salovaara, I. (2016) Participatory maps: digital cartographies and the new ecology of journalism, *Digital Journalism*, 4 (7), 827–37.

Salvatore, R. D. (2003) Local versus imperial knowledge: reflections on Hiram Bingham and the Yale Peruvian expedition, *Nepantla: Views from South*, 4 (1), 67–80.

Salvatore, R. D. (2005) Library accumulation and the emergence of Latin American studies, *Comparative American Studies*, 3 (4), 415–36.

Salvatore, R. D. (2006). Imperial mechanics: South America's hemispheric integration in the Machine Age, *American Quarterly*, 58 (3), 662–91.

Saracevic, T. (1975) Relevance: a review of and a framework for the thinking on the notion of information science, *Journal of the American Society for Information Science*, 26 (6), 321–43.

Saracevic, T. (2007) Relevance: a review of the literature and a framework for thinking on the notion in information science. Part III: Behavior and effects of relevance, *Journal of the American Society for Information Science and Technology*, 58 (3), 2126–44.

Savolainen, R. (2007) Information source horizons and source preferences of environmental activists: a social phenomenological approach, *Journal of the Association for Information Science and Technology*, 58 (12), 1709–19.

Schatzki, T. R. (1996) *Social practices: a Wittgensteinian approach to human activity and the social*, Cambridge University Press.

Schatzki, T. R. (2000) The social bearing of nature, *Inquiry*, 43, 21–38.

Schatzki, T. R. (2017) Sayings, texts and discursive formations. In Hui, A., Schatzki, T. and Shove, E. (eds), *The nexus of practices: connections, constellations, practitioners*, Routledge, 126–40.

Schmidt, R. (2017) Reflexive knowledge in practices. In Hui, A., Schatzki, T. and Shove, E. (eds), *The nexus of practices: connections, constellations, practitioners*, Routledge, 141–54.

Schneider, S. M. (1997) *Expanding the public sphere through computer-mediated communication: political discussion about abortion*. Doctoral dissertation, Massachusetts Institute of Technology.

Schunk, D. H. (1998) Peer modelling. In Topping, K. and Ehly, S. (eds), *Peer-assisted learning*, Routledge, 185–202.

Scott, J. (2000) *Social network analysis: a handbook*, 2nd edn, Sage.

Scott, J. C. (1990) *Domination and the arts of resistance*, Yale University Press.

Secker, J. and Coonan, E. (eds) (2012) *Rethinking information literacy: a practical framework for supporting learning*, Facet Publishing.

Shenk, D. (1997) *Data smog: surviving the information glut*, Harper Collins.

Skupin, A. and Fabrikant, S. I. (2003) Spatialization methods: a cartographic research agenda for non-geographic information visualization, *Cartography and Geographic Information Science*, **30** (2), 99–119.

Sonnenwald, D. H. (1999) Evolving perspectives of human information behavior: contexts, situations, social networks and information horizons. In *Exploring the contexts of information behavior: proceedings of the Second International Conference in Information Needs*, Taylor Graham.

Sonnenwald, D. H., Wildemuth, B. S. and Harmon, G. L. (2001) A research method to investigate information seeking using the concept of information horizons: an example from a study of lower socio-economic students' information seeking behavior, *The New Review of Information Behavior Research*, **2**, 65–86.

Sotelo, L. C. (2010) Looking backwards to walk forward: walking, collective memory and the site of the intercultural in site-specific performance, *Performance Research*, **15** (4), 59–69.

Spry, T. (2001) Performing autoethnography: an embodied methodological praxis, *Qualitative Inquiry*, **7** (6), 706–32.

Steinerová, J. (2010) Ecological dimensions of information literacy, *Information Research*, **15** (1).

Tagliaventi, M. and Mattarelli, E. (2006) The role of networks of practice, value sharing, and operational proximity in knowledge flows between professional groups, *Human Relations*, **59** (3), 291– 319.

Taylor, G. J., Martel, L., Karunatillake, S., Gasnault, O. and Boynton, W. (2010) Mapping Mars geochemically, *Geology*, **38** (2), 183–6.

Thompson, D. (2008) *Counterknowledge*, Atlantic.

Thompson, K. M. (2007) Furthering understanding of information literacy through the social study of information poverty, *Canadian Journal of Information and Library Science,* **31** (1), 87.

Thoreau, H. D. (2006) *Walden*, Yale University Press.

Tippett, J. (2005) Participatory planning in river catchments, an innovative toolkit tested in Southern Africa and North West England, *Water Science and Technology*, **52** (9), 95–105.

Tippett, J., Handley, J. and Ravetz, J. (2007) Meeting the challenges of sustainable development: a conceptual appraisal of a new methodology for participatory ecological planning, *Progress in Planning*, **67** (1), 9–98.

Tippett, J., Farnsworth, V., How, F., Le Roux, E., Mann, P. and Sheriff, G. (2009) *Improving sustainability skills and knowledge in the workplace: final project report*, University of Manchester Sustainable Consumption Institute.

Tippett, J., Farnsworth, V., How, F., Le Roux, E., Mann, P. and Sheriff, G. (2010) *Scaling-up: learning to embed sustainability skills and knowledge in the workplace*, Final Project Report, University of Manchester Sustainable Consumption Institute.

Tuominen, K., Savolainen, R. and Talja, S. (2005) Information literacy as a sociotechnical practice, *Library Quarterly*, **75** (3), 329–45.

Valentine, B. (2001) The legitimate effort in research papers: student commitment versus faculty expectations, *Journal of Academic Librarianship*, **27** (2), 107–15.

Walsh, A. (2014) SEEK!: creating and crowdfunding a game-based open educational resource to improve information literacy, *Insights*, **27** (1).

Walsh, A. (2015) Playful information literacy: play and information literacy in higher education, *Nordic Journal of Information Literacy in Higher Education*, **7** (1), 80–94.

Walton, G., Barker, J., Hepworth, M. and Stephens, D. (2007) Using online collaborative learning to enhance information literacy delivery in a Level 1 module: an evaluation, *Journal of Information Literacy*, **1** (1), 13–30.

Walton, G. and Cleland, J. (2017) Information literacy: empowerment or reproduction in practice? A discourse analysis approach, *Journal of Documentation*, **73** (4), 582–94.

Walton, G. and Hepworth, M. (2011) A longitudinal study of changes in learners' cognitive states during and following an information literacy teaching intervention, *Journal of Documentation*, **67** (3), 449–79.

Wandersee, J. H. (1990) Concept mapping and the cartography of cognition, *Journal of Research in Science Teaching*, **27** (10), 923–36.

Watson, M. (2017) Placing power in practice theory. In Hui, A., Schatzki, T. and Shove, E. (eds), *The nexus of practices: connections, constellations, practitioners*, Routledge, 169–82.

Webster, L. and Gunter, H. (2018) How power relations affect the distribution of authority: implications for information literacy pedagogy, *Journal of Information Literacy*, **12** (1).

Webster, L., and Whitworth, A. (2017) Distance learning as alterity: facilitating the experience of variation and professional information practice, *Journal of Information Literacy*, **11** (2).

Webster, L. and Whitworth, A. (2019) Power and resistance in informed learning. In Ranger, K. (ed.), *Informed learning applications: insights from research and practice*, Emerald, 115–31.

Wengel, Y., McIntosh, A. and Cockburn-Wootten, C. (2019) Co-creating knowledge in tourism research using the Ketso method, *Tourism Recreation Research*, **44** (3), 1–12.

Wenger, E. (1999) *Communities of practice: learning, meaning and identity*, Cambridge University Press.

Wenger, E., White, N. and Smith, J. D. (2009) *Digital habitats: stewarding technology for communities*, CPSquare.

Westrem, S. D. (2001) *The Hereford Map: a transcription and translation of the legends with commentary*, Brepols.

Whitworth, A. (2001) Ethics and reality in environmental discourses, *Environmental Politics*, **10** (2), 22–42.

Whitworth, A. (2009) *Information obesity*, Chandos.

Whitworth, A. (2014) *Radical information literacy: reclaiming the political heart of the IL movement*, Chandos.

Whitworth, A. (2015) Using mapping to facilitate innovation in libraries. In Walsh, A. and Clement, E. (eds), *Inspiring, innovative and creative library interventions: an i2c2 compendium*, Innovative Libraries.

Whitworth, A. (2017) Lessons from the Borg cube. Keynote speech, *European Conference for Information Literacy*, St Malo.

Whitworth, A. (2019) The discourses of power, information and literacy. In Goldstein, S. (ed.) *Informed Societies*, Facet Publishing, 25–45.

Whitworth, A., Torras i Calvo, M. C., Moss, B., Amlesom Kifle, N. and Blåsternes, T. (2014) Changing libraries: facilitating self-reflection and action research on organizational change in academic libraries, *New Review of Academic Librarianship*, **20** (2), 251–74.

Whitworth, A., Torras i Calvo, M. C., Moss, B., Amlesom Kifle, N. and Blåsternes, T. (2016a) Mapping the landscape of practice across library communities, *portal: Libraries and the Academy*, **16** (3), 557–79.

Whitworth, A., Torras i Calvo, M. C., Moss, B., Amlesom Kifle, N. and Blåsternes, T. (2016b) How groups talk information literacy into being. In *European Conference on Information Literacy*, Springer, 109–18.

Whitworth, A., Torras i Calvo, M. C., Moss, B., Amlesom Kifle, N. and Blåsternes, T. (2016c) *Bibliotek i Endring: final project report.*

Whitworth, A. and Webster, L. (2019) Digital and information literacy as discursive mapping of an information landscape. *Proceedings LILG-2019 conference*, Frankfurt.

Willard, B. (1989) *The Forest: Ashdown in East Sussex*, Sweethaws Press.

Williamson, D. and Connolly, E. (2009) *theirwork*: the development of sustainable mapping. In Dodge, M., Kitchin, R. and Perkins, C. (eds), *Rethinking maps: new frontiers in cartographic theory*, Routledge, 97–112.

Wilson, P. (1983) *Secondhand knowledge: an inquiry into cognitive authority*, Greenwood Press.

Withers, C. W. J. (2009) Place and the 'spatial turn' in geography and in history, *Journal of the History of Ideas*, **70**, 637–58.

Wittgenstein, L. (1953) *Philosophical investigations*.

Wogan-Browne, J. (1991) Reading the world: the Hereford mappa mundi, *Parergon*, **9** (1), 117–35.

Wrong, D. (1995) *Power: its forms, bases and uses*, Routledge.

Zimmerman, M. S. (2018) Information horizons mapping to assess the health literacy of refugee and immigrant women, *Proceedings of the Association for Information Science and Technology*, **55** (1), 963–4.

Zurkowski, P. G. (1974) *The information service environment: relationships and priorities, Report presented to the National Commission on Libraries and Information Science*, Washington DC.

Zurkowski, P. G. and Kelly, J. (2014) *Zurkowski's 40-year information literacy movement: fuelling the next 40 years of action literacy*, All Good Literacies Press.

Index

Note: 'maps' and 'mapping' have not been separately indexed: the whole book is concerned with these concepts. Some other key terms, particularly 'information landscape' and 'information literacy', have been indexed selectively rather than exhaustively.